CONFERRING

CONFERRING

The Keystone of Reader's Workshop

Patrick A. **Allen**

Foreword by Debbie Miller

Stenhouse Publishers

Portland, Maine

Stenhouse Publishers
www.stenhouse.com

Credits

Pages 115–116: William Stafford, "You Reading This, Be Ready," from *The Way It Is: New and Selected Poems*. Copyright © 1998 by the estate of William Stafford. Reprinted with the permission of Graywolf Press, Saint Paul, Minnesota, www.graywolfpress.org.

Page 140: "The Other Side of the Door," from *The Other Side of the Door* by Jeff Moss, copyright © 1991 by Jeff Moss. Used by permission of Bantam Books, a division of Random House, Inc.

Page 153: John Fox, "When Someone Deeply Listens to You," from *Finding What You Didn't Lose: Expressing Your Truth and Creativity Through Poem-Making*. Copyright © 1995 by Jeremy P. Tarcher, Inc. Used by permission.

Library of Congress Cataloging-in-Publication Data

Allen, Patrick, 1960-

Conferring : the keystone of reader's workshop / Patrick A. Allen ; foreword by Debbie Miller.

p. cm.

Includes bibliographical references and index.

ISBN 978-1-57110-768-8 (alk. paper)

1. Reading--Evaluation. 2. Communication in education. 3. Teacher-student relationships. I. Title.

LB1050.42.A43 2009

372.48--dc22

2009024561

Cover design, interior design, and typesetting by Designboy Creative Group

Keystone cover art by Sophie, with Tammy Edwards

Manufactured in the United States of America

PRINTED ON 30% PCW
RECYCLED PAPER

15 14 13 12 11 10 9 8 7 6 5 4 3

To my father, Glenn.
1904–1988

With love and affection.

So . . . *What do you think?*

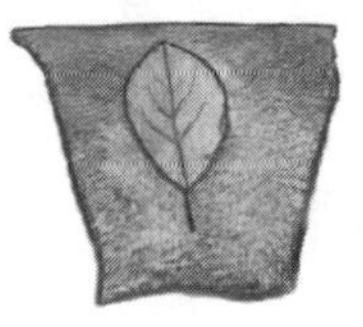

CONTENTS

Foreword *by Debbie Miller* vii
Acknowledgments ix
Prologue: *Why Confer?* xii

Introduction: *Why a Keystone?* 1

PART 1: *What Brings About a Good Conference, Anyway?* **7**
Chapter 1: *Counterfeit Beliefs About Conferring* 8
Chapter 2: *Conferring Goals and Guiding Principles* 21
Chapter 3: *Building the Environment for Conferring—Five Requisite Ashlars* 37

PART 2: *What Are the Essential Components of Conferring?* **93**
Chapter 4: *The RIP Model—Bringing Thoughtful Structure to Our Conferring* 94
Chapter 5: *Cultivating Rigor, Nurturing Inquiry, and Developing Intimacy* 117

PART 3: *What Emerges from Our Reading Conferences?* **155**
Chapter 6: *Conferring Walk-Aways* 156
Chapter 7: *Conferring Ain't Easy* 175

Conclusion: *Adieu* 191

Appendix 195
Bibliography 203
Index 209

FOREWORD

by Debbie Miller

Conferring with children is an art. It's an active process wherein we sit side-by-side with children, put ourselves in the moment, listen carefully, and reflect and respond in ways that encourage and nudge them forward as learners. I believe that conferring is one of the most significant actions we take as teachers: it serves to individualize our instruction, move children from guided to independent practice, and provide daily opportunities to know—*really* know—our students. When teachers and children confer about books and big ideas, it puts us both in the active roles of teaching and learning.

Yet, as Patrick Allen writes, "Conferring Ain't Easy"! Learning just what to say and what not to say, and knowing just what to do and what not to do, takes time, practice, persistence, and patience. It takes knowing children *and* ourselves as readers, learners, and thinkers. Patrick's right—conferring isn't easy. But really, is there anything in our profession that is?

In *Conferring: The Keystone of Reader's Workshop*, Patrick has written about conferring with readers in a way that no one has before. It's a smart, in-depth, and accessible read that just might change how you see yourself (and your students) as a teacher and a learner. Patrick knows that there is something "lasting about sitting down next to a child and having a conversation as fellow readers." I know that, and I expect you do too. But there's a big difference between knowing something and making it happen, right? Lucky for us, that's just what Patrick has done—he's helped us develop and hone our side-by-side work with children.

In this book, you'll learn how to create a classroom culture that honors and builds upon each student's uniqueness and strengths. You'll learn how the structure of a conference facilitates its process. Perhaps most important, throughout the book Patrick includes "Ponderings"— questions that not only serve to shape your thinking but also explore ways to adapt and internalize Patrick's hard-won experience and make it yours. Ultimately, *Conferring* asks us to dig deeper with our kids and to gently nudge them forward as they become independent, inquisitive, problem-solving thinkers who know the joy and power of what it means to be a reader.

Patrick and I have been friends for years. We met through our work at the Denver-based Public Education and Business Coalition, and it was there we began to think about children, teaching, and learning in new ways. I've spent time in Patrick's classrooms over the years. Whether he's teaching inside the building or outside in a mobile room, it usually takes me a while to find him. That's because he's *with* the children, crouched down beside them, listening, learning, and teaching with his head and his heart. I am honored and delighted to introduce you to Patrick A. Allen and his most excellent book, *Conferring: The Keystone of Reader's Workshop*. Happy reading!

ACKNOWLEDGMENTS

I've often hesitated in beginning a project because I've thought, "It'll never turn out to be even remotely like the good idea I have as I start." I could just "feel" how good it could be. But I decided that, for the present, I would create the best way I know how and accept the ambiguities.

—*Fred Rogers, 2003*

When I read Fred Rogers's wise words, I think he must have read my thoughts. And, it is with utmost respect that I humbly recognize those who have made writing this book such a blessing. You are the mortar that holds this book together.

Thank you, first and foremost, to my mom, Freda, and my dad, Glenn—your foundation is the bedrock on which I continue to build; I miss you both. And, thank you to my nine siblings, especially Doris and Joy, for your love and encouragement. You both, along with Dan, Glenn, George, Margo, Marlene, Jim, and Peggy, created a lasting legacy for the Allen family.

Thank you to Lori Conrad, whose collaborative spirit meanders through this book—we have done some great thinking together, haven't we? To my treasured friends Randi Allison (twenty-four years and counting), Cheryl Zimmerman, and Mimi Brown for reading initial drafts and offering suggestions, providing clarity, and validating specifics—your unwavering trust and friendship make me a better person. Thank you to my best friend, Troy Rushmore, and dear friend Janice Gibson for your faithful kindness—without the "critical triangle" where would we be?

Thank you to the rest of the Friday Freaks—Missy Matthews, Susan Logan, Kristin Venable, Karen Berg, and Ilana Spiegel (along with Troy, Randi, Cheryl, and Lori)—without all of you the first Friday of each month wouldn't be nearly as full of laughter and learning, would it? When we get together, I always know I'll leave a bit wiser. Thank you to Jim Becker, my other *brother*—keep on running for Him.

Thank you to Cris Tovani for always listening, sharing laughs, and nudging me forward. Thanks to Ellin Keene for continuously extending my understanding and thinking—I have loved being a groupie all these years, and I value our friendship. Thank you to Debbie Miller for writing the foreword; it is truly an honor to call you my friend, and I have appreciated learning from and with you. And, thank you to all of my Public Education and Business Coalition

(PEBC) colleagues—past and present—for your cutting-edge brilliance and commitment to teaching, learning, and professional development. Your collective voices create lasting change in the hearts and minds of teachers everywhere.

A special thank-you to all the PEBC staff developers who have facilitated countless groups of visitors to my classroom and focused the observations and conversations so eloquently—every one of you stretch learning to extraordinary limits (thanks to Judy Hendricks for organizing it all). Conferring was a topic of import with each visit, wasn't it?

It is my involvement in the PEBC that has afforded me the pleasure of meeting some of my reading and writing heroes and friends (many of whom are quoted throughout this book). Each of you has made me a better teacher through your wisdom and experience, and for that, I'm forever grateful.

Thank you to the administrators I have had the privilege of working with over the years. Particularly Laura Penn Harmon, my first principal—your "go for it" attitude helped mold a collection of teachers and school leaders who stand up for what we believe and understand that we teach to honor children and their thinking. It has been a pleasure to work with many incredible teachers—from Mountain View to Cherokee Trail to Frontier Valley. Thank you, as always, to Judy Gilkey; my fondest teaching memories include you—I cherish your friendship.

Thank you to the staff at Stenhouse. To Bill Varner, whom I now call my friend, it is a pleasure to work with you—I hold your patience, humor, and insight in highest esteem. So . . . *What's next?* Thanks also to Philippa Stratton, who wrote these words to me years ago: "You can't not want this . . . are you with me?" I am, and I sincerely thank you for inviting me into the Stenhouse family, albeit with detours and plenty of thinking time (writing *Put Thinking to the Test* with my coauthors gave me the final prod needed to get this book going). And to the rest of the Stenhouse staff, including Jay Kilburn, Chris Downey, Nate Butler, and Rebecca Eaton—you take remarkable pride in your work, and I appreciate your support.

Thank you to those whose voices are heard throughout this book; many ideas were lifted from our conversations and e-mails (your words added depth, honesty, and richness when it was needed most). Your perceptions and belief in children inspire me. And, thank you to the educators and staffs who have invited me to collaborate with your schools; it has been a treat working with each of you (notably my friends in Kent, Washington, and Casper, Wyoming—it's been, well, almost paradise). The most rewarding part of traveling is the friendships I have made that will last for many years to come.

Thank you to the children with whom I have had the pleasure of conferring. Your voices are paramount. Fred Rogers also said, "What seems to matter most is the way we show those nearest us that we've been listening to their needs, to their joys, and to their challenges" (2003, 73). Thanks for the opportunity to listen. It has been my sincere pleasure to be your teacher.

And to my own children, Graham, Anneke, Jensen, and Lauryn—when God gave each of you to your mother and me, we knew how much our lives would be enriched, but we didn't know how much we would be enveloped in love. We are so proud of each one of you! And, to my wife (and second editor), Susan: when I saw your brown eyes and gorgeous smile for the first time, I was smitten! If it weren't for you sharing your enthusiasm for teaching with me, my passion for teaching wouldn't have come to fruition; you led me down the right path. Your patience and grace continue to bring me blessings beyond number. I love you.

PROLOGUE: WHY CONFER?

"You know, my eyes ain't too good at all. I can't see nothing but the general shape of things, so I got to rely on my heart. Why don't you go on and tell me everything about yourself, so I can see you with my heart."

And because Winn-Dixie was looking up at her like she was the best thing he had ever seen, and because the peanut-butter sandwich had been so good, and because I had been waiting for a long time to tell some person about me, I did . . .

And the whole time I was talking, Gloria Dump was listening. She was nodding her head and smiling and frowning and saying, "Hmmm," and "Is that right?"

I could feel her listening with all her heart, and it felt good.

—Kate DiCamillo, 2000

What Do Their Teachers Know About Them?

The picture shows my own children: Graham, Anneke, Jensen, and Lauryn—probably the four most important reasons I have come to write *Conferring: The Keystone of Reader's Workshop*. I have seen the power of the influence of teachers who got to know each of my children. I have experienced the connections between home and school that occur when a teacher takes the time to build that personal foundation through conferring. Each of my children can easily name the teachers who regularly sat down, one-on-one, to get to know him or her as an individual, as a learner, a reader, a writer, a thinker.

I want the children in my classroom and the children in your classrooms to leave our auspices with some of our words in their heads and a whole lot of our caring in their hearts (and if we gather some important, documental data about them along the way, all the better). Over the years, my own children have given me reason to believe that I had to get better at conferring and had to make reading conferences a regular part of my reader's workshop.

Which Teachers Did That for My Children?

Each of my children has had several teachers who have taken the time to get to know them as learners, as individuals. But for each child, a specific teacher comes to mind.

For Graham, it was Ross Ericson, his high school architecture and sci-tech teacher. For four years, Graham had Mr. Ericson for a variety of classes. During Graham's high school years, our family's dinner conversations usually included at least one Mr. Ericson story. "Today, in class when I was talking to Mr. Ericson about . . . he helped me clear up my thinking and understand that . . ." Graham tells me that when he was learning to use ProENGINEER to design and draft his projects, Mr. Ericson was often sitting side-by-side with him explaining the software, asking questions, monitoring his progress, and encouraging his independence. Whether Graham was developing a prototype in the plastics lab, creating a scale balsa wood house, or reading text about a construction topic, it was Mr. Ericson who was right there with him—learning along the way.

For Anneke, it was Meredi Miller, her teacher in kindergarten, first grade, and second grade. For three years, Anneke had Mrs. Miller helping her stretch her thinking, uncover her passions, and strengthen her self-confidence. It was Mrs. Miller who was Anneke's kindred spirit. She knew our daughter inside and out, forward and backward. Because Mrs. Miller took time to talk and listen to Anneke, Anneke flourished—especially in reading. To this day, Mrs. Miller tells us specific stories of our daughter's primary years.

For Jens, it was Denise Johnson, his middle school gifted and talented teacher with whom he took three semesters of advanced humanities. When Ms. Johnson talked to us about Jens, she could explain his learning style and his quirks. She began each interaction with us by saying, "Today, when I was talking to Jens about . . . ," and with amazing insight she painted a portrait of him as a learner. Ms. Johnson worked as a liaison between Jens and his core classroom teachers, so that they could better understand him. He was a bit laissez-faire about the mundane tasks sometimes required of middle schoolers. But Ms. Johnson nudged him to read, encouraged him to take risks, and provided opportunities for him to "go deeper" into text.

For Lauryn, it was Jo Franklin. Mrs. Franklin, like me, opens her classroom to local and national visitors for the Denver-based Public Education and Business Coalition (PEBC), who come to see "thinking strategy" instruction. She understands the power of conferring. Many first-grade teachers spend the majority of their time working with small reading groups, but Mrs. Franklin spends the bulk of her time kneeling down, child-by-child, learning about who they are as readers, writers, and thinkers. She stretched Lauryn's intellect and let her dwell in in-depth study, especially nonfiction (tigers and polar bears were favorites). Mrs. Franklin created a safe, trusting environment in which Lauryn could blossom and grow. Even today, if Lauryn has free time at school, she loves to wander back to first grade to visit Mrs. Franklin and her students. Lauryn learned a lot from Jo about the importance of quiet reflection, thoughtfulness, listening, and a love of learning for learning's sake. Lauryn fell in love with reading because of Mrs. Franklin.

What Would Their Teachers Know?

Would they know that Sam is a University of Colorado fan and reads sports statistics on the Internet every morning before school? He can rattle them off, *and* he knows what the statistics mean! Would they know that Sam is growing a bit tired of *The Magic Tree House* books because they all sound the same?

But that his favorite parts in this series are the nonfiction parts—the interspersed facts, the details!—because it's "like the newspaper"?

Would they know that Maclaine creates images in her head constantly and that she "just can't keep them out"? And that she worries about her brother because she thinks he doesn't get sensory images at all? But that when she closes her eyes she can "see" exactly what's happening? The words paint pictures in her mind and help her understand and remember the details of the text.

Would they know that Hannah loves to read picture books because they help her as a writer? That she's made the leap to "reading like a writer"? She wants to read more nonfiction but gets pulled back to the "blue buckets" (all narrative books in my classroom are in blue baskets) because they seem to call her name! Would they know she loves a captive audience? And that she's reading a "really old book" she found in one of the paperback buckets and that it just "caught her eye"?

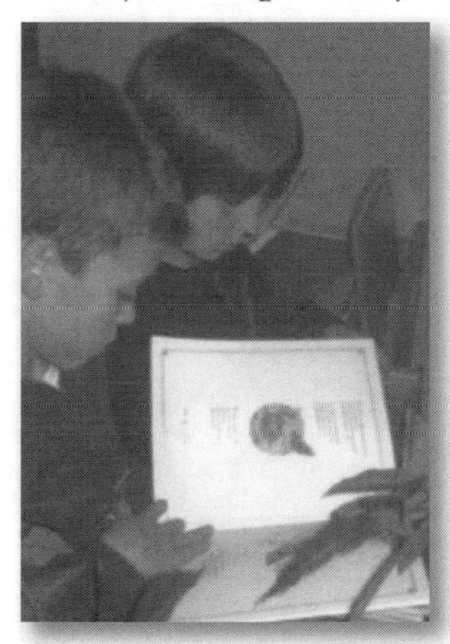

Would they be able to talk about Joey and his thinking about book choice—his depth, his coming to know himself as an active reader instead of a passive reader? That he is destined to be a spy . . . bird-watcher . . . reporter? And that he can help other readers "make really wise choices"? That he says he used to be a "fake reader," but now that he understands metacognition, he sees what he named the "cogs" moving in his brain while he reads?

I knew. I knew because, like my own children's teachers, there is something lasting about sitting down next to a child and having a conversation as fellow readers. True fellowship, shared coming to know. And while there are many instructional practices, routines, processes, and rituals that help lay the foundation for thoughtful reading instruction, it is conferring that I've chosen to explore in this text. I believe that it should be the keystone of reader's workshop. And, based on my experience, that's why I chose to pursue this writing project.

I end this prologue with a Helen Keller quote. When I first read this quote, it reminded me of how important well-established rituals and routines are to our teaching. It reminded me of conferring. Anne Sullivan, Helen's teacher, obviously spent important time "talking" with her about her learning:

> She realized that a child's mind is like a shallow brook which ripples and dances merrily over the stony course of its education and reflects here a flower, there a bush, yonder a fleecy cloud; and she attempted to guide my mind on its way knowing that like a brook it should be fed

by mountain streams and hidden springs, until it broadened out into a deep river, capable of reflecting in its placid surface, billowy hills, the luminous shadows of trees and the blue heavens, as well as the sweet face of a little flower.

Any teacher can take a child to the classroom, but not every teacher can make him learn. (Keller 2003, 33)

Introduction:

Why a Keystone?

This book is about conferring. Conferring with young readers.

For me, conferring has always been at the heart of my reader's workshop, much like the keystone has been important to stonemasons and bricklayers throughout history. Long before I began writing, I thought the keystone was a perfect metaphor in which to shape and construct my thinking. I have used it often as I've talked to colleagues about the importance of conferring. Regular opportunities to confer with readers must become a daily ritual in our reader's workshops.

Why compare conferring to a keystone? Recently, I was talking to my oldest sister, Joy, about my students. During our visit, our conversation turned to our father. She reminded me of Dad's talent as a bricklayer—a true craftsman. Being the youngest of ten children, I turn to Joy for family stories (she's thirty-one years older). "What you're describing, this work you're doing, it's a craft in itself. I always knew you were a lot like Dad—both fine craftsmen." After I hung up the telephone, I thought a little more about my father's craftsmanship . . .

Dad was born in 1904 in Ness City, Kansas. Ness City is famous for its limestone. If you drive through this country hamlet, the landscape is speckled with white stone posts holding barbed wire tight and straight. Outcroppings of limestone are abundant on the treeless plains, just under the sod, and these unique posts have dotted the prairie since the 1870s. Like many resourceful pioneers, the settlers used what they had and made the most of it. As lasting proof of pioneer ingenuity and creativity, limestone posts and buildings remain—important foundations to regional history.

The windows of the Ness County Bank Building are arched. Each arch contains a keystone—a symmetrical, wedge-shaped stone at the center of each arch. The central voussoir of an arch is said to hold the arch's weight. The truncated keystone is often the final stone placed to close the arch. The keystone is the reason we are able to see craftsmanship that has endured for decades.

Dad became a master bricklayer and stonemason, and the fact that he was born in Ness City is an ironic coincidence. Our environment often influences our learning.

Throughout Kansas, California, Utah, and Colorado evidence of his skill as a craftsman remains; intricate walls of homes and buildings stand firm and straight, walls that he helped build. These walls serve as a testament to his craft. The walls survive because of his dedication and commitment to his craft.

When Dad turned seventy-two, he decided to build a chimney up the side of our house for a wood-burning stove (much to my mother's chagrin, he planned to remove one of the living room's only two windows). I remember sitting with him at our worn kitchen table as he sketched out the chimney plans, pulled out his supply list, and looked at the notes he'd compiled in his pocket-sized notebook. He read his notes to me and thought aloud about the process of bricklaying. He shared his drawings and talked through his supply list in detail. I listened and watched.

Then he turned to me and asked me one question: "What do you think?"

What did I think? What did *I* think? I knew nothing about bricks and mortar. I couldn't tell a London trowel from a Philadelphia trowel. I didn't know a "running bond" from a "course." The only time I had used a level was when I walked around the house watching the magical bubble move mysteriously in the glass window as I placed Dad's wooden level on various surfaces around the house; I didn't understand the level's real purpose, I just thought it was cool. But, his sketches intrigued me (though I had no idea how the chimney would eventually look, let alone any inkling about its construction), and I was curious.

He looked me in the eye and asked me a second time, "What do you think?" And he waited. I sat there perplexed—thinking and wondering what he wanted me to say.

I knew absolutely nothing about bricklaying. There I was, sitting at our kitchen table, looking into the eyes of my father. He waited patiently for my answer. The spark in his brown eyes told me that he was expecting a response. There was a sense of sincerity in his inquiry.

"I'm not sure what I think," I said. "It sounds like a lot of hard work. I like the drawing, and I think the chimney is a great idea. I think that having a woodstove in the living room on cold winter days will be nice. But I have so many questions. There's so much I don't understand."

"Are you willing to learn?" he asked.

"I'm willing to watch," I said. "And ask more questions! Then maybe I'll learn."

"You think about your questions and maybe jot them down. I'll try to help you find the answers," he replied. "But just remember to ask them. We'll see how this project goes. I haven't built anything in a while, but this will be a lot of fun! Kind of an adventure." He was so enthusiastic.

It was the first time I remember him asking me to work side-by-side with him on a project. "Okay," I said. "When will we start?"

"Well," he replied, "we'll start tomorrow. Be up and ready at 7:00 A.M. and we'll get this project going."

At that moment, I got nervous and queasy. I realized he was inviting me into unfamiliar territory. He was sharing unfamiliar content and stretching my intellect into a new realm. He was ready to apprentice me to something he'd spent his life perfecting. He was genuinely interested in my opinion, my thinking, my understanding. He sincerely cared about my ideas. I trusted him.

I couldn't wait to get started.

The next day I was up and ready to begin.

As weeks passed, our conversations continued. Each morning Dad and I would meet at the north end of the house, trowels in hand, wheelbarrow at the ready, bricks organized and stacked. Then we'd talk. We'd ponder. He'd demonstrate. Dad would question, assess, measure. He would think aloud as he worked. Side-by-side, I was learning a new craft from a master.

But what was he really doing? He had studied his craft for his entire life. Now he was building the foundation for me.

Over time he taught me how to mix mortar and carry the hod, how to set bricks and pay attention to the pattern, how to use the mysterious level . . . but it was the one-on-one conversations that became the keystone of our work together.

Purposeful conversations that provided me with meaningful instruction—rich in strategy, inquiry, vocabulary, and skills.

Purposeful conversations that stretched my thinking and monitored my understanding.

Purposeful conversations about the process and the product.

Purposeful conversations that made me want to learn more, to do more.

Purposeful conversations with a specific goal in mind.

That first question, "What do you think?" has stuck with me all these years. Now, some thirty-five years later when I visit my hometown, I drive past my parents' house, long since sold to new owners. I remember my last walk through the empty house with peeling paint and missing window screens. The once-green lawn is bone dry and covered with leaves. The trees are untrimmed and unkempt. The wild roses, peonies, and tulips lining the property have all but disappeared.

However, the chimney still stands straight and tall. It was the last thing I took a picture of before I said goodbye to my childhood home. It was no longer the home of my youth, but tucked deep in my mind was that time I had shared with my father, the learning we had done together.

So why reminisce all these years later? I remember not only the house and the environment, but also the conversations. Our talks were indeed the keystone, the strength of working together—of being together.

Isolated skills aside (and there were many), it was the rigor, inquiry, and intimacy that stuck with me. All the changes to the house and yard could never overshadow our work together on that chimney.

And, that indelible memory is what leads me to the idea of comparing the reading conferences we have during our daily interactions with young readers to a keystone. The very word *keystone* comes from the Latin *clavis* for "key." *Key* meaning imperative, vital, essential. These are the same words I would use to describe the importance of conferring in the reader's workshop.

I believe that the reading conferences we have with children are the strength of our instruction. So, as I sit to write a book about conferring, the keystone metaphor immediately pops into my brain. Thanks, Dad.

So . . . What Do You Think?

This question not only permeated my initial thinking, but also will remain a mantra I use throughout this book. This text will comprise three main sections, each section highlighting specific constructs that strengthen my reading conferences. In turn, I hope conferring with readers will become the keystone of all our reader's workshops.

Part 1: "What Brings About a Good Conference, Anyway?" describes my historical perspective of conferring and the role conferring plays in my reader's workshop. In Chapter 1, "Counterfeit Beliefs About Conferring," I investigate some of the myths we have developed around the notion of conferring. In Chapter 2, "Conferring Goals and Guiding Principles," I explore my own burgeoning understanding of conferring and the role of reading conferences in the reader's workshop. In Chapter 3, "Building the Environment for Conferring—Five Requisite Ashlars," I focus on the environmental factors and classroom constructs necessary to make conferring become a living, breathing part of the reader's workshop.

Part 2: "What Are the Essential Components of Conferring?" recounts the purpose and structure of my reading conferences. In Chapter 4, "The RIP Model—Bringing Thoughtful Structure to Our Conferring," I propose and describe a specific structure I have developed to follow during reading conferences. In Chapter 5, "Cultivating Rigor, Nurturing Inquiry, and Developing Intimacy," I focus on three specific contexts in which conferring can flourish.

Part 3: "What Emerges from Our Reading Conferences?" examines the specific outcomes of reading conferences. In Chapter 6, "Conferring Walk-Aways," I synthesize several specific instructional points that result from making conferences an everyday part of the reader's workshop. The final chapter, "Conferring Ain't Easy," examines several premises I've developed as I've grappled with reading conferences and the role they play in my classroom.

Throughout the book, I've interspersed "ponderings": important questions that came to mind as I was writing. Thinking points. Ideas worth investigating. It's my hope that opportunities to ponder will nudge you to reflect on your own teaching, define your own beliefs, strengthen the foundation of your own reading conferences—perhaps even take a few minutes to write in your notebook.

I have also placed snippets called "keystone points" throughout the book. I hope that these points will provide insight into the interactions I have with the readers in my classroom or insights others have considered in terms of reading conferences. Perhaps each notion will provide a thinking point to help you contemplate your own reading conferences.

So, here we go. Let's talk conferring.

When a child asks you something, answer him, for goodness' sake. But don't make a production of it. Children are children, but they can spot an evasion quicker than adults, and evasion simply muddles 'em.

—Harper Lee, 1960

PART 1

WHAT BRINGS ABOUT A GOOD CONFERENCE, ANYWAY?

As we begin to orchestrate various question types in the pursuit of understanding, we expand our capacity to think and act in smart ways.

—James McKenzie, 2004

Conferring helps me share my thinking and to share what I know to other people. When I read to somebody, I really think of what I'm reading. Conferring really makes me think that I know what I'm doing and it makes me feel really smart. It helps me be more confident and it helps me understand the text.

—Lexee, Third Grade

Chapter 1

Counterfeit Beliefs About Conferring

I remember when my friend and colleague Lori Conrad and I met to plan a presentation on conferring with readers. Scones and lattes in hand, we set to work (we always do our best thinking over coffee, it seems). We had our conferring notebooks, anecdotal records, professional texts, and favorite conferring quotes spread out on the table. We were hoping to synthesize years of conferring work into a two-hour presentation.

When we spent time in others' classrooms, Lori and I noticed that many teachers were conferring with writers, but fewer were having similar interactions with readers. Teachers were talking to children about their writing, but not always taking the time to have the short, meaningful types of reading conferences we were having with the children in our classrooms. Why were we seeing so few regularly occurring reading conferences?

As we started to outline our presentation, Lori said to me, "There are a lot of misconceptions out there about conferring with readers. I hear them pop up when I talk to teachers about the power of conferring."

I nodded in agreement and added, "*I don't have time; I don't know what questions to ask; It's too hard; I don't know what to write in my notes; I don't even* take *notes; I don't know how to go deep . . .* These excuses are myths that have developed about such an important instructional construct. Teachers have internalized lists of reasons about why conferring can't or won't work. There has been such a focus on small groups of late. Reading conferences are less tangible, but not less important. I think people just think they're too hard. The lists of 'can'ts' or 'won'ts' are the things people need help sorting and understanding. We know conferring is effective, but there's so much to learn."

"You're right," Lori said. "There's a difference between legitimate wanting to learn and making excuses."

"Learning to confer is an art; we know that. It's not easy; it takes practice," I said. "But it's one of the most important and beneficial instructional moves I use with my students."

Then a lightbulb went off. "That's how we should start," we said together.

Lori said, "Let's start out by sharing some of the conferring myths we've uncovered in our work with students and adults."

"Should we call them myths? A myth is more like a legend or a tall tale," I said.

We both laughed. We'd heard plenty of reasons why conferring takes a backseat to other instructional practices. "What about counterfeit beliefs?" Lori suggested.

"Counterfeit beliefs. I like that."

We started talking about the film *A Private Universe*. You remember it, don't you? Many of us saw the film in one of our college methods courses. If you didn't, it is an interesting commentary on what happens when learners develop and maintain long-held beliefs that lead to misconceptions in their understandings of a concept. In the film, graduating Ivy League seniors were asked to explain what causes the seasons. The graduates thought that "eccentricity in Earth's orbit" made it warmer when it was closest to the sun and that the moon's phases were caused by Earth's shadow. And when ninth graders at a nearby school were asked the same questions, they had similar misconceptions.

Then students had an opportunity to test their ideas and justify their reasoning. The results? If students saw their ideas proven wrong they would do one of three things: (1) immediately let go of their old ideas and accept the new ones, (2) try to blend the old and new, or (3) revert to their previous learning.

In college, before we became classroom teachers, we may have found the film a bit humorous, but our humorous reaction changed to a state of being flabbergasted. We started asking, "Why don't students grasp these concepts?" Even the brightest students have long-standing misconceptions that endure despite what they were taught by their teachers. And, in our methods classes we had conversations about instruction and assessment, trying to identify the causes of having students leave our classrooms with mistaken thoughts, ideas, or notions about their learning.

I know that conferring helps me see if it is a good book choice.
C.J.

Student Keystone Point

In our experiences, Lori and I saw the misconceptions about the power of conferring running rampant. The very definition of conferring—discourse, consultation, discussion, comparison, viewpoints, deliberation, talk—was somehow getting lost in translation. If *confer* means to bestow a gift, we hoped that participants would better understand conferring as a result of our workshop.

Jeff Wilhelm says that many teachers still rely on an "information-transmission" approach, focusing mainly on the *what*, which he believes is insufficient for powerful understanding (2007, 9). Wilhelm contends that if we focus on only the *what* of learning, it leads to "shallow learning and even misconceptions" (2007, 9). Educational psychologists know that "if misconceptions exist, meaningful classroom learning requires experiences that help to restructure existing knowledge" (Murphy and Mason 2006, 307).

Perhaps teachers were doing the same thing with the notion of conferring with readers. The misguided concepts Lori and I noticed about reading conferences needed to be restructured. Murphy and Mason point out that "*Conceptual change* refers to revisions in personal mental

PONDERING: If you have developed counterfeit beliefs about conferring, where did they come from? How would you describe and discuss your misconceptions about conferring?

representations; revisions that are often precipitated by purposeful educational experiences" (2006, 307). Lori and I felt that nudging teachers to revise their misconceptions was our best option.

So what did we come up with? Here is our list of counterfeit beliefs. Which ones do you believe? Which ones have you actually said, or thought, at one point or another?

Counterfeit Beliefs About Conferring

1. If I meet with small groups, I don't have to meet with individuals. It's easier to meet with small groups.
2. If I don't meet with every student every day, I'm not doing a good job.
3. If I don't do a running record during each and every reading conference, I'm not really assessing my students' reading ability.
4. If I don't talk about all the errors a student is making while he or she is with me, I'm not being diligent.
5. I have to take an expert stance in each conference.
6. I need to focus on skills and fluency; comprehension comes later.
7. When I'm talking to a child about his or her learning, I'm *conferencing*.
8. I need to confer with every student the same number of times for the same amount of time each week.
9. I need to give the rest of the class something "to do" so they'll stay busy and leave me alone so I can confer.
10. I've tried _____'s conferring suggestions and recommendations and they just didn't work out.

Now before you close the book and say, "Wait a minute, I agree with number nine or number two," let the statement weigh on your mind a bit. Think about each statement carefully. Spend some time pondering. Can you see why these ideas might be considered misguided?

For Lori and me, these statements represent a synthesis of conversations we have had with each other and with many teachers with whom we have worked. And, though a bit tongue-in-cheek, these statements do represent the kinds of "excuses" we hear fellow teachers, district curriculum directors, and pundits use on a regular basis to delegate conferring to undocumentable and rhetorical fluff. The truth is, we believe each statement is, indeed, a falsehood—a myth!

I think some misconceptions are simply reactions to fear. Conferring is new territory for many of us; for some of us it has become old hat. In this age of accountability, we have to look carefully at the ways we assess students—and conferring with readers is of utmost import. Together, perhaps we can manifest the power of conferring.

It is my hope that these counterfeit beliefs will be dispelled or revised as you read this book. And, it is my hope that some of our fears or apprehensions about conferring subside. By sharing my own classroom conferring experiences, I trust that you will rethink your connections to a "myth" or two on our list (assuming you read one to which you've made a connection). I have.

And, while I won't directly address each statement in isolation, you'll find each myth discussed and perhaps dispelled in context (remember the best learning happens in context). That said, I would like to dispel one "myth" right away: number seven. My pet peeve (and Lori's too). The word is *conferring*. When we have a reading conference (or any other conference for that matter), we are *conferring. Confer* is a verb meaning to consult together, compare opinions, or carry on a conversation. It is active.

The conference itself is a noun. *Conferencing* is holding a series of meetings or conferences. Things.

So, we have a conference or a series of conferences over time—the conference is the meeting itself. When we are actually sitting shoulder-to-shoulder talking with readers, we are conferring. We are conferring with individuals, and sometimes small invitational groups, engaging in behaviors to uncover a reader's metacognitive moves, understandings, or reflections. Conferring with readers. Not conferencing with readers. Phew, I feel so much better having alleviated that confusion right away!

So, what should we do with this list? I think each of us needs to examine the list closely. If one of these "excuses" is getting in the way of our conferring with readers on a regular basis, we need to examine the *why* behind the statement. *Why* do we believe it? If you find a statement you agree with, reflect upon it. If you find a statement you disagree with, reflect upon that also.

If, like Lori and me, you find each statement somewhat fatuous, eliminate it from your vernacular. We have!

So, What Emerges in a Conference?

If we eliminate these counterfeit beliefs, what do we believe? Good question, eh?

When I began to think more intensely about reading conferences, I asked myself, "So, what emerges in a conference?" I realized that if I was going to use reading conferences in my classroom as a major instructional practice to collect information and data about the readers I am teaching, I'd best spend some time in good (or should I say wise?), old-fashioned inquiry. I needed to think closely about what I thought might emerge from my side-by-side work with young readers. I needed to study what my background knowledge and background experience led me to believe.

First, I created a web. At the center of the web, I wrote one question: What emerges in a conference? I thought it was a grand question for my inquiry and my answers might provide some insight into my own purposes for having reading conferences. I had to analyze the purpose and the outcomes for the readers in my classroom that I expected to emerge during my reading conferences. Moreover, I thought it would help me develop a rationale for putting reading conferences on my A-list—the instructional practices for which I am willing to fight, my lines in the sand. I thought it might just help me name my own thinking and, by naming my thinking, might improve my instructional prowess.

Shall we try it out? Look at the web in Figure 1.1 (also in the appendix). Create a similar web in your writer's notebook or your reflection notebook. Now ruminate about the question, What emerges in a conference? for a few minutes.

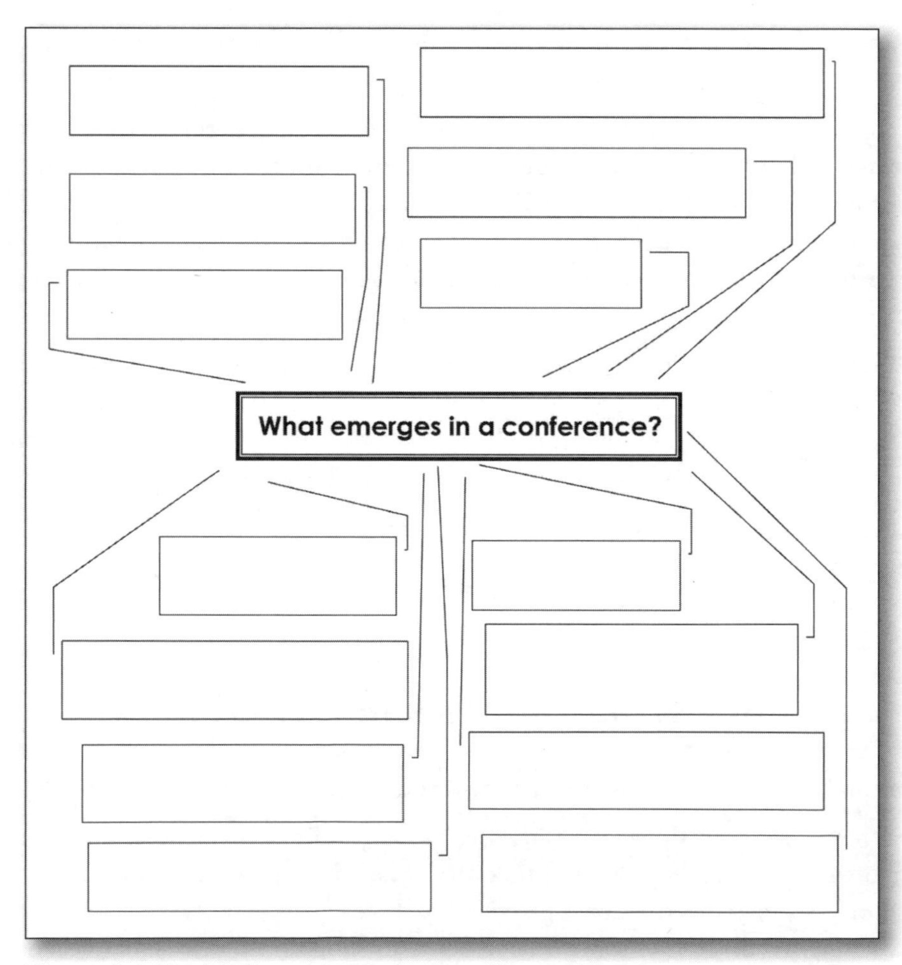

Figure 1.1 Blank What emerges in a conference? form

Take some think time—there are fourteen blank spots on the web. Think carefully about the entries you might expect to show up and materialize on your web. Think about your own attempts at conferring—the good, the bad, and the ugly. Think about your students and what they have taught you. Think about the types of conferences you have had with *your* fellow readers in book clubs, study groups, or while browsing in your local bookstore. Take your time.

PONDERING: What might emerge from your reading conferences? What do you hope will emerge?

Now begin to fill in the blanks. Try not to "double book." Let's say you write "graphophonics" in one branch of the web; don't put "sound symbol relationships" in another space. Don't focus on responses that are too similar. Try to create a more varied and diverse list; the sky's the limit (well, okay, the fourteen spaces on the web are the limit).

Try to identify the critical attributes of reading conferences—current state, right now in your classroom.

Now, set this book down until you are finished with your graphic. Think crossword puzzle or Sudoku mentality—don't look at my web until you've finished your own web. Experiment a bit. There are no right or wrong answers.

PONDERING: How did it go? Were you able to fill in the entire graphic? When you look at your responses, what are you contemplating, thinking about, or wondering?

I have inserted a copy of my initial completed graphic (see Figure 1.2) for you to peruse. Compare your web with mine. I am sure yours is much more thoughtful, more apropos. After all, mine was completed some time ago and my thinking has transformed a tad.

Rereading my initial web, I realize there are attributes I might revise if I did it today; my schema has changed and expanded. But I think it is important to show you my original thinking. When visitors watch me confer, they say, "I could never think that fast on my feet!"

I say, "Yes, you can. Take it slowly. Experiment. Get your hands dirty. Strengthen your foundation." Think of learning to confer with readers as a journey, an adventure, and a challenge. Conferring is nudging children toward independence. Our webs reflect those nudging points. Orchestrate the pursuit of understanding!

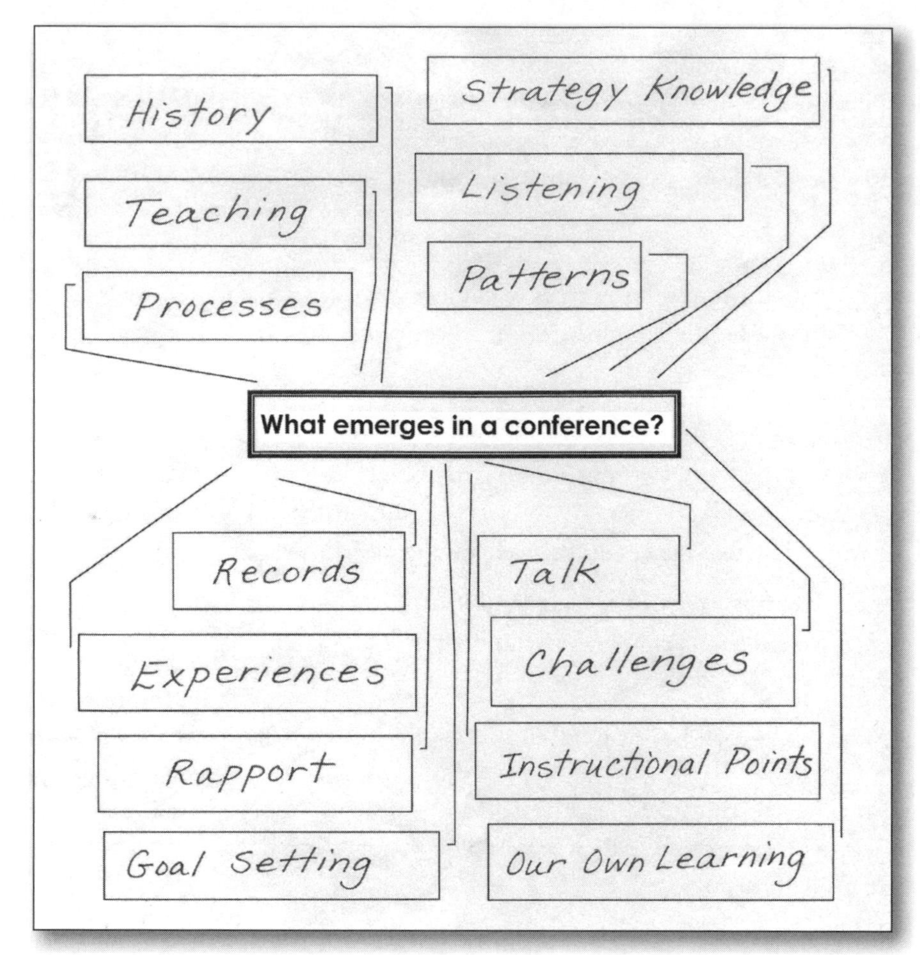

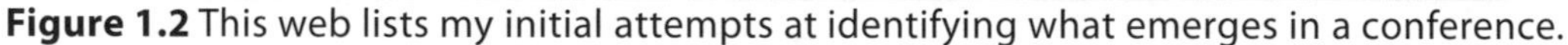

Figure 1.2 This web lists my initial attempts at identifying what emerges in a conference.

Discussing conferring, Peter Johnston writes,

> The more independent literate activity that goes on in the classroom, the easier it is to observe it, and the more consistent evaluation will be . . . The notion of *independence* is critical. Teachers obtain the most useful information in one-to-one conferences with students, and from stepping back and watching how students make choices and manage their literate activity when they are self-directed. (1997, 9–10)

So if we want to develop independence, we have to risk close examination of our own conferring practices. Here is an explanation of each of my fourteen points. After each statement and explanation you will find a few questions we might ask ourselves as we contemplate the implications of each of the fourteen ideas. Revisiting each statement helped me to clarify the statements on my web.

Strategy Knowledge—Reading conferences provide the perfect opportunity to assess and uncover students' use of the thinking strategies being taught in our crafting lessons in reader's workshop. A conference might lend itself to the pursuit of strategy application and understanding. We should listen for the language of strategies permeating our conferences.

We might ask:

- How is the conferee explaining his use of thinking strategies?
- How does the conferee explain his metacognitive process as it relates to a specific thinking strategy?
- What strategies are becoming engrained and applied? What is the proof?

Goal Setting—An outcome of every reading conference is for the reader to walk away with a plan, or goal, in mind (either one she decided upon, one chosen together, or one that you as the teacher chose). Using the gradual release of responsibility, we must guide her toward the next important step in her reading process.

We might ask:

- What goals does the conferee set for herself?
- What goals does the conferrer set for the conferee?
- What goals can be set for the whole class as a result of an individual conference?

Processes—Sitting shoulder-to-shoulder provides a perfect situation for delving into a reader's thinking and helping him describe his metacognitive stance. Looking into a reader's eyes and listening can provide the most intensive, yet unobtrusive, way to uncover specific characteristics of the reader's process, both surface structures and deep structure systems.

We might ask:

- How does the conferee describe the act of reading?
- What metaphor does the conferee create to describe his reading process?
- What does the conferee's process say about his learning style?

Patterns—Looking for emerging patterns provides us with rich assessment data. Patterns of growth or noticeable misconceptions provide us with natural teaching points. Specific patterns that emerge over a period of time provide a detailed portrait of the reader.

We might ask:

- What instructional patterns are being seen in the conferee?
- What is the conferee consistently showing the conferrer about ways her reading is changing over time?
- What growth patterns are noticeable?

Records—One of the key elements of effective conferring is being able to leave a conference with documentation (written or recorded). One of the most challenging aspects of conferring is record keeping, but it is also one of the most beneficial. Effective reading conferences can provide specific and anecdotal documentation of a reader's strengths and growth areas. Our records serve as a source of how well a reader is responding to interventions we may provide. Our records offer important assessment and evaluation data.

We might ask:

- Who are the records really for? What is their purpose?
- How will the information we gather be used? How could it be used?
- In what ways will the records be shared with the conferee? How will they be shared with others?

Experiences—When we are hoping to understand a reader's strengths and growth areas, we also have to understand a bit about his past reading experiences. What are the milestones and the paths each reader takes before we sit down with him during a conference? Our experiences define who we are, and a reader's experiences define him.

We might ask:

- How have conferring experiences changed over time?
- What characteristics are gleaned about the conferee's previous literacy experiences?
- What reading experiences did the conferee find most rewarding?

My goals are finding my way in, naming what they're doing well, and then inviting them to see themselves as smarter in some way.
Lori Conrad
Fifth-Grade Teacher

Teacher Keystone Point

Instructional Points—Instruction is paramount to every reading conference. It is our classroom instruction that changes a conversation to a conference. We use the actual conference as a tool to stretch and strengthen the abilities of each reader. We should be able to identify visible characteristics of classroom instruction living outside the conference that then meander through the context of every conference. Listening for personal application of specific skills and strategies is important to make sure the reader is making a connection to classroom instruction.

We might ask:

- What would help the conferee progress most efficaciously?
- What would challenge the reader to stretch her thinking?
- What are the conferee's next steps?

Teaching—Teaching relates to the specific point of instruction within each conference. Purpose is uncovered during the reading conference, and teaching the reader about clarifying and conscientiously defining his purpose is crucial. Within a reading conference, we limit the "teaching" to the task at hand without overwhelming the reader.

We might ask:

- What is the conferee's purpose? Who is the decision maker?
- What does the conferee need from the conferrer at that moment?
- What is one thing the conferee will leave the conference with and be able to apply immediately?

History—We gain a historical perspective of the reader during each conference. Throughout the year, over time, we add to the reader's history. We look for chronological improvement and an explanation of growth over time. We challenge each reader to reflect about her progress and developmental milestones.

We might ask:

- How does this conference compare with previous conferences?
- Have any negatives transformed into positives over time?
- What historical perspectives are being gleaned about the conferee as a reader?

Listening—We must learn to listen. Listening is the fundamental frame of reference in a reading conference. The more time we spend listening, the more time the conferee spends talking. The more the conferee talks, the more clarity we have about his reading strengths and growth areas.

We might ask:

- Who does most of the talking? What are we talking about?
- When should the conferrer jump into the conversation?
- How does the conferee explain his thinking or understanding? What does the conferrer hear?

Talk—Talk about process and talk about content lie at the heart of each conference. Talk relegated to question/answer leads to bland, unproductive conferences. Talk rich in both deep and surface structure language contributes to the depth of the conference. The conferee's talk is of utmost importance.

We might ask:

- What are the reading "words" or "sense of language" evident in the conference?
- Who does most of the talking?
- How can we extend the talk from the conference into the classroom?

Rapport—Conferences are preeminent when a sense of trust and tone of respect permeates the classroom. If there is little sense of community, it is harder to make conferences work. Building rapport from the get-go is the key to composing sessions that allow for reading conferences to occur and thrive.

We might ask:

- What did the conference reflect about the conferrer's rapport with the conferee?
- What did the conversation reflect about the relationship between the conferrer and the conferee?
- What issue of trust needs to be further developed or explored?

Challenges—Like every ritual and routine, conferences have their share of challenges. The question is, What is in place to allow the unexpected to happen? When we are ready for challenges, we are able to deal more effectively and efficiently with specific teaching of the reader. We have to recognize that we will face challenges as we learn to confer.

We might ask:

- How do we handle conferences that seem to slip away from our intended goals?
- What outlets do we establish for conferees who are struggling?
- What challenges might we expect? What might we face as we confer with students?

Our Own Learning—We need to put ourselves in the position of the conferee. What are the types of situations we like to engage in as a reader? When we have a conversation about our reading, we want it to be authentic, natural, and nonthreatening. We want to better our reading lives by interacting with other readers. How we learn to navigate text and how we build understanding should be reflected in our interactions with readers in our classrooms based on our interactions with *our* learning peers.

We might ask:

- How does the conference impact the conferrer's learning beyond the short time we are together?
- What is the conferrer learning about his own reading process while he's talking with a student about her reading process?
- What is the conferrer getting better at doing? What are continued areas of growth in relationship to conferring?

Reread the statements on your web. Are there any you would change immediately?

After you have settled on your final fourteen, go back and write brief statements describing each of them; just a sentence or two or three.

PONDERING: How would you characterize each of the descriptors on your web? What questions might you ask about each descriptor?

Now, go back and add a few questions to each statement. See if you can add more specificity to your deliberate thinking and understanding by identifying your curiosities and wonderings. The questions can guide you as you reflect on each statement and descriptor. The purpose is not to create a list of questions to ask as you confer. However, your questions might be a helpful added step and lead to specific questions you might ask students. When I wrote my questions, I tried to think specifically about the reader.

Where Do We Go from Here?

In the next chapter, I explore more specifically my "coming to know" conferring as a key instructional practice in my day-to-day reader's workshop.

I have thought about conferring a lot. I have practiced it a lot. Conferring takes time to explore, time to practice, and time to reflect upon as a conferrer. Coming to know conferring has been a journey, but when you spend time and intention on an instructional practice, the benefits are well worth the effort. I have had to define my beliefs about conferring, become mindful of what reading conferences offer my students, and think about the specific attributes of day-to-day life in the classroom that allow conferring to flourish—to become a keystone.

Student Keystone Point

I leave you with a piece written by one of my former students. Clearly, ten-year-old Sara has personalized strong beliefs about herself as a reader, many honed and strengthened by the individual conferences we shared. Sara's words describe the type of reader I believe all children can become—she worked hard at it!

I have changed as a reader in tons of ways. Way back in July I came in as a reader who only knew how to predict, question, and read words basically. Now I can infer, determine what's important, gather clues, come away with an Ah-ha, etc. Mr. Allen made this change in my life of reading for me. I think it's a very good change too. I can now read a book without saying "What was this book about?"

The strategy I use the most is giving my opinion about the text. If I were to go over my reading responses there would probably be my opinion in almost every one. For example [if the book said], *Thomas said it was his and his grandfather's business to know why Aunt Linzy didn't get married.* [I would think] "I OBJECT your honor! It is not grandfather's nor Thomas' business." In my life I usually give my opinion. I think I'm starting to write like I talk. Writing like you talk is a special thing only a few people can do. It is like talking to animals when no one else can.

My attitude toward reading is a wall that won't break. It's straight and tough. When meaning breaks down the love of reading keeps the wall standing. Imprinted on the wall are strategies and the words I love to say, "I love reading!"

My reading is like a pirate's love for gold. He searches for the perfect map. Starts exploring. Gets confused somewhere along the trail. Finds his way back and sometimes finds his treasure and sometimes is lost in the underground ocean.

My reading life is like this—a pirate loves gold and I love books. He searches for the perfect map; I search for a perfect book. He gets confused and lost; I come to a part I don't understand. He finds his way back and I *understand.* Sometimes he never finds his way, but I always find true meaning in a book. That's just reading.

When we confer with students, we're not standing above them or even leaning over, we're sitting right beside them, shoulder to shoulder. We're digging deeper now, working hard to individualize our instruction and support children as they apply what we've taught them in large- and small-group settings.

—Debbie Miller, 2008

My favorite time of reader's workshop is when you sit down and talk to me. It's like you really care. You listen. I feel important. You and Mr. Rushmore are both "book guys" and I think I'm gonna be one too.

—Nick, Third Grade

Chapter 2

Conferring Goals and Guiding Principles

Not long ago, I was sitting with my friend and colleague Randi Allison, having coffee at a favorite coffee shop. We often meet to chat about family and friends, learners and learning.

I have worked with Randi for more than twenty years, and she's one of the people I most trust. Don Graves tells us, "If you have even one colleague with whom you can share ideas, readings, and questions, you can draw from that enough energy to maintain your motivation and ability to grow professionally" (2002, 9).

Randi is one of those energy-giving people. She and I don't always agree, but I always know that when I leave one of our conversations I will leave with a bit more energy.

On this particular day, we were talking about a former student's latest accomplishment and sharing recent children's literature finds from our local bookstore. We were laughing about the antics of our family members. We were enjoying the panoramic view of the Rocky Mountains in the distance. It was an unusually springlike winter's day, and we were basking in the Colorado sunshine. (Where else can you sit outside in February, catch rays, and see snow-capped mountains?)

I was telling Randi about the writing some friends and I had completed. I was telling her that I was revisiting some initial writing I started several years ago and how I was ready to tackle it, but I was still having some trouble finding my focus. I told her my editor thinks it's quite possible I "think too much." I was rambling. She was listening.

As our conversation continued, the topic turned away from my writing to one of our retired teaching friends, Lois, who was receiving yet another round of cancer treatments. Randi said, "Remember Lois's classroom? You always knew what she believed. When you walked into her room, you always knew she was there for children. You just sensed something special. She had one purpose in her classroom—to challenge her students' thinking." I nodded in agreement.

Lois was amazingly tough, but not in a boisterous, gloves-on, ready-for-the-ring way. She was more reflective and determined. Quiet. Humble. Honest. Real. At the ready.

When Lois was teaching, she fought for children. Always refining her practice. Always looking through an insightful lens. Always sharing her fresh thinking with others.

Later, after leaving the classroom, her toughness turned to taking on mutant cells, probes, tests. Same strength, different focus. Lois had the uncanny knack of focusing in on the positive, even to the end. She fought the good fight, first for her students and then for herself and her family.

As a beginning teacher, I remember sitting in her classroom watching her teach, wondering if I could ever connect with my students the way she did. In Lois's classroom, the focus was always on children and their learning in whole group, small groups, or as individuals. It was Lois's interactions with individual students—those times she sat down one-on-one with learners—that left an indelible mark in my mind. Interactions that were authentic, thoughtful, and rich. So individualized.

In the midst of our talk, I gazed off for a moment, thinking about Lois and her determination.

PONDERING: Think about a teacher who has influenced you. What was it that made an impact on your teaching?

Out of the blue, Randi looked at me and asked two questions that almost blew me out of my chair. She posed, "What are *your* guiding principles? What are *you* willing to fight for?"

I stared at her. Dumbfounded.

For twenty-plus years Randi and I have learned together—about readers, about writers, about thinkers. And, although our conversations often focused on lines in the sand and philosophical underpinnings, this was the first time a colleague had come right out and specifically asked me those questions.

I stared at her for a moment longer. Still dumbfounded.

She stared back. I knew she was expecting a response. Her body language told me that she wasn't going to turn her attention to anything else until I came up with an answer. She turned to face me and leaned in a bit. She looked me in the eyes. She waited. I knew she wouldn't let me off the hook. I gave her my standard answer: "I don't know."

"I hate when you say 'I don't know'!" she replied. "Because I know that you *do* know. What do you think?" She waited again, looking me directly in the eyes. She'd heard my pat answer before.

I thought for a moment.

"Wow, Randi. This feels like a job interview. Those are tough questions. How would you answer?"

"I asked you first!" She waited.

"You sure did," I thought to myself. I rattled off an answer about every child being a learner, authenticity in the classroom, the necessity of using a workshop structure, thinking strategy instruction, the importance of building community. I thought that if I gave her an answer, any answer, she would accept it and we could continue with our coffee and conversation.

"You should really think more about those two questions!" she responded. "It's something we should all think about. It's something that we don't think about enough. But if you're going to do more writing, you really should be able to answer them!"

> The more I confer, the more I trust my ability to listen.
> Cheryl Zimmerman
> Seventh-Grade Teacher
>
> Teacher Keystone Point

When I got home I sat down at my keyboard and typed out Randi's two questions—in bold red ink. I printed them and taped them above my computer screen. And those questions hang there today.

What are *your* guiding principles?
What are *you* willing to fight for?

Every time I check an e-mail, I read those two questions. Every time I type a letter to my students' parents, I read them. Every time I take a book off my bookshelf, I read them. Every time I sit down to write, I read them.

Guiding Principles Worth the Fight

Randi's two questions haunt me! I thought of taking them down, until I started thinking about why they haunt me.

I have let them linger, and I have been mulling them around since that February day. The questions Randi asked gave me energy. They gave me the energy to make purposeful decisions about what is important to my teaching. I left that coffee date slightly confounded. Catch and release. Randi reminded me of my father a bit!

Since that time, I've come to identify several of my guiding principles. And conferring is one of them: the strength, power, and necessity of conferring in the reader's workshop.

Randi's grilling stretched my intellect to new depths. Together, we reflected a bit, she challenged my thinking, and I left with a plan lingering in my mind. Randi had demonstrated the perfect conference for me.

Of course, Randi wasn't sitting beside me focusing on a piece of text. We weren't discussing a cueing system. We weren't focusing on the use of a particular thinking strategy. She didn't bombard me with a thousand questions (just two really important ones). But, Randi had taken me through the very process I use with the readers in my classroom. She empowered me to think about my own learning.

Conferring is a keystone of effective instruction. Without conferring, my reader's workshop flounders. If I do not have time each day to meet one-on-one with readers, I don't have a clear picture of each reader and who he is becoming as a reader. It is a key instructional strategy that strengthens the community of readers. My "conference" with Randi became a critical aspect of rethinking my long-shelved writing project.

With the help of my colleague Lori Conrad, I've come to realize that conferring:

- Mirrors rich conversations
- Shepherds developing readers and writers
- Provides an authentic context for ongoing assessment and responsive teaching

Why Confer?

Teaching is the art of changing the brain.

I don't mean controlling the brain, or rearranging it according to some "brain manual." I mean, creating conditions that lead to change in a learner's brain. We can't get inside and rewire a brain, but we can arrange things so that it gets rewired. If we are skilled, we can set up conditions that favor this rewiring, and we can create an environment that nurtures it.

An art, indeed!

—James Zull, 2002

When I read this quote, it made me ponder the important role conferring plays in my reader's workshop. As a conferrer, it is my role to create the conditions necessary to help readers adapt and develop their own skills and strategies as they explore text. It's my role to nurture students to think through text using strategic problem solving. It's my role to create the situations necessary for learners to think about the metacognitive moves they make as they grapple with the intricacies and nuances of text. It's my role to have students understand the importance of "reading with meaning" as well as developing specific skills that allow fluent readers to adapt their flow depending on their purpose for reading.

It is my shepherding that helps students define themselves as readers. I want our conferences to mirror the conversations I have with my peers as we talk about our reading. At the end of a conference, I want to have some documentable data to support a reader's growing understanding. We both have an important role in the conferring process.

During reader's workshop in our classroom, there are four ultimate goals for my students:

1. I want readers to *understand* more clearly.
2. I want readers to *remember* more completely.
3. I want readers to *extend meaning* more consistently.
4. I want readers to make their reading experiences *memorable* more often.

Beginning on the first day of each school year, I start familiarizing students with these statements. Our early crafting sessions in reader's workshop center on these concepts.

I want students to realize from the beginning of the school year that reading is more than just barking at print, getting each word correct, being fluent without attaching meaning to the text. I want students to know that choosing books should be more about their purpose than mine. I want them to know that, as readers, they can slow things down—students should be afforded the time to go deep into a study of a thinking strategy in a variety of text. I want students to understand that their depth of thinking inevitably makes them better readers, writers, and thinkers.

Conferring helps me get deep thoughts out and share them.
M.H.

Student Keystone Point

Our beginning crafting sessions also focus on the question, What does it mean to be a wise reader? (see Figure 2.1). Notice that I don't say "good" reader. I want my students to know that even readers who struggle periodically (and who doesn't?) can be wise. All readers can make wise decisions about what they read, about what they're thinking about as they read, and about the choices they can make to get better. I wrote a quote in my notebook once that reads, "Knowledge is gaining and storing information. Wisdom, on the other hand, is knowing how to act on that knowledge."

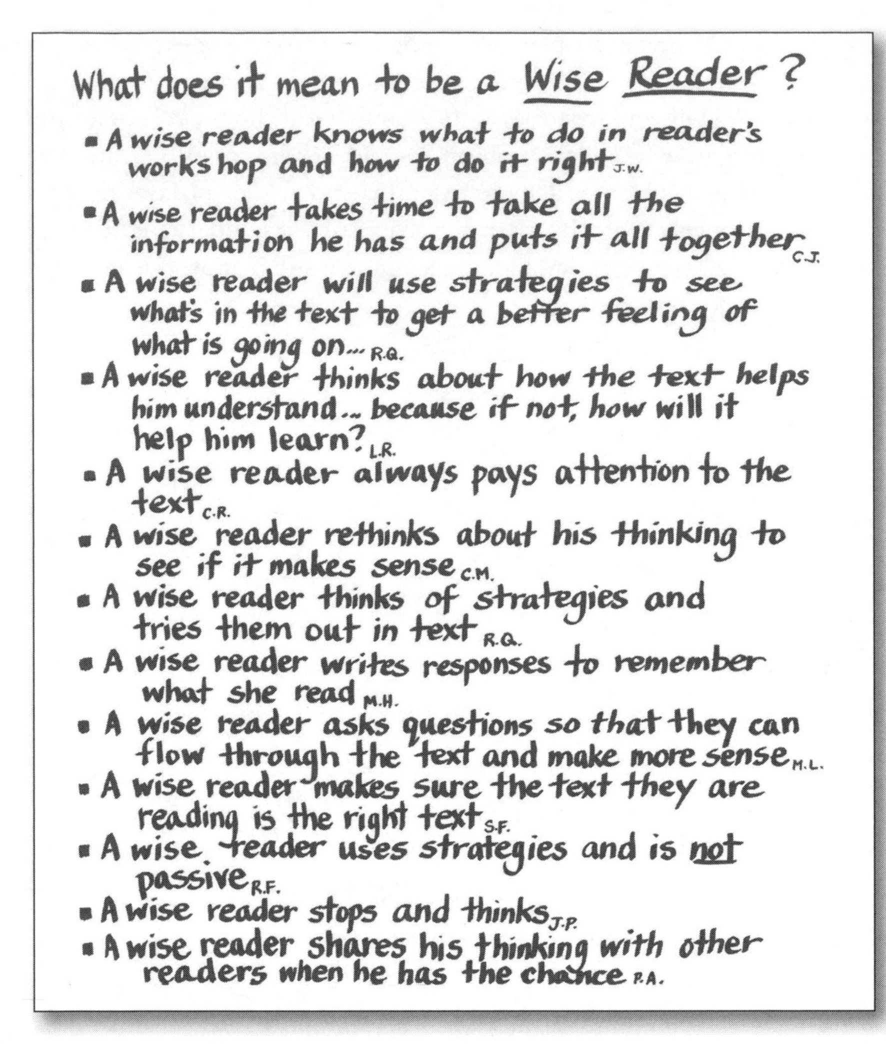

Figure 2.1 Students' beginning-of-the-year thinking about what it means to be a wise reader

That's what I want students to do as readers, to realize and understand that reading is an active meaning-making process. When I sit down to confer with a reader, I want our time together to be productive, authentic, and relevant.

Fortunately, I can start talking to my students about rich thinking early on in the school year because Troy Rushmore, my second-grade teammate, sends students to me already well grounded as readers and writers. A colleague who speaks "the same language" ensures that students will have a strong grasp of the intricate underpinnings of workshop structures (crafting, composing, reflecting), which provide the framework for classroom discourse: students will know how to make wise book choices; students will have some experience identifying and varying purpose and audience; students will have strong thinking strategy knowledge; students will have a toolbox full of ways to respond to text; and students will come to me knowing how conferring works.

PONDERING: What do your students bring with them as readers? How could you go about finding out?

Troy and I have worked closely over the years to develop a collegial relationship grounded in talk about students and their learning. We've come to believe that whatever he can do to strengthen literacy rituals and routines with his second graders can't help but strengthen the rituals and routines used in my third-grade classroom.

When I called my third graders to the carpet for one of our first gatherings of the year, one of my students looked up and said, "You know what, Mr. Allen? I was a little scared about coming to third grade, but when I walked into the room I realized there was nothing to be scared about. Your room and Mr. Rushmore's room feel so much alike. It feels like we're gonna be diving deeper in the same pool." (This is a metaphor Troy and I both talk about with students—about taking our learning deeper rather than dog-paddling along the surface.)

When I asked my students to write to me a bit about how they feel while working in our classroom, Scott wrote about the classroom environment. He wrote, "Mr. Allen's and Mr. Rushmore's rooms are kind of the same. And they don't have the big lights on—they have perfect lights right now. They have so many books (which I love)."

"Being a part of a community is special to me because I will not be lonely. Being a part of community feels great, I have a family that loves me," Mason wrote as he explored the idea of community.

Marlee said about the classroom environment, "What helps me work better is that all of the lights are off and I feel better with them off and just having the lamps. All of the books make me feel good because I just don't have to pick one or two books to read, I get to read different ones. With all of the books and other things that just makes me feel good because that means that I'm being taught right."

And, that is exactly what I want my students to understand, that learning is about continuity, not starting over. That the environment, the sense of community, and the instructional practices between classrooms can and should be similar. But more important, students know that I'll be doing my best to understand who they are as readers. Students come to know I will help them develop a "sense of agency" in their learning—helping them discover useful strategies and engaging them in how to learn (Johnston 2004, 8). That I'll be helping them dive deeper into an already rich pool of rigor and learning. Individual conferences are one of the most effective ways I've found to accomplish these goals.

I think Katie Wood Ray described this notion brilliantly in *Study Driven: A Framework for Planning Units of Study in the Writing Workshop* (although she was talking about writers, it also applies to readers):

> One thing we've realized is that depth in writing [reading] work is made possible more by what stays the same year after year than by what is different from grade level to grade level. When students encounter

> whole new ways of doing things every year, whole new stances to teaching and learning, whole new notions of what writing [reading] means and what writing [reading] is supposed to be when it's good, it takes a long time to get anything very meaningful or deep because there is so much time spent wallowing in the newness of it all.
>
> Whenever I think about this, I can't help but picture scenes from the book and movie *Holes* where you can see the young boys surrounded by all their shallow holes. There is no way for the boys to dig deep, to dig, say, to China, because every day they have to start digging a new hole. I think this is what is happening to a lot of children in schools. Every year they start digging a different hole in a different classroom with a different agenda, so they can only get so far before they have to start all over again. Imagine how different it would be if each year, students could continue digging into the same "hole" they dug into the year before? Imagine the depth they would find in their work as the years of digging deeper went by. The challenge, of course, is for whole schools of teachers to agree on what hole should be dug. (2006, 183)

Digging the Hole Deeper

Because students are used to many familiar rituals and routines, our discussions at the beginning of the school year can focus on these four questions:

1. What does it mean to *understand*? As readers, what does understanding look like?
2. What does it mean to *remember*? As readers, what might remembering look like?
3. What does it mean to *extend meaning*? As readers, what might extending meaning look like?
4. What does it mean when something is *memorable*? As readers, what does memorable look like?

These four questions become principles that guide our reader's workshop conversations—as we craft, compose, and reflect as readers. These concepts become the common ground, or red thread, of our learning—as we learn as a whole group; as we meet in small, interest-based groups; as we meet one-on-one in conferences. Ron Ritchhart describes the red thread as "a metaphor to connecting, binding, and uniting" or "finding a central commonality across different situations" (2002, 181–182).

Our discussions, no matter what thinking strategy we are exploring, boomerang to one of these four concepts. And, because students know about being "wise readers," this new language helps dig the same hole a bit deeper and strengthens our commonalities.

The time we take to explore these four concepts is really about focusing on their purpose as readers. As students begin to define *purpose* for themselves, they can filter their thinking through remembering, understanding, extending meaning, and making reading experiences memorable.

And how better to reinforce these concepts than through effective, individual conferences? Conferences in which I can nudge students to take a different learning stance while continuing to define themselves as young readers. Conferences in which students build on their previous experiences as readers.

PONDERING: What are your goals for your readers? What guides your instruction? Do you have a red thread that connects reading experiences?

Learning to Confer

Like my conversation with my father, Randi's "What do you think?" did exactly that—it made me think. And, it made me realize that conferring and the ability to confer is a crucial and often neglected component in reader's workshop.

I don't specifically remember learning to confer. It is a practice that I discovered early on in my career and something I've tried to improve each year. I do know it has taken hard work, practice, and reflection.

One of my first exposures to conferring was in November of 1987 when I attended a workshop by Donald Graves given in my school district. Ellin Keene worked as a literacy specialist in our district at the time and arranged for Don to meet with selected teachers from throughout our district. Prior to the workshop, Don sent us a letter asking us to prepare for our time together. In the letter, he asked us to:

> Conduct some interviews with children about literacy and learning. Choose three children whom you would call low, middle, and high ability in your room, or a room you have selected. Interview these three children and ask them to respond to the following.
>
> - Tell me about learning to read. How did you do it? What do you need to know how to do in order to be a good reader?
> - Tell me about a good reader in this room. How does he/she read? How do they do it?

- Tell me about some books you've read. Are the books in here? You can get them if you like (if this is convenient). Tell me about two of your favorites.
- Tell me about learning to write. How did you do it? What do you need to know how to do well in order to be a good writer?
- Tell me about a good writer in this room. How does he/she write? How do they do it?
- What do you plan to read next? What do you plan to write next?
- What do you think you need to learn next in order to be a better reader? Better writer?
- Would you please tell me how people learn in this room? Please take me around the room and tell me how people use the various items in the room. What are some things you can do on your own? Some things that you can only do with the teacher or with his/her permission?
- Tell me about something you know a lot about. That means that people come to you and ask you about it. It may be something you know that's outside of school, or inside school.
- Tell me about someone who knows a lot about one subject or thing in this room. That means that people come to that person to find out about it, or they just know a lot about it.

Donald ended his letter with the statement, "I am hoping that these interviews will open the door for discussion about the literacy learning of the children and us. Children's perceptions about literacy and how our rooms function will be useful information to us all." The letter goes on to say, "Be sure to start your journal by writing down what the children say in response to the questions they are asked. As close as you can record the actual words used by the child, the data you have will be more useful to you."

Now, here I am, more than twenty years later, realizing that that letter was the nudge I needed to sit down and talk to children about their thinking—to open the door. In 1987, Don was asking me to confer, gather "data" and information, and discuss literacy learning. He was asking me to sit down with my students and talk, shepherding them as developing readers and writers. He was asking me to develop an authentic context for ongoing assessment. He was teaching me how important it was to get to know the learners in my care.

Those initial interviews helped me realize that sitting down one-on-one with a child had to become a natural part of my reader's and writer's workshop. I knew then that with practice I could expand conferring into the reader's workshop. And, I've been doing it ever since.

It was Donald Graves who, in the same workshop, said, "It is the learner's perception of who they are and what they can do that has the greatest effect on what they learn." Isn't it amazing how that quote holds true today?

When I first began to confer with readers, I remember having a laminated list of questions with me as I talked to them, conferring checkpoints if you will (see Figure 2.2). It was a

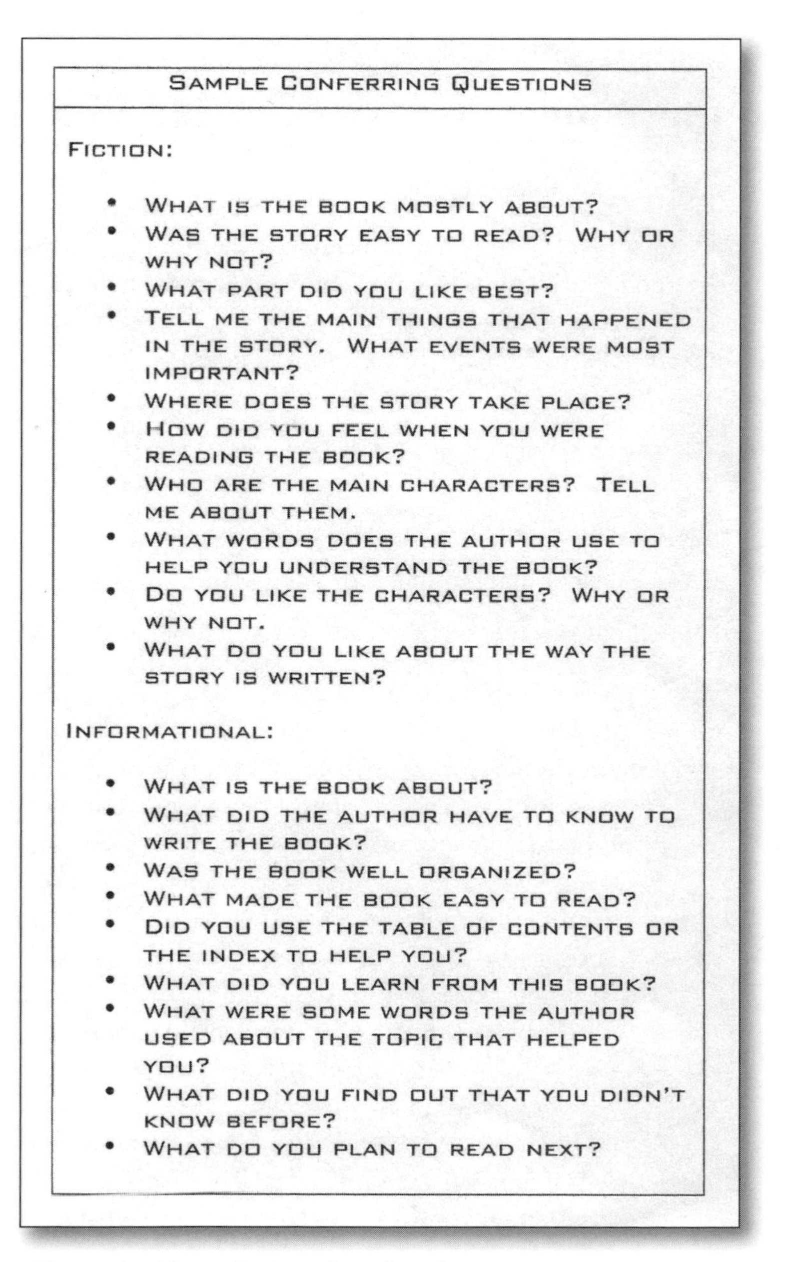

SAMPLE CONFERRING QUESTIONS

FICTION:

- WHAT IS THE BOOK MOSTLY ABOUT?
- WAS THE STORY EASY TO READ? WHY OR WHY NOT?
- WHAT PART DID YOU LIKE BEST?
- TELL ME THE MAIN THINGS THAT HAPPENED IN THE STORY. WHAT EVENTS WERE MOST IMPORTANT?
- WHERE DOES THE STORY TAKE PLACE?
- HOW DID YOU FEEL WHEN YOU WERE READING THE BOOK?
- WHO ARE THE MAIN CHARACTERS? TELL ME ABOUT THEM.
- WHAT WORDS DOES THE AUTHOR USE TO HELP YOU UNDERSTAND THE BOOK?
- DO YOU LIKE THE CHARACTERS? WHY OR WHY NOT.
- WHAT DO YOU LIKE ABOUT THE WAY THE STORY IS WRITTEN?

INFORMATIONAL:

- WHAT IS THE BOOK ABOUT?
- WHAT DID THE AUTHOR HAVE TO KNOW TO WRITE THE BOOK?
- WAS THE BOOK WELL ORGANIZED?
- WHAT MADE THE BOOK EASY TO READ?
- DID YOU USE THE TABLE OF CONTENTS OR THE INDEX TO HELP YOU?
- WHAT DID YOU LEARN FROM THIS BOOK?
- WHAT WERE SOME WORDS THE AUTHOR USED ABOUT THE TOPIC THAT HELPED YOU?
- WHAT DID YOU FIND OUT THAT YOU DIDN'T KNOW BEFORE?
- WHAT DO YOU PLAN TO READ NEXT?

Figure 2.2 My preliminary list of conferring questions

good strategy for me as I embarked on this notion of "interviewing" readers. But it didn't last long (in Chapter 4, I'll describe the conferring format I've developed). The questions weren't horrible, but what I discovered was that the predetermined questions were vague, content and structure driven, floating on the surface, typical "answer at the end of the chapter" questions, and contrived. There was no inquiry. There was no passion. There was no purpose. I was trying to teach the reading rather than the reader.

Honing Conferring as a Thinking Routine

I've been trying to improve my reading conferences ever since. I came to realize that conferring with readers is truly an art. As I've sat beside students over the years to iron out the language, the structure, and purpose of conferring, it has become apparent that our reading conferences don't depend on us taking the lead. We don't have to ask a thousand questions. We have to encourage students to develop the capacity to take the lead in their conferences. After all, who are they for?

In his book *Intellectual Character: What It Is, Why It Matters, and How to Get It*, Ritchhart says that to identify thinking routines, we must ask these three questions:

1. How are ideas discussed and explored within this class?
2. How are ideas, thinking, and learning managed and documented here?
3. How do we find out new things and come to know in this class? (2002, 93–94)

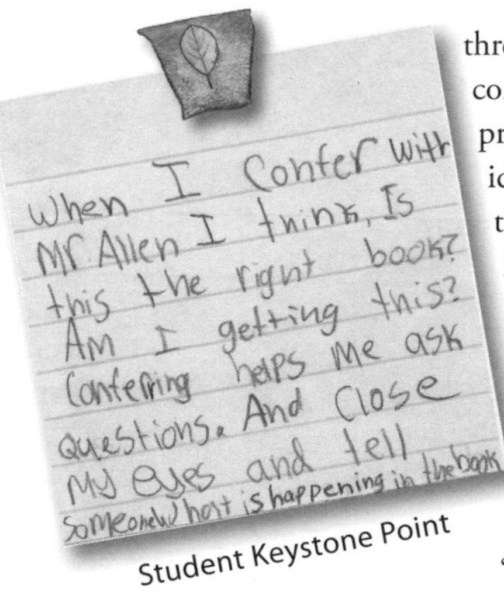

Student Keystone Point

When I filtered the notion of reading conferences through these three questions, it occurred to me that conferring can and should be considered a nonnegotiable routine in our classrooms. Conferring provides an opportunity for my students and me to discuss and explore ideas together—everything from word-level strategies used to uncover the meaning of unfamiliar words to understanding how sensory images can deepen a reader's understanding of text. Conferring helps me uncover a reader's learning in a manageable, thoughtful way while leading to documentable data—everything from how he or she is determining the attributes of a character's emotions to how book choice is affecting the reader's understanding of the text he or she is reading. Conferring helps me find out new things about the reader and provides an intimate opportunity for a shared "coming to know"—everything from the variety of texts a student chooses to his or her burgeoning understanding of how the life cycle works during a read of nonfiction. Conferring naturally becomes a thinking routine that is valued and appreciated by both my students and me.

Recently, I asked my students to write to me about the classroom, conferring, and our learning community. In the following narrative, Sydney reminded me of just what an important thinking routine conferring is:

> Mr. Allen's room is my favorite. I like the dim lights because they're calm and peaceful so I can think better. He has lots of different reading level books so I can find a book that fits just me. He really teaches us to think deep down into the text and infer and determine so many other things. It's not just reading on the surface of the book.
>
> When my teacher talks to me I learn. You have to give him all your best thinking. Show him how smart you are. Everybody is smart in their own way, so don't be afraid to stand out in a crowd!
>
> We really fit together as a classroom. We aren't afraid to share our thinking with each other. We all make connections with other people's thinking. Whenever someone shares their thinking it sets a spark in someone else's mind and they add on their thinking and that's how they make a connection!

Why Should We Confer?

A visitor to my classroom once asked me, "Why should we confer? Why is it so important? Why do you choose conferring over small-group work?"

I wrote the following passage in my notebook later that evening as I pondered his questions:

> *Conferring is the keystone of my reader's workshop. I find that when I sit down with a reader, I'm better able to get a handle on his/her emerging understandings and thinking than I am when I work with a small group. I love the shoulder-to-shoulder, eye-to-eye commitment that we make to one*

another during each and every conference. There's something special about making discoveries, hashing out thinking, wondering . . . together. It's the kind of moment that I want my own children to have with their teachers, the kind of moment where nothing else in the world matters but the reader. The kind of moment where a teacher listens. It's that important. I venture to guess that if we all spent a little more time getting to know our students as individuals, we'd have a lot less trouble getting them to do the hard work we're asking them to do. It's my line in the sand. It's my favorite time of the day.

Since then, I've come to believe that I confer:

- ◐ To uncover a reader's *attitudes*—what students think of reading and themselves as readers
- ◐ To discover a reader's *stamina and work ethic*—how students manage their reading lives
- ◐ To explore a reader's *process*—how students go about composing as readers
- ◐ To record a reader's *diet*—what students choose to read and why
- ◐ To form a relationship of *intimacy and rigor*—how students are interacting with text
- ◐ To gather data for *assessment and evaluation*—how students describe what they know and are able to do

What are *your* guiding principles?
What are *you* willing to *fight* for?

PONDERING: Why do you think it is important to confer? What would you add to this list that's missing?

I am so glad Randi asked me these questions. I think I've begun to answer them.

When I asked my colleague Missy Matthews about conferring with young readers, she said:

I think conferring with young readers sets the stage for how we define "understanding." This is the chance we have to show them that our thinking is what really matters. And, each and every one of their thinking matters. We can only do this by conferring.

> I find myself thinking aloud to model the language I would use to describe my thinking more with younger readers. When I do this, I make sure to ask if they'd like to see how another reader (or writer) might talk about his/her thinking or whatever I'm demonstrating. I want them to still be in charge of the conference, even if I think aloud a bit.

In order for our conferences to matter, they must become one of the principles that guide our instruction. If we want students to "define understanding" or "remember details" or "extend their thinking" or "make their reading experiences memorable," we have to provide an opportunity each day for this to happen with the readers in our workshops who are there waiting . . . waiting for us to guide them as readers. To encourage them to dig the hole a little deeper.

PONDERING: Think about your own conferring. What's your historical perspective as a conferrer? What are you thinking about now, or differently, that you were not thinking about before?

Traditional classrooms are like corn fields. The farmer plows the whole field at one time. One type of corn is planted with a standard distance between the rows and between the seeds within the rows. Every row receives the same amount of fertilizer. Each plant should look about the same and will be harvested at the same time. A very simple structure.

My classroom is more like a prairie. The grasses, insects, mice, and hawks coevolve. Each species is dependent on countless others and also on soil and climate. A prairie is difficult to establish, but in place it endures—a very complex structure.

—Mark Wagler

(quoted in Mooney, Mooney, and Holt 1996)

Community means to have ownership. We have time. We have thinking strategies. We have reflecting. We have conferring. We pause and consider. We say "What do we need to do and what is our purpose?" We have our brains to work.

—Kelly, Third Grade

Chapter 3

Building the Environment for Conferring— Five Requisite Ashlars

Have you perused a teaching-oriented bookstore or the exhibit hall of your state's annual literacy conference recently? I have. Each time I walk up and down the aisles, I spot at least twenty surefire resources guaranteed to help expedite the creation of the classroom environment or community, many seemingly promising certain automaticity to the process. Titles often read something like *Creating a No-Nonsense Literacy Workshop*, *101+ Activities to Make Your Workshop Work*, or *Classroom Communities Made Easy*. Titles jump out at us with shiny, graphically designed covers. Many have a red apple insignia glaring from the cover (to remind us that we are teachers perhaps).

We read the words *fast, simple, proven*. And, if you are like me, you're *almost* tempted to stop when words like *easy* or *guaranteed* or *foolproof* jump out at you in bold print and bright colors. Dangling carrots. But, like me, hopefully you're seldom fooled into spending $19.50 for a book that will end up collecting dust on your shelf or sell for 50 cents at your next tag sale. Rather, you remember it's nonsensical to think that any resource can instantly create classrooms we work so hard to develop—especially if it's marketed to be fail-safe.

Like you, I have learned, and know, that creating a "culture of thinking," a classroom way of life in which literacy learning thrives, is not uncomplicated, foolproof, or fast. Creating a culture of thinking, in which all members develop a sense of trust and safety, is hard work and, like the prairie ecosystem, sometimes difficult to establish without persistence, patience, and practice.

Conferring helps make sure I am doing what we talk about on the floor and to understand what I'm doing as a reader.
L.R.

Student Keystone Point

Over the years, I've been fortunate enough to spend time in some amazing classrooms—classrooms where conferring with readers takes on an important and prominent role. Take our friend Debbie Miller. Perhaps you've seen the photographs of her classroom in *Reading with Meaning* and said, "I want to learn in that classroom." Debbie explains to us how she masterfully created the learning environment for her students. The photographs do not do her classroom justice. It was absolutely one of the most beautiful and literate places. The interactions Debbie had with her students were always purposeful.

Take my colleague Cheryl Zimmerman. Cheryl's students understand the importance of literacy learning, and the routines she and her students have developed are flawless. There is something about the feeling in her classroom that causes anyone who has spent time watching her and her students work together to wonder, "How could I do that with my students?" There is a true sense of "children first."

Take my teammate Troy Rushmore. I step into his classroom and watch him interact with his students always with amazing depth. In his classroom, thinking takes precedence over ordinary, run-of-the-mill tasks. Troy's is a classroom where children feel safe and honored. His work with his students piques my curiosity each time I pop my head in or sit, listen, and watch him work.

Take my Wyoming pal Dana Berg. Dana teaches first grade in Casper, Wyoming, and walking into her classroom is like taking a breath of fresh air. There is something about the environment that she has created that makes me stop and just look around for a moment; I want to breathe in the warmth. It is a serious place to learn tempered with beauty.

And, I have tried to make sense of it. What do these amazing teachers do to create the types of learning environments in which all students can learn and prosper?

Debbie taught me that beauty and organization are essential. If we want our classrooms to be places that reflect our intentions, we have to be purposeful about how we set up our environment. And, it was not just the physical beauty of her classroom, but also the inner beauty created by listening in as Debbie sat down to talk with a child about his reading. The interaction.

Cheryl teaches me that a quiet voice, sincerity, and passion are critical. Listening to Cheryl's teaching reminds me how the language we use with children elicits deep thinking. She is precise, soft-spoken, and chooses words that reflect clarity. The language.

Troy teaches me that we must be trustworthy and sincere in our work with our students. He plans his reading instruction based on his daily interactions with readers. Troy reminds me that quirks should be honored, depth can be reached, and kindness is contagious. The honesty.

Dana teaches me that classrooms should honor and value children as "little people" (her favorite term). Dana stretches her students' thinking to extraordinary limits simply by "putting it out there" for them to explore. She allows children to "play in the sand" with thinking before asking them to build sand castles around a specific thinking strategy. The hope.

These four classrooms serve as mentor classrooms for me. Each teacher inspires me. A sense of intimacy floats between teacher and students. Inquiry and rigor permeate each teacher's interactions with his or her students. There are certain commonalities—rituals and routines, language, structures—that strengthen the foundation of learning. Consistent structures are in place to provide time for conferring, purpose for conferring.

Should we not spend some time in the classrooms of colleagues we want to emulate? Should we not ask ourselves, "What are they doing that I might be doing in my classroom?"

Although my classroom ultimately reflects my beliefs, there are bits and pieces of learning from Debbie, Cheryl, Troy, and Dana (and many other mentors) breathing in my classroom that further allow thinking to thrive. And, while I consider all four teachers as mentors, I have nudged them a bit along the way too.

I like to keep the environment simple. In my classroom, there are spaces for readers to work, an organized classroom library, and walls covered with fabric and bordered with "kid-made" borders with lots of blank space ready to hold student thinking as the year progresses. There are certain constructs serving as mortar to hold the workshop together. Spending time with teachers like Cheryl, Troy, Dana, and Debbie nudges me to keep learning, to keep improving my craft. In my classroom, children are encouraged to remember, understand, extend meaning, and make reading experiences memorable. Most important, spending time with Debbie, Cheryl, Dana, and Troy enhances my understanding of the importance of conferring as an instructional keystone.

PONDERING: Which colleague(s) do you want to emulate, to learn from? What will you do to create learning opportunities with that person?

Isn't that the best way to learn? Not by purchasing flashy, surefire programs, but by using "mentor classrooms" to apprentice ourselves to the colleagues we trust most. If we spend time learning from one another, we can observe the interactions, listen for the language, hear the honesty, and relish in the hope.

Creating an environment in which students can thrive as thinkers relies on my interactions with fellow teachers. What sits at the heart of everything I do: authenticity. I remember hearing Shelley Harwayne once say to look at everything we do through "the lens of authenticity." Identifying the key elements and behaviors necessary to create a workshop that is predictable, yet flexible, is time well spent. Strong cornerstones allow reading conferences to thrive and develop.

Thoreau said, "Let your affairs be as two or three, and not a hundred or a thousand" (2005, 46). It has been important for me to identify the essential rituals and routines that help students learn and grow as scholars. An effective classroom, particularly a well-running, workshop-oriented classroom, requires a lot of preparation and planning at the forefront. The results are worth the time and effort. We can, and should, strive for the types of learning environments where complex things can prosper and develop over time, but that are not so bogged down with clutter, rhetoric, and mandate that students are not afforded the opportunity to achieve success.

A lot has been written about instructional settings that work—what it takes for a classroom to run smoothly, effectively, and efficiently. Some educators refer to it as community, some educators refer to it as voice, some educators refer to it as environment. Whatever the designation, we need to identify the essentials in which we couch our thinking and our students' thinking. If we want to have time to confer, and confer well, we have to create environments rich in ownership, stamina and endurance, and independence.

PONDERING: Think about the environment of your classroom. What works? What doesn't? What would you like to change this year?

The Thinking Strategies and Conferring

The overarching umbrella of my work is the thinking strategies outlined in other professional books like *Reading with Meaning* by Debbie Miller; *I Read It, But I Don't Get It* by Cris Tovani; *The Literate Kindergarten* by Susan Kempton; *7 Keys to Comprehension* by Susan Zimmerman and Chryse Hutchins; *Strategies that Work* by Stephanie Harvey and Anne Goudvis; and of course, *Mosaic of Thought* by Ellin Keene and Susan Zimmerman and *To Understand: New Horizons in Reading Comprehension* by Ellin Keene. In *Put Thinking to the Test* (coauthored with Lori L. Conrad, Missy Matthews, and Cheryl Zimmerman), we explored an inquiry study of how the thinking (comprehension) strategies relate to the types of thinking students do on standardized tests.

Throughout the school year, my students and I do in-depth thinking strategy studies, spending four to six weeks on each strategy. My students learn to ask questions; create mental images; draw inferences; synthesize new learning and ideas; activate, utilize, and build background knowledge (schema); determine the most important ideas and themes; and monitor for meaning and problem-solve when meaning breaks down.

The thinking strategies provide a framework for my instruction, and I plan my year around them. They provide the underpinnings for my instruction. My work with the Public Education and Business Coalition based in Denver, Colorado, has helped me put the thinking strategies into practice in my classroom. This book focuses on the keystone of conferring, not on strategy instruction. However, without the language of the thinking strategies floating through the classroom, conferring would seem less relevant. It is the language of strategies that I hope my students will use independently in their reading, and this language is uncovered during reading conferences.

The cognitive strategies, behaviors if you will, guide my teaching. They serve as a filter for my interactions with children and as a stronghold of my instruction. Throughout this book, I will refer often to the strategies themselves.

PONDERING: Are you familiar with the thinking behaviors themselves? To what degree? Where will you go to find out more about them?

When I open my classroom to visitors, they see strategies at work in reader's workshop. The strategies remind us that "talk is the sea upon which all else floats" (Britton 1970, 164)—during whole-group crafting lessons and in individual conferences. But I've realized thinking strategy instruction involves more than asking questions, making a connection, deciding on a theme, and so on.

Like Troy, Cheryl, Dana, and Debbie, my classroom reflects my philosophical underpinnings, and thinking strategies play a major role. But to encourage the conferring conversations I have with children during the reader's workshop, there are other factors worth investigating.

I believe that before we start talking about the thinking strategies themselves (or any other reading skills) with students, we have to have several factors operating in our classroom. We have to slow down the pace a bit and get some other balls rolling. For conferring to be a natural part of my classroom, I have identified five instructional ashlars:[1]

- Defining Trust, Respect, and Tone
- Strengthening Endurance and Stamina
- Discussing Purpose and Audience
- Exploring the Gradual Release of Responsibility Model
- Focusing on the Structure of Reader's Workshop

---

1. An ashlar is a building stone cut more or less true on all faces adjacent to those of other stones, permitting very thin mortar joints. Dressed stonework was used in ancient Greece and is still used by bricklayers and stonemasons today.

As my students and I plan and improve the inner workings of our literacy workshop, exploring these five elements is well worth the effort. As you read about these five *ashlars*, please keep in mind the following quote that Lori Conrad and I developed while planning an inservice on reader's workshop:

Authentic rituals and routines

lead to

committed, proficient, independent readers and writers

while _false_ rituals and _artificial_ routines

lead to

classroom mindlessness and uninspired,

dependent readers and writers.

Ashlar 1: Defining Trust, Respect, and Tone

I have identified three notions as strong bulwarks in my classroom. Conversations with my students reflect these three principles.

The notion of *trust*.

The notion of *respect*.

The notion of *tone*.

Naturally, intense work happens as the year progresses to constantly strengthen a climate of "rigor, inquiry, and intimacy" necessary for effective literacy work. I believe that a sense of trust, respect, and tone can ensure that my classroom is primed and ready for literacy learning to flourish.

How? Weeks before the school year begins, I spend time exploring my insights around these three principles. I consider the physical aspects of the classroom that will provide the best opportunities for authentic interaction. I dwell on specific rituals, routines, and constructs that best support my students' growth as readers and thinkers. I read or reread the work of other mentors such as Donald Graves, Shelley Harwayne, Ellin Keene, Franki Sibberson, Karen Szymusiak, Debbie Miller, Katie Wood Ray, Don Murray, and Cris Tovani; I talk to my peers; I revisit notes and anchor charts from previous years; I write in response to my thinking in my notebook.

I identify my role and my students' roles in our shared "coming to know." I identify the ways in which we can develop our interactions with text and how our response to each other will structure the work we do throughout the year. Perusing one of my writer's notebooks, I discovered the following reflection:

> *Today I started to talk to my kids about tone, trust, and respect. These three ideas have been floating through my mind for the past few weeks. I just reread Ralph Peterson [Life in a Crowded Place] and my mind has been racing. Such a wise man. I realized that we, I, jumped in too fast. We need to slow things down.*
>
> *I decided we have to stop and contemplate these ideas again, together. I'm asking my kids to work as wise readers and we haven't spent enough time talking about what it should sound like, look like, feel like . . . I think our discussion is going to lead to a much more effective workshop . . .*

What I have discovered since jotting that entry in my writer's notebook is that spending time exploring these concepts with my students does lead to a shared coming to know. Trust, respect, and tone meander through the ins and outs of the framework of the workshop itself—whether it be as readers, writers, or mathematicians. Each construct has its specific function.

I continued to explore each of these notions in my writer's notebook; here is what I discovered:

The Notion of Trust

Trust is a definite hallmark. If we expect students to honor the thinking they do for themselves and the thinking they do for those with whom they have relationships, we have to assume that, given opportunities to respond to one another, trust will become the vanguard of our interactions. I want students to have confidence in, and reliance upon, the other members of the classroom. I want students to behave responsibly and honorably when classmates are sharing thinking—in pairs, in small clusters, and during whole-group interactions. A literacy workshop cannot function without trust. Trust in the classroom ensures that great care will be exhibited in classroom interactions. Trust is the sieve through which our interactions [student to text, student to student, student to teacher] are filtered. Trust leads to fellowship. Fellowship leads to effective conferring.

The Notion of Respect

Respect is paramount. Classroom interactions must be melded with consideration and thoughtfulness. I want students to naturally create recognition of their unique abilities and notice the abilities of others in the classroom. As they interact with each other, I want students to be considerate and thoughtful members of the classroom. Respect in the classroom ensures individual points of view will be honored—in whole-group interactions, small-group interactions, and when conferring. I value the commonalities and diversities of each member of the classroom. Respect can be thought of as the appropriate interactions that merge thinking collectively among peers. Respect leads to reverent response, particularly one-on-one talk.

The Notion of Tone

Tone is fundamental. As individuals, why and how we say something in response to those with whom we learn serves as an indicator of our attitude toward the thinking and feelings of fellow learners. As members of a literate community, the tone that permeates our literacy workshop can dictate an individual's willingness to become an active learning participant. I want students to realize that the tone of the literacy workshop determines how well the workshop functions. I want students to notice the distinction tone plays in the midst of conversations and interactions with one another. A productive tone in the classroom ensures our workshop will function more fruitfully. Tone can be thought of as the plainsong that permeates the workshop, the subtle nuance or quality that provides the backdrop for our workshops. Tone allows time to confer to become a reality.

PONDERING: What comes to mind when you think of the notions of trust, respect, and tone as they relate to your classroom? How would you define each construct?

Development of Trust, Respect, and Tone

Defining these three notions is fairly concrete, simple. But how on earth do we help our students internalize trust, respect, and tone as mainstays in our workshop? How do we infuse the magnitude of each so that they become seamless aspects of the classroom itself? I have come to realize that classroom conversation at the forefront, and throughout the year, is key!

My students gather around the park bench in my classroom, sitting as a group in the carpeted gathering area. Our first few gatherings are met with typical beginning-of-the-year apprehensions about third grade. I choose to wrap each notion around student apprehension.

We discuss each notion, over a period of days, trying to relate each to real-life situations or trying to create a metaphor in which each notion can manifest itself meaningfully. Our initial discussions naturally evolve into clarification of the behaviors we can draw upon throughout the year. They are grounded in talk and conversation—especially during reading conferences. The following guiding questions can serve as a springboard to discussions about trust, respect, and tone.

Guiding Questions to Elicit the Notion of Trust

To develop a sense of confidence with one another, our beginning workshop conversations might begin by delving into questions like the following:

What does it mean to trust someone?

How do you know when someone trusts you as a learner?

Think of a time when you knew that you were trusted. How did that feel?

Think of someone you trust. What qualities do they have that allow you to trust them?

What kind of "talk" happens when you are with someone you trust?

Guiding Questions to Elicit the Notion of Respect

To develop a sense of esteem for fellow learners, critical to the function of our workshop, we might explore the following:

What does it mean to respect something?

When your parents say, "Be respectful," what do they mean?

Who is someone you respect? How did they earn your respect?

What kind of language do we use when we are showing respect for someone else?

Think of something that you've done to encourage respect. What were the actions that made that happen?

Guiding Questions to Elicit the Notion of Tone

The overall feel of our workshop induces the most productive and lasting work if we take the time to chat about the following:

What does it need to sound like when you're working as a reader or writer?

Think about a classroom in which you felt you were an active member. What did it sound like, look like, feel like?

When someone walks into our classroom during reader's or writer's workshop, what would you like them to notice?

How will we talk to one another? What should that sound like? What language are we going to use?

Describe a classroom that "feels right" to you. What are the qualities it has that make it feel that way?

The questions themselves can be explored in a variety of ways. They can take the form of a notebook entry, using the question as a springboard for an initial "quickwrite" (Rief 2003, 8)—writing for ten minutes, in-depth about one topic. Gathering students at our feet, reader's/writer's notebooks in hand, we pose a question and spend time reflecting in our notebooks (building fluency as writers).

Everyone writes. The rules are simple: (1) your pencil must be writing words on the page (I used to say, "Your pencil should be moving," but you can only imagine how kids define *moving*) and, (2) you shouldn't stop until time is up (a colleague taught me to say, "Please finish the word or thought you're on and then look up at me"; this gives students the sense that we're never "done" and that they can always come back to their writing after we have left the gathering area to work independently). Sometimes a seed is planted that serves as fodder for later writing.

During our crafting session, sometimes we simply jot down our thinking on a 4-by-6-inch lined sticky note or a sentence or two on a small sticky note, a brief synthesis of our thinking. I often collect students' sticky notes and attach them to an anchor chart that lives as part of our ongoing study, and I use them to assess their understanding of our discussions. But more important, I use their comments as a door into their cognition during initial reading conferences early in the year.

My father always said, "You can't talk about nothin' if you want people to listen." He was right. Giving learners a chance to jot down their thoughts and sharing those ideas teaches children three things:

1. My thinking is important enough to write about.
2. My thinking can lead to rich conversation.
3. My thinking is valued.

Our beginning conversations lead to a classroom where a scholarly feeling evolves, mutual respect develops, and communal trust lasts. Our beginning conversations during reading conferences allow me to further develop each of these notions.

Significant Physical Aspects of the Environment

Defining the concepts of respect, trust, and tone encourages me to begin to contemplate specific attributes of the classroom, again the "lens of authenticity." It is with that phrase in mind that I ask myself the following questions as I strive to create the environment in which our thinking and learning are to be nurtured.

◐ If someone walked into our classroom, who would he or she say owned it?

I want my students to take ownership in our workspace, to know that it is our classroom, not just mine. I am careful to place my area in a distant corner of the room so that there is more room for students to move about and so that their desks and workspaces take prominence. Although I make logistical decisions about where furniture is placed, there is always opportunity to change. I want every visitor who comes into our classroom to sense that the room belongs to learners. If our students have a sense that the classroom belongs to everyone, it encourages community and adds depth to the types of response that occur.

When Mr. Allen confers with me it helps me focus better on my text. It helps me use new strategies in my reading. It helps me get more important things out of my text.
AD

Student Keystone Point

◐ What needs to be in place for the room to function effectively?

I think about the format of the workshop. I think about the setup of our classroom library (poetry in purple baskets, nonfiction in red baskets, fiction in blue baskets), and our system for finding appropriate text to read. I think about areas in the room for students to gather as a whole group or in small clusters and where they will work independently (and where I will sit when I confer with them). I think about how we will make the decisions necessary to have a smoothly running workshop.

◐ Have I added a personal touch?

My students know me well. Ask them now and they can tell you which book I'm currently reading, my current writing project, my plans for the weekend, my family stories . . . and they know because I believe it is imperative that I invite them to get a glimpse into my life. They see pictures of my four kids. They notice the colorful placemats under book baskets, the lamps, and the strings of lights above their work areas. My friend Chryse Hutchins says, "It is more than just lamps," and I agree. It is the lamps and more! Personal touches set a milieu of comfort.

◐ Is this a room that I would want my own children to be a part of?

I never thought about this question before I was a parent. Now I think about it all the time.

Often when I'm sitting with my students, gathered around the chart paper or the document camera projecting a piece of text we're working on together, I wonder if my son Jens is being asked to gather around his teacher to contemplate a particular thinking strategy or to discuss the qualities of a wonderfully written piece of text, or I wonder if my daughter Lauryn is listening to a lovely book by Patricia MacLachlan and being asked to mull over a memory it sparks or a sensory image it creates. It is with the eyes and ears and voice of the teacher I want my own children to have, that I interact with my students, especially as I sit with them one-on-one.

- Will the room be conducive to silence or conversation?
  Silence is not always golden. The types of interactions that allow for mindful work sometimes have a buzz about them. Sometimes percolating thought requires silence, time to think, time to ponder—an idea, a text, or a concept. Sometimes allowing a thought to percolate requires quiet interaction through conferring. I want our classroom to offer times of silence and times of talk. Learners need both. A student needs time to shape his or her thoughts in order to respond wisely.

- Does the room look like a teacher supply catalog blew up? Is there room for learning to grow?
  Our room has blank space on the walls strategically placed throughout the room. Rarely will you find a poster supplied by our local teacher supply center. My funds are better spent purchasing books. Besides, I do not think students pay attention to posters that say "How to Choose a Good Book" or "Ten Things That Readers Need" if they come prelaminated with a circle of cartoonlike children holding fake books. Rather, I think that the language and the thinking that adorns our walls should be that of the children. And, it takes time. I never feel the need to fill the walls with "stuff" until we've had the time to bring it together as a group of learners. The walls should be a public display of their ideas.

- What will times of movement look like—chaos or calmness?
  Logistical, I know. But often I have visited classrooms where there was no area to gather as an intimate group on the floor without clamoring to move desks and tables away. I stand at my door and peruse the room and look carefully at the route to the pencil sharpener, the route to the writing paper, the route to the various sections of the classroom library. When I say, "Friends, it's time to meet me in the gathering area," or use music as a transition, I don't want a stampede. I want the classroom to flow so that learners can work diligently and purposefully. I want the classroom to flow so that students meeting in book clubs can move calmly without disruption. I want the classroom to flow so that students can meander. Chaos leads to unproductive time; unproductive time leads to ineffectiveness.

- How low can you go? How are materials arranged?
  I try to put things in the reach and view of children. I learned this lesson from my mother-

in-law; she absolutely despises walking into someone's home seeing pictures hung so high you have to crane your neck to look at them. "Eye level, eye level, eye level"; I have heard her say it more than once! The same should hold true for our classrooms. If it is meaningful information, students should be able to see it easily. If students are encouraged to revisit previous learnings on charts you created together, they are more apt to reuse them while working independently if they are hung more at their level.

◐ Is an authentic literacy atmosphere the focal point of the room?
Shelley Harwayne once said she hates walking into a classroom and seeing the wastebasket first. She wants to see books. What's more authentic than baskets of books? That is what I want people to notice when they walk into my classroom. I love when visitors say, "Where did you get all these books?" I love when visitors notice the charts in the classroom as evidence of the mindful work we do as readers or writers. I love when visitors comment on the "real" feeling they get when they walk in the door. If we encourage authenticity, we are apt to get more authentic responses during our conferences.

◐ What would my wife say if she walked into the room?
This is one of the most important questions I ask myself. My wife, Susan, is an educator and tends to be a bit more blunt with me than my colleagues. When she asks, "Have you thought about moving that bookcase there?" or "Do you think that's a good spot for that table?" she causes me to reflect. Because she's the person who knows me best and whose opinion I value the most, I often try to predict her reactions before her first visit to my classroom each year. She is the one who taught me that books needed to be organized, labeled, and accessible. She is the one who taught me that purpose is everything; if it does not have a purpose, do you need it? She is the one who taught me that a classroom that is calm and appealing serves as an invitation for students to share their thinking more readily.

◐ Does the room reek of "cute" or reverberate thinking?
Thinking is hard work. Cuteness isn't. If someone walks into my classroom and says, "That is so cute!" I immediately ask myself about thoughtfulness. If someone is observing me teach and says, "Your kids are so cute!" I immediately ask myself about thoughtfulness. If someone says, "That is such a cute idea!" I immediately ask myself about thoughtfulness. I don't want my classroom to mirror strong evidence of the quality of "cuteness." I want my classroom to reverberate with a sense of thinking.

◐ When they walk in the classroom, do my students get a feeling or sense of responsibility, ownership, and awe?
I love the word awe. *In our classroom, I want to have a positive spin, more a sense of "Ahhhhh!" and even of reverence. I want students to walk into the classroom knowing that*

they will be asked to think hard, to work diligently, and to know that scholarship coupled with thought is at the forefront. They have to take ownership and responsibility in the learning community.

- Why? How come? So what? Goodbye?
  These last questions speak to the "stuff" that we tend to collect as teachers. Is there anything more disdainful than the doldrums of having to fill in a worksheet that has been copied for so many years that it is barely legible? Get rid of it! Clear out old files and cabinets. Ridding ourselves of "stuff" helps keep our classrooms organized and productive.

To further build a sense of trust, respect, and tone, I think about the following criteria: Ownership, Exploration, Demonstration, Time, Response, and Belief. These are all aspects important to encourage an environment full of trust, rich in respect, and judicious in tone. If I want thinking to sustain itself over a long period of time, across many workshops (and if I want this thinking to surface regularly during reading conferences), the following foundations are essential:

Trust, Respect, and Tone: Essential Foundations

Ownership: The learners in our classrooms need to be discerning about . . .	◐ The materials they choose to read and write ◐ Their use of time ◐ The strength of the community and collegiality
Exploration: The learners in our classrooms should be regularly investigating . . .	◐ New and enhanced learning ◐ Authentic contexts and experiences ◐ Behaviors of thinkers
Demonstration: The learners in our classroom should habitually be observing . . .	◐ Models of effective thinking ◐ The practice of the "craft" of thinking ◐ A variety of social settings
Time: The learners in our classroom should be lingering and dwelling . . .	◐ In fodder that takes them a "mile deep" ◐ With the ability to "muck around" ◐ In situations that extend thinking behaviors
Response: The learners in our classroom should be receiving regular feedback . . .	◐ About what they *can* do ◐ With opportunities to reflect ◐ During formal and informal invitations to share
Belief: The learners in our classroom must be entrusted . . .	◐ To stick with a task over a period of time ◐ To use their literate occasions wisely ◐ To think deeply

Ashlar 2: Strengthening Endurance and Stamina

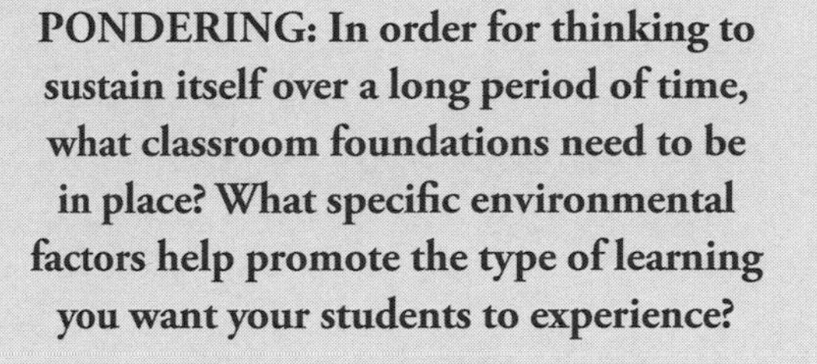
PONDERING: In order for thinking to sustain itself over a long period of time, what classroom foundations need to be in place? What specific environmental factors help promote the type of learning you want your students to experience?

I look at the photo in Figure 3.1 and laugh. I've seen that look on so many people's faces. That look of "Help me!" When I show it to my friends, we laugh out loud. We've all felt that way, ready to give up. We've all seen our students with that same look too. But it's our job to strengthen stamina and build endurance in our students.

My friend and fellow educator Jim Becker is a marathon runner. He just turned fifty and will soon run in his fiftieth marathon. He is one of the most focused, stamina-filled people I know. Give him a bike with a square wheel and he will ride it until it's smooth and to his liking. Recently I asked him about his passion for running, "What motivates you to put your body through this? Why do you run like you do?"

He answered, "I run for many reasons. I run so I don't have to buy a new wardrobe. I run because I think it will save money in health care. I run so that I don't feel so guilty when eating an old-fashioned doughnut. I run because I am all alone for thirty to forty minutes, and I can think, pray, ponder, plan, problem-solve, laugh, and sometimes cry. I run because it feels good when I'm done. I run so that I can see things that few people are awake to see, like shooting stars and the red fox in the neighborhood. I run because it is an accomplishment just to get out the door. I run so that the discipline of running carries into other areas of my life. All these things keep me engaged and lacing up my shoes every morning at 4:45 A.M."

Figure 3.1 Riding a square-wheeled tricycle is no easy task.

"Have you ever felt like giving up? How do you keep that stamina going, race after race, day after day?" I asked.

"Oh yeah. The races that particularly test my stamina are the ones in which I have fallen apart. In Boston in 2007, it was a windy, rainy, horrible race day. In fact, it was almost canceled; no one had ever seen such poor conditions. Darned nor'easter, but the race went on as scheduled. At mile twenty, something went wrong. No reason. I just ran out of gas, and I've never forgotten that moment. No way was I not going to finish the Boston Marathon! So . . . I slowed down even though my body wanted to stop right there. In a time like that, a runner wills his body forward, thinking one step at a time, one light post at a time, one block at a time. If you think about there being six more miles in those conditions, you can easily just step off the course and lie down. But, I finished the race. Not pretty, but I finished."

"How do we build stamina and endurance to become wise readers?"

It is early in the school year and I write this question on the chart tablet. With students gathered at my feet, I share two quotes I have also written on a chart:

Endurance and to be able to endure is the first lesson a child should learn because it's the one they will most need to know.

—Jean-Jacques Rousseau

It's not just the home runs, but stamina, the way the game is played. Little things don't matter—speed, stealing bases . . .

—Joe Morgan

"These two quotes really caught me eye. Follow along as I read them to you. I'll read them once for your head. Now take just a minute or two to reread them to stick them in your heart. Take your time and think about them for a moment. Choose the one that strikes you the most." As students read the quotes, immediately two hands shoot up in the air.

I add, "If you're dying to talk or you'd like to respond, please open your notebook, write down today's date, and jot yourself a few notes. We'll give everyone a few minutes to think before we chat."

I open my notebook and begin to jot down my thinking. From the onset of the school year, I want my students to know that I will never ask them to do something I'm not willing to do myself. As I glance up, I notice several students writing a quote down in their notebook. Some students are rereading the quotes. Some students are watching their classmates and me, noticing that we are taking this task seriously, and they begin to jot down some thinking in their notebooks.

For most of my students, *stamina* is a familiar term. They have learned about it previously. In second grade, they investigated and synthesized things that "Build Stamina" and things that "Break Stamina Down" as readers, writers, and thinkers (see Figure 3.2). They understand that in order for wise work to occur as readers they've got to strengthen and increase their stamina. They understand the importance of having a purpose, having their "tools" at the ready, and finding a just-right place to work as readers. Especially during composing time, this type of "knowing what to do" enhances the venue for conferring.

Their earlier work with stamina leads perfectly into our third-grade study of endurance.

"Boys and girls, tell me what you're thinking."

My students take turns sharing their experiences with stamina:

"Last year, Mr. Rushmore talked to us about stamina a lot," Alex says.

Stamina

The ability to do something or "carry on" for a long period of time.

What builds our stamina?	What breaks down our stamina?
~ trying it out...thinking, how would this work for me?	~ not trying, not attempting.
~ carefully thinking about your needs–knowing your needs.	~ not knowing your needs or knowing them but deciding to ignore those needs.
~ knowing or figuring out your next steps.	~ not knowing your next steps.
~ gathering all your tools.	~ not thoughtfully gathering your tools... work, get tools work, get tools.
~ finding a wise place to compose.	~ finding a place to work... then moving, moving again.
~ knowing your purpose then making decisions.	~ being a passive learner–not caring.

Figure 3.2 Second graders in Troy's room create a "Stamina" chart. They determine what builds stamina and what breaks it down.

Jack adds, "Yeah, whenever we were working we'd look up at our chart whenever our stamina was low."

"We spent time talking about it. Almost every day we'd hear Mr. Rushmore say, 'Boys and girls, check your stamina.' And we did," Mackenzie interjects.

"I'm glad you know so much about stamina and what it does for you as learners," I say. "During the next few weeks, we're going to spend some time talking about endurance." I write the words *Learning with a Spirit of Endurance* on a chart. "This year, we're going to spend some time investigating this idea of endurance, which means the same as stamina, but we'll look at it through a different lens. It's a synonym. Let's see if we can figure out what else it might mean."

"A synonym is a word that means the same thing as something else," Jaryd says.

"You're exactly right. A synonym is a word that means the same thing as another word. Like meanings. Let's focus on these three words—*learning*, *spirit*, and *endurance*." I underline them on the chart. Together, my students and I brainstorm synonyms for each word (with very little teacher input, I might add) and here's what we come up with:

Learning: discovering, understanding, changing, knowing, exploring, reward, looking, passing on, thinking, trying, remembering, listening, focusing, coming to know, choice, growing, experimenting, sharing.

Spirit: enthusiasm, joy, energy, outlook (positive), belief, trust, pride, excitement, happiness, passion, bursting, sharing, purpose, vigor, trying, praise.

Endurance: stamina, fortitude, strength, stick-to-it-ness, willingness, fight, not giving up, taking risks, courage, agility, powerful, bravery, honor, skill.

Our initial chart shows me that my students do have a lot of background knowledge flowing through their minds. What if they didn't? This would be a perfect time to share some of my ideas. Listing just a few synonyms and leaving it at that . . . using our chart as a growing list as our study continues. Returning to it often so that students' thinking fills it.

I learn that my students definitely know the essentials of stamina. "I can tell you know a lot about stamina already. This year, we're going to name it 'endurance,' and for the next week or two we're going to try to figure out what it actually means for us to *learn with a spirit of endurance* and how we'll bring that learning into our workshops as readers, but also as writers, mathematicians, and thinkers. How's that sound?" Then, after brainstorming and recording a list of Reader's Responsibilities (a laminated chart we change each day) for composing time, my students set about doing their reading work. I set about conferring.

The next day, I hand each child a 3-by-5-inch sticky note. "For the next couple of weeks, our crafting lessons will focus on this idea. We're going to be listening for 'signs of stamina' or 'signs of endurance' together. These sticky notes are for you to collect your thinking. Each day we'll get a new one and we'll discuss the 'signs' we uncover. We're going to be looking at several texts. When we're finished, we'll pull all our thinking together."

I begin our study of learning with a spirit of endurance by reading Jennifer Armstrong's book *Spirit of Endurance: The True Story of the Shackleton Expedition to the Antarctic*. My students are excited about this book from the moment I hold it up. There is something intriguing about the cover (the book is oversized, and its cover has a dramatic painting of a small ship being tossed about in the white-capped waves), and relating this book to our study of endurance makes the idea of endurance more meaningful and relevant. Keeping the gradual release of responsibility in mind, I use this text as the first opportunity to do a think-aloud (I am not expecting too much jotting on the sticky notes, but want students to have a means to record their thinking from the onset of our study—I have discovered that when students have a place to record their thinking they are more invested in the conversation). This text sets the course for our study of endurance.

As I read, I stop periodically to identify excerpts from the text that indicate a sign of endurance for me as a reader. I notice, "Right here it says, 'he was determined to set a new Antarctic record: to lead the first-ever trek across the frozen continent' [p. 3]. That's telling me that he has determination, a word I would use to describe endurance" or "'For weeks, *Endurance* navigated through a crazy patchwork of ice' [p. 9]. I'm wondering if *time* has something to do with endurance—they are willing to spend a lot of time on this mission."

PONDERING: How does conferring encourage stamina and endurance? What is the connection between developing stamina and having time to confer with students during reader's workshop? How do you build a sense of endurance in your readers?

As I continue, I stop to share my own thinking and invite students to turn to the person next to them and share the notes they have taken or the words they have heard that lead to a sense of endurance. I am building discourse—the same language that I will use with students as I confer during their reading is the same language we use during crafting. And, although our crafting is not focused on a particular thinking strategy or "reading" skill, I am demonstrating how readers think inside their heads as they read, I am demonstrating talk and the language readers use when they have text-based conversations, and I am giving them a window into the idea of endurance (which they hopefully will synthesize into their own reading experiences).

When we finish reading and thinking together about *Spirit of Endurance* (which takes more than *one* crafting session), I ask my students to share their discoveries, and we create the chart shown in Figure 3.3.

Our study of endurance continues for the next week or so. During each crafting session of reader's workshop, I introduce another text that deals with the topic of endurance.

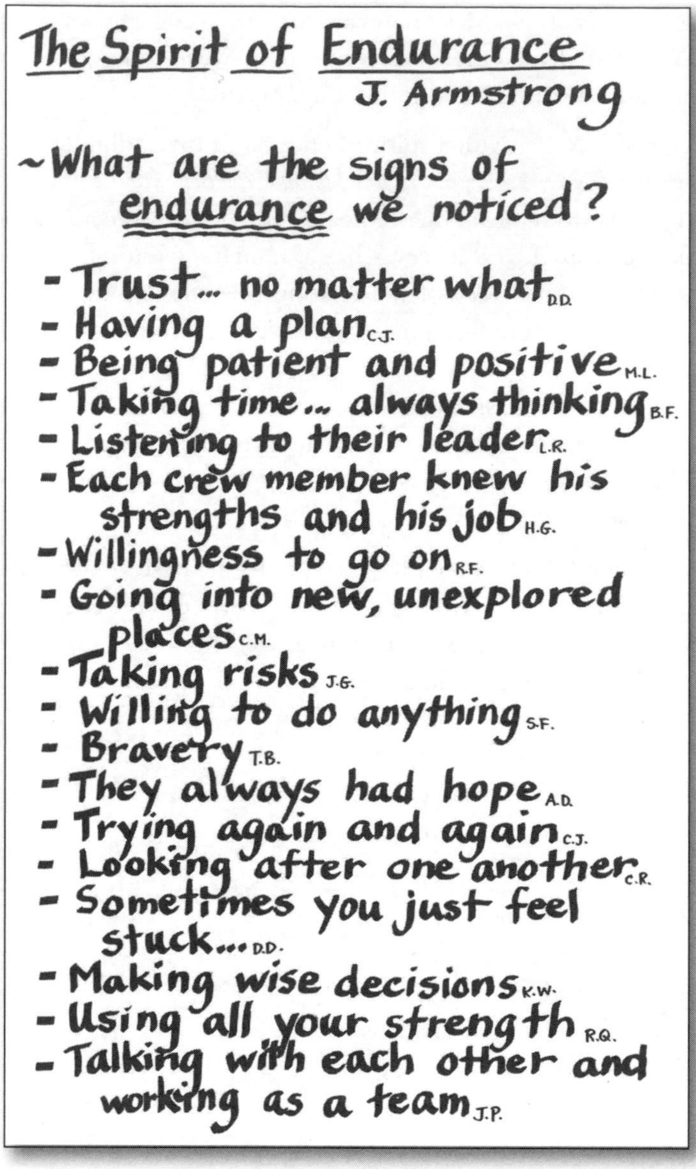

The Spirit of Endurance
J. Armstrong

~What are the signs of endurance we noticed?

- Trust... no matter what D.D.
- Having a plan C.J.
- Being patient and positive M.L.
- Taking time... always thinking B.F.
- Listening to their leader L.R.
- Each crew member knew his strengths and his job H.G.
- Willingness to go on R.F.
- Going into new, unexplored places C.M.
- Taking risks J.G.
- Willing to do anything S.F.
- Bravery T.B.
- They always had hope A.D.
- Trying again and again C.J.
- Looking after one another C.R.
- Sometimes you just feel stuck... D.D.
- Making wise decisions K.W.
- Using all your strength R.Q.
- Talking with each other and working as a team J.P.

Figure 3.3 The signs of "endurance" that students noticed and identified

The following are a few examples of titles we investigated and documented on charts during our study. I have listed the title and some of the "signs of endurance" students noted during each read (specific words from the text, ideas they surmised, general thoughts, and so on):

Winners Never Quit! by M. Hamm	◐ If you give up, try again ◐ Support from your team ◐ Never quit ◐ Trying hard ◐ Playing every day
Odd Boy Out: Young Albert Einstein by D. Brown	◐ Thinking about one thing for a long time ◐ He wanted more information about what he focused on ◐ He thinks before he talks ◐ He let things flow and linger through his mind ◐ He did math everywhere ◐ He loves puzzlements ◐ He never quit math ◐ Always wanting to learn more ◐ He always wonders ◐ He let things linger ◐ He knew what he liked ◐ He had wonderings of all kinds
Wilma Unlimited: How Wilma Rudolph Became the World's Fastest Woman by K. Krull	◐ Trying something in front of other people ◐ Helping others ◐ She practiced even when it hurt ◐ She kept trying ◐ She'd rather do things that seemed impossible ◐ Power of concentration ◐ She forgot about her fears ◐ In a fraction of a second, she blazed across the finish ◐ Working together ◐ She believed in herself ◐ She was unlimited ◐ She competed in a "man's" sport ◐ She taught others

High as a Hawk by T. A. Barron	◐ Getting hurt, but continuing ◐ She kept going for her mother ◐ She was a young age ◐ To see a hawk ◐ Her legs moved at different speeds ◐ Leading ◐ Specific time limit ◐ Getting thorns ◐ Wobbly rocks ◐ In the dark ◐ Climb in the snow ◐ Endured weather
Walk On! A Guide for Babies of All Ages by M. Frazee	◐ Not giving up ◐ Taking time ◐ Trying to find good things about what you're doing ◐ Blocking voices ◐ Trying something you've never done before ◐ Learning how to walk ◐ Having support ◐ Taking steps ◐ Believing in yourself ◐ Letting go ◐ Beginning when you're ready ◐ Walking
Sky Boys: How They Built the Empire State Building by D. Hopkinson	◐ Bravery ◐ Willingness to work ◐ When they were finished it was the tallest building ◐ Working together ◐ Trusted one another ◐ Started in the morning and worked into the night ◐ Took shifts ◐ Never gave up ◐ Worked in all kinds of weather ◐ Overcame their fear

Two Bobbies: A True Story of Hurricane Katrina, Friendship, and Survival by K. Larson and M. Nethery	◐ Sticking together ◐ Waiting for a rescue ◐ Trying to break the chain ◐ Getting a brand-new home and family ◐ Kept trying to look for their family ◐ Going with no food or water ◐ Knew they would get help ◐ Trust
The Secret Remedy Book: A Story of Comfort and Love by K. Cates	◐ Stay at someone's house for a month ◐ Finish something before time runs out ◐ Reading something again and again ◐ Doing whatever it takes ◐ Dreaming of great things ◐ Protecting a wild thing ◐ The promise ◐ Trying to taste something new ◐ Trying new things ◐ Trust ◐ Feeding, finding, or noticing something you've never seen before ◐ Walking as far as you possibly can ◐ Being patient

After we read each book, share our thinking with one another, jot some notes in our notebook, and so on, and after we spend time learning what it means to *learn with a spirit of endurance*, I invite my students to choose three books that made the greatest impact on them as a learner and fill out a form with three columns labeled with the following (see Figures 3.4 and 3.5):

Book Title

Signs of Endurance

What these signs tell me as a learner . . .

Why? These forms give me fodder for conferring with my students during our beginning-of-the-year conferences when we are grappling with book choice, developing our endurance as readers, and so on. I'm able to bring student thinking to the conference to help guide their conversations as readers. I'm also gathering a little assessment data along the way related to our initial study of endurance.

Thinking about Endurance – Books We've Shared Name ______________________

Book Title	Signs of Endurance	What these signs tell me as a learner...

Figure 3.4 Blank Endurance form (also in appendix) used by students to synthesize our study

During our study of endurance, I try to collect a variety of texts that might enhance our investigation. Peruse your classroom library, read a few titles, and build your own collection of books that instill a sense of stamina and endurance. Some other titles I might use:

Alice Ramsey's Grand Adventure by D. Brown

The Hickory Chair by L. Fraustiano

Hank Aaron: Brave in Every Way by P. Golenbock

The Raft by J. LaMarch

A Frog Thing by E. Drachman

Just Like Josh Gibson by A. Johnson

Mr. George Baker by A. Hest

Firefly Mountain by P. Thomas

Thinking about Endurance – Books We've Shared Name Mikayla

Book Title	Signs of Endurance	What these signs tell me as a learner . . .
High as a Hawk	•riding in the dark •being led •not quiting •when it hurt her heels she just kept on going	To not quit on what I am doing as a reader. To be led into what we are working on.
Odd Boy Out	•he was focused on one thing at one time •he thinks before he says it •finds out more about what you're focused on •he was always practicing everywhere	To not give up, but find out more about something. And to think more before I say what I want to say.
Walk On!	•having support •taking time •falling down, and trying again •begin when you are ready—not when someone tells you to go.	To go when I am ready not when someone tells me to go like in writing. To take time and get some support from other readers.

Figure 3.5 Completed Endurance form; Mikayla records her synthesis after exploring several books that demonstrate and illustrate stamina and endurance.

Gleam and Glow by E. Bunting

Necks Out for Adventure: The True Story of Edwin Wiggleskin by T. B. Ering

Women Daredevils: Thrills, Chills, and Frills by J. Cummins

Teedie: The Story of Young Teddy Roosevelt by D. Brown

The Girl on the High-Diving Horse by L. High

Girl Wonder: A Baseball Story in Nine Innings by D. Hopkinson

Amber on the Mountain by T. Johnston

Keep On! The Story of Matthew Henson by D. Hopkinson

Maxwell's Mountain by S. Becker

A River of Words: The Story of William Carlos Williams by J. Bryan

Throughout our study, I have a basket of books labeled "Books About Endurance," and I invite my students to find other texts that have characters that "learn with the spirit of endurance." I also invite them to look through their own books at home for stories that might represent stamina or endurance. I want my students to discover the signs of endurance they run across in their own reading—in books, magazines, newspapers, and other texts. It is my hope that students will discover that this spirit can make its way into our reader's workshop as a result of their own investigation.

My friend Cheryl has the following John Ruskin quote in her classroom: "The highest reward for a person's toil is not what they get for it, but what they become by it" (Guthrie 2003, 19). When I read this quote, it reminds me of how important it is to help build endurance in our readers. We must focus on stamina and endurance

- if we want our students to become independent, mindful readers.
- if we believe that "Endurance and to be able to endure is the first lesson a child should learn because it's the one they will most need to know."
- if we believe that our reader's workshops should be places where conferring can thrive.
- if we want our students to become more intellectually engaged during reader's workshop and we want to have the time to spend our energy on conferring.

I end this section with my student's chart of "A Spirit of Endurance as Readers" (Figure 3.6) —the things that build it and the things that take it away. Without endurance during our reader's workshop, our conferences will waver and be less likely to be effective.

Ashlar 3: Discussing Purpose and Audience

In *Put Thinking to the Test*, my coauthors and I introduced readers to our investigation of purpose, ownership, and accountability, which we refer to as the "Purpose Triangle." In the section "Who Decides in a Workshop?" we wrote, "We've come to think of it [the triangle] as a way to represent the many decisions thinkers make, during school and across their lives" (2008, 43). We learned that "through inquiry, explicit instruction, practice, and feedback, we can help our students develop a flexible and widely applicable understanding of ownership, purpose, and accountability" (2008, 45).

Since *Put Thinking to the Test* was published, the triangle has continued to evolve. As part of our early crafting sessions, my students and I develop our understanding of purpose and audience as readers (as well as writers and mathematicians). I've also come to realize that simply by helping students become cognizant of both purpose and audience they become more flexible in how they "go after" text. My students understand that being able to adapt their

A spirit of ENDURANCE as Readers...

↑ Things that strengthen or increase ~	↓ Things that lower or decrease ~
• Keeping your purpose in mind	• Being "lazy"
• Constantly being alert or metacognitive	• Not "thinking about your thinking"
• Being flexible ~ trying new strategies	• Getting distracted from trying
• Knowing what to do at the right time	• Faking your purpose, pretending
• Focusing	• Fooling around
• Staying "in your work" and not bothering others	• Move and talk, move and talk, move and talk...
• Listening to others and to yourself	• Not listening or hearing
• Practicing and concentrating	• Checking out or giving up

Figure 3.6 Third graders' "Spirit of Endurance" chart; students identified what strengthens and decreases their endurance as readers.

thinking, based on the triangle (see Figure 3.7), allows their attempts with burgeoning literacy strategies and skills to become more purposeful—more deliberate. It wasn't until I started having these conversations with my students that they realized that they were in control of their learning. I think my students used to do everything veiled in mystery. Don Graves nudges us to ask learners, "Who's that for?" When I ask my students that question and when I teach them about purpose and audience, I see students who are more intellectually engaged in decision making. They know they are in the driver's seat when it comes to the complexity and explicitness of their own literacy.

But where did this triangle idea originate? How was it conceived?

Figure 3.7 Our "Purpose Triangle"; we ask ourselves, "Why am I doing this?" and "Why do I think it will work?"

Several years ago, during one of her visits to my classroom, Cheryl Zimmerman and I developed the "Purpose Triangle." I invited Cheryl to come watch our reader's workshop and record some of my reading conferences. Cheryl is one of those peers who always stretches my thinking, and this visit was no exception.

Originally I wanted Cheryl's help in refining some of the rituals and routines in my reader's workshop. I wanted her to help me think more clearly about the goings-on in my classroom—especially my reading conferences. Cheryl was intrigued with the triangle graphic I was using during a study of "Asking Questions" with my third graders. While debriefing the visit, she mentioned that the triangles I was using to symbolize our study of questioning could be used easily in other parts of our reader's workshop. Our conversation that day went something like this:

Cheryl: I was struck by how your students knew exactly what they were doing and to whom they were accountable. They recognize their purpose so clearly. Each time you conferred, kids could tell you why they chose the text they were reading. They were pretty clear about why they were reading the book they had chosen and who they were reading it for.

Patrick: You're right; we do a lot of talking as a class about what we are doing and why we are doing it. And, whom we're doing it for. I learn so much about the reading decisions my kids are making.

Cheryl: It's so important that we help our kids identify their purpose. It's not easy though. So often they feel like they're doing things just for us.

Patrick: They do. But they also have to realize that their thinking changes, depending upon their purpose. There's a sense of flexibility, of adaptability, that readers often overlook. We don't always have to decide their purpose for them; we have to help them take ownership. We have to empower them to be decision makers as readers. That's what I try to do in my reading conferences, get at those decisions. And, it varies from reader to reader, ability to ability.

Cheryl: They have to be so flexible. And we have to encourage them to recognize how important the decisions they make can be—each time they choose a book, each time they read independently, each time they talk with us about their reading.

Patrick: I'm struck by how they come to understand how the decisions they make as readers can, and should, change depending on what they're doing. Sometimes they read because they want to do their best work for us—the people with whom they have a relationship.

Cheryl: Sometimes they know they're reading for someone they'll never meet—like test makers. And they have to adapt their thinking to fit that purpose in a given situation at that moment on that particular day.

Patrick: And, of course, they have to realize that sometimes they're just reading for themselves. It's their choice. The decisions they make are just for them. And isn't that really our goal?

Our conversation continued. Cheryl and I agreed that this was territory worth exploring. We would have to do a bit more thinking about this idea of redefining purpose and audience. Ownership takes time to develop and entrusting that responsibility to our students makes for an important instructional linchpin. And, our one-on-one time with students is the perfect time to nudge them.

Cheryl left my classroom that morning with our conversation and an inquiry question in mind: "What if we applied this triangulation model to purpose and audience?"

Later that evening, she synthesized our discussion and drafted our first formal look at the Purpose Triangle. When her e-mail arrived with the triangle attached, I knew that we had to spend some time talking about it with our students. Since that time, our focus on helping learners make decisions about purpose and audience has evolved into a critical aspect of the work we do with the learners in our classrooms. The revised thinking that Cheryl and I did together is represented in the triangle pictured in Figure 3.8.

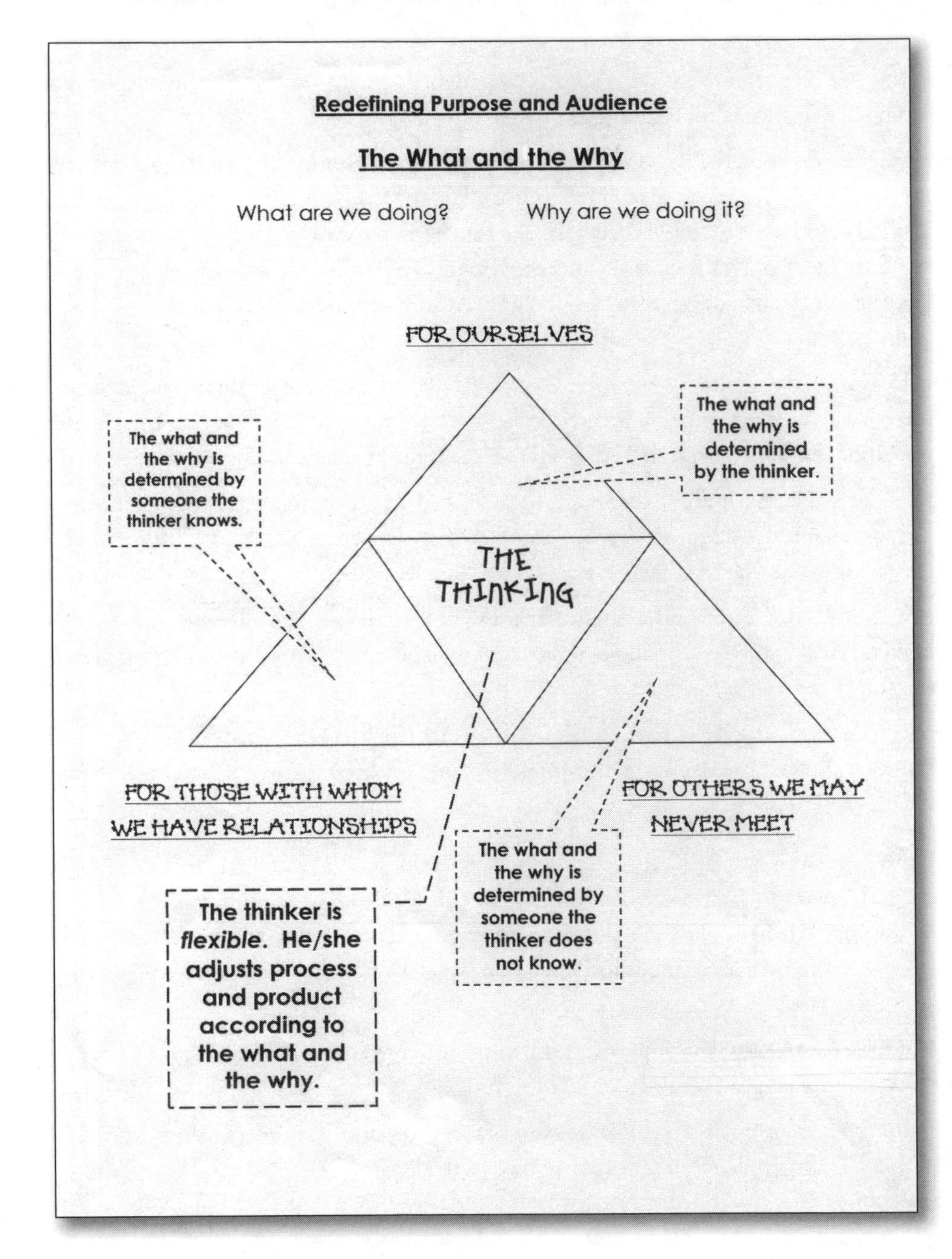

Figure 3.8 Redefining Purpose and Audience

> **PONDERING: When was the last time you invited a colleague to sit in on your reader's workshop? What new thinking evolved from your time together?**

Our Purpose Triangle takes a prominent position in our classrooms. Both Cheryl and I refer to it often. We use it as an instructional tool—during crafting lessons, during small-group work, and during individual conferences. In my classroom, I have come to realize that throughout the year—whether crafting about the sensory images we're creating in a favorite picture book, determining the most important details in a released testing item, asking questions about a piece of poetry, synthesizing new thinking from a nonfiction text—my students can become flexible in defining their purpose, knowing their audience, and exploring the depth at which they go after a piece of text and make it their own.

I recognize that reading with a purpose and audience in mind propels readers to become more authentically engaged in the text they are reading. If a reader is always hand-fed his purpose, without the opportunity to make decisions of his own accord, I know that the depth and breadth of his understanding is hindered or compromised. As teachers, it is our job to notice when students need a push from us or when they are able to make that choice independently. A reading conference is the perfect venue to explore purpose with a reader. My students and I know:

Figure 3.9 Choice plays an important role in reader's workshop.

Particularly during reading conferences, it is beneficial to encourage students to consider the following:

- Who are you reading this for?
- Tell me a little about the decisions you're making as a reader. What is causing you to make those decisions?
- When you're reading this type of text, what is your purpose?
- How are you reading this text differently than the last text you read?
- What would you say to someone who asked you why you're reading this text?
- Can you help me understand some of the decisions you're making as a reader?

PONDERING: How often do you record your reading conferences? Play them back? Listen to the questions you ask? When you listen in on your own conferring, what do you notice?

Remember the laminated list of questions I kept within reach when I conferred? I am wondering how the depth of my conferring might have changed had I thought more about these types of questions; they seem much more explicit and thoughtful than questions like "How do you think the character is feeling?" or "What is the most important event so far?"

Why? Because now my focus is on the reader and his ferreting of his understanding. Purpose and audience often should be focal points for our reading conferences. If our students are not able to identify their purpose, their reasons for reading a particular piece, or who they are reading it for, are they at a disadvantage? If we are the ones always making the decisions, are we not doing them a disservice? If we are doing all the work, are we guiding students toward independence?

A reader should always ask himself: Am I reading this for me? Am I reading this for someone with whom I have a relationship? Am I reading this for someone I will never meet?

If he is able to ask, and answer, one of these questions, his metacognition and understanding will be enriched. When I read *People* magazine, I read it differently than I read a driver's license manual to pass the written portion of my driving test. My purpose and audience change. I am flexible and adapt my thinking to match that purpose. It is similar with our students; they learn to develop the same flexibility. I love when I am conferring and I say, "Tell me a bit about the decisions you made when you chose this text," and a student can articulate the reasons he chose the book, what he hopes to accomplish as a reader, and what he will do when he is finished reading to extend meaning. He has a clear purpose. Purpose is important.

The National Reading Panel's report mentions purpose, grounding it in understanding:

> In the cognitive research of the reading process, reading is purposeful and active. A reader reads a text to understand what is read and to put this understanding to use. A reader can read a text to learn, to find out information, or to be entertained. These various purposes of understanding require that the reader use knowledge of the world, including language and print. This knowledge enables the reader to make meanings of the text, to form memory representations of these meanings, and to use them to communicate information with others about what was read. (2000, 4–5)

In *Strategies That Work*, Stephanie Harvey and Anne Goudvis discuss purpose:

> When we were kids, we obediently kept our noses in our school books without knowing why we were reading or what we were expected to

> get out of it. We were passive readers, because we didn't believe we had much to do with anything in the text or that our thoughts and opinions mattered. . . . The truth is we weren't very engaged and remember very little, since we viewed ourselves as ancillary to the whole reading process. . . . We teach kids to think about their purpose as well. If they can't tell us why they are reading something, we may all need to go back and reconsider what we are doing and why we are doing it. There is one purpose that never changes, however. The purpose of reading is always understanding. (2007, 25)

And, in *Do I Really Have to Teach Reading?* Cris Tovani focuses on the issue of purpose. She reminds us that:

> The purpose readers set for themselves as they read affects comprehension in several ways. First, it determines the speed of the reading. If readers are scanning the phone book for a name, they can read very quickly. If they are reading a math word problem, they most likely read slowly to catch important information. Purpose also determines what the reader remembers. When readers have a purpose, they tend to remember more of the text. (2004, 52)

On our triangle, Cheryl and I have identified three specific categories in which readers can couch their decisions as readers. Focusing on "Who decides?" allows students to better answer two basic questions (gleaned from Stephanie and Anne's quote):

1. What am I doing?
2. Why am I doing it?

PONDERING: When you think about purpose and audience, what do you consider?

In order to answer these questions, I teach my students that the what and the why change according to their purpose and audience (it's important to note that this works within a wide variety of text—poetry, narrative, nonfiction, and tests).

We read . . .

For Ourselves. The thinker determines the what and the why.

For Those with Whom We Have Relationships. The what and the why is determined by someone the thinker knows.

For Others We May Never Meet. The what and the why is determined by someone the thinker does not know.

Always at the center of the triangle is "The Thinking." The focal point of our triangle is the thinker and his thinking. The reader adjusts the process and the product according to the what and the why and, ultimately, creates meaning. Meaning allows a student to remember, understand, extend meaning, or make a reading experience memorable. The reader takes ownership and develops flexibility. We use our reading conferences to help us better understand the decisions the reader makes as he navigates and negotiates the text. We use our reading conferences to help students recognize their purpose, encouraging them to think about "What am I doing?" and "Why am I doing it?"

PONDERING: Think about the last thing that you read by your own choosing. What was your purpose? What were you hoping for as a reader?

Reading for Ourselves

Let's say a student is reading a self-selected text during composing time. He is reading the text because *he* has chosen to read it—maybe from a recommendation, maybe because he is intrigued by the author, maybe because it "just felt right." But ultimately his purpose, his experience with the text, is his. As a conferrer, I might spend time trying to get at the heart of book choice, how his purpose is changing, or how he is reading with his own purpose in mind. Knowing that the student has a text in his hand of his own choosing, for his own purpose(s), for his own enjoyment or learning, makes me more cognizant of the route the conference will take.

Conferences take on a student-led tone. The reader's purpose is his own, and perhaps he is reading with a little less specificity—although he is still trying to be metacognitive.

When a reader chooses to read a text for his or her own purpose—be it to build schema around specific content or to try out a new strategy or perhaps just to enjoy the piece—the conference may take on a "tell me and explain to me" tone. When a child is reading for his own purpose (see Figure 3.10), the conferring I do has more to do with encouragement, uncovering, or discovering something about the reader.

Of course, this type of conference is not a free-for-all. I, too, have a purpose in mind, but when the thinking is coming from the reader I feel a need to use that as a hook. I really want to get in the mind of the reader and see what he is thinking about at that moment.

I might say:

- Tell me a little about the decisions you made when you chose this text and what you are thinking now.
- What are you noticing about the way you are reading this text?
- What are you thinking? How is this choice working for you?

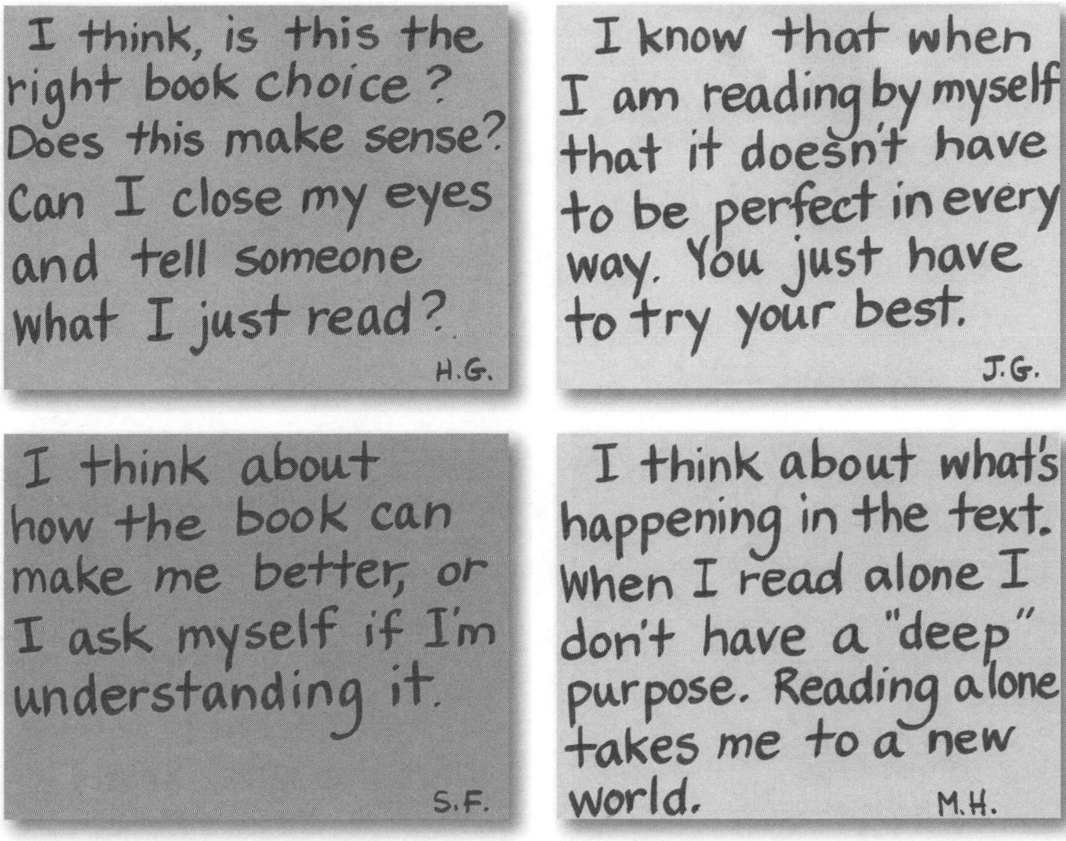

I think, is this the right book choice? Does this make sense? Can I close my eyes and tell someone what I just read? H.G.

I know that when I am reading by myself that it doesn't have to be perfect in every way. You just have to try your best. J.G.

I think about how the book can make me better, or I ask myself if I'm understanding it. S.F.

I think about what's happening in the text. When I read alone I don't have a "deep" purpose. Reading alone takes me to a new world. M.H.

Figure 3.10 Students identify how their purpose changes when reading is a personal choice.

Reading for Someone with Whom You Have a Relationship

> **PONDERING: When you are reading something for someone you know, how does your purpose change? What do you think about as you read?**

Let's say a student is reading a text that I've encouraged him to read—perhaps because of content, perhaps because of level, perhaps because of interest. He is reading because he knows that someone else has encouraged him to read the text. His purpose changes (see Figure 3.11). And, while he might be just as passionate about the text as if he had chosen the piece, in the back of his mind he's thinking about the reasons someone has asked him to read it.

If he is reading for someone with whom he has a relationship and that person is asking him to read, summarize, or to respond in some fashion, the flexibility of thought changes. As a conferrer, I hope to invite a student to be more explicit in explaining his understanding. He might be asked to support his thinking with evidence from the text. He might be asked to

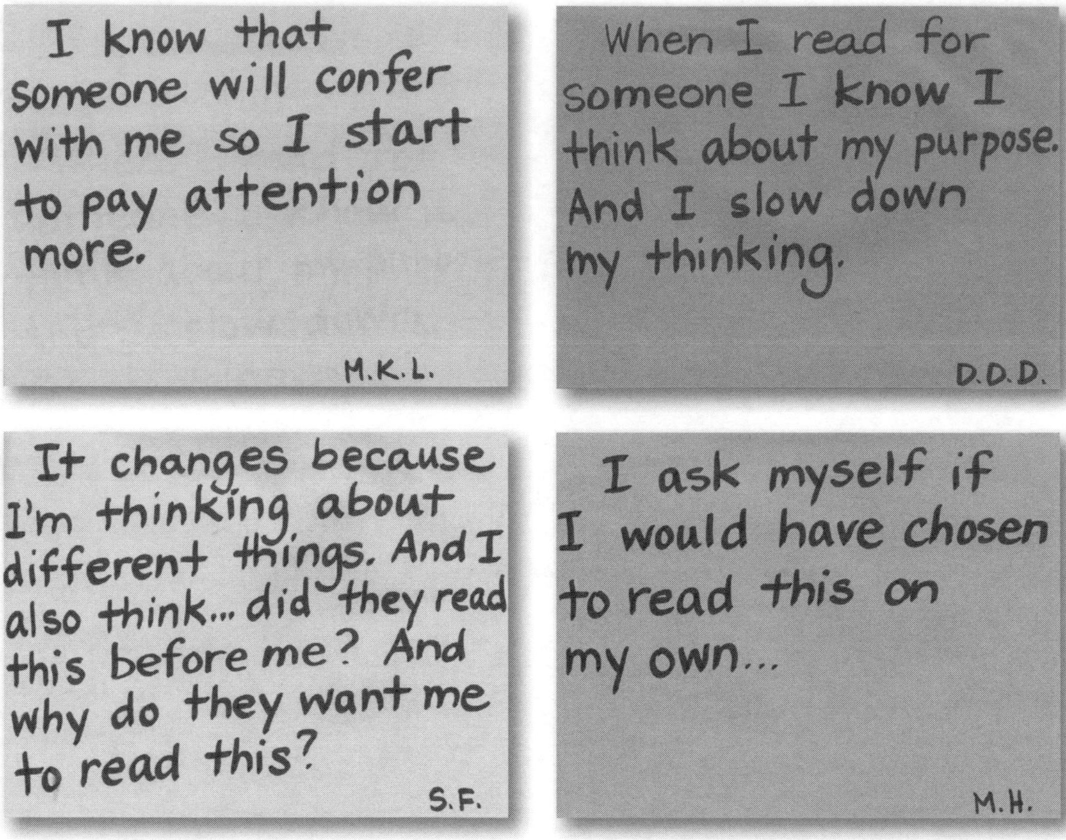

Figure 3.11 Learners recognize the various ways they adapt their purpose when reading for someone they know.

expand on his thinking as he talks about his understanding. He might focus on his process, strategies, or wonderings.

Situations within the reader's workshop vary. Let's say he is required to read a passage to demonstrate his fluency and will get a chance to reread the piece and respond to his understanding of the material. If he's reading a passage as part of a reading inventory, he is more likely to slow down, distill important details, and focus on the content of the text as well as his process as a reader.

When conferring about a text that someone you trust has encouraged you to read, conferences take on a "let's think about this together" tone. The reader knows that he has more responsibility to "prove" his understanding. The reader takes on a "Here's what I am reading . . ." and "Here's what I plan to do with my understanding . . ." attitude. His purpose is focused on whom he is reading the piece for and why he is reading the piece.

"What will I do with this information?" might be the question floating through the reader's mind. If I am conferring with a student and he is reading a text I have helped him select, I focus our conversation on that audience (implied at times, clearly explained at times).

I might say:

- Tell me what you were thinking when you first saw this text.
- What decisions are you making as a reader? Who are you thinking about as you read?
- Describe for me what you're trying to remember. How are you deciding what to keep and what to let go?

Reading for Someone You May Never Meet

Let's say a student is taking a standardized test. He is alone; he is in total control. He opens the test booklet and knows that for the next sixty minutes he will be responsible for reading passages, answering questions, and checking to make sure he has answered each question carefully. Purpose and audience take on a new tone.

While I cannot confer with him on testing day, I can be certain that he has had plenty of opportunity to talk with me, reader-to-reader, before he is left to his own devices. When we read for someone we may never meet, our purpose requires a tremendous amount of clarity and independence. We are in the driver's seat.

PONDERING: Read a sample test item. What strategies are you using? How would you confer with students to help them understand the specific skills you use when you're reading for an outside audience?

For eight years I taught swimmers. It was always my goal for a swimmer to take on the deep end without me swimming beside him; that was when I knew I had been an effective swimming instructor. Independence. I would stand on the side of the pool and watch, knowing I had spent plenty of time before that day demonstrating strokes, swimming side-by-side with the swimmer, watching him try each stroke out in the shallow end. And, while teaching swimming is not quite as complex as teaching readers, the same notions hold true—to know there will be a time you have to stand on the side and watch, hoping you have helped the swimmer strengthen all of his skills and strategies for that special moment when he can swim in the deep end alone.

Our metacognitive skills have to change based on the time and purpose of the text we are reading. Conferences prior to the time of actual independence ("reading for someone I will never meet" situations) take on a "What if . . ." and "When you . . ." tone. Our conferences cannot occur in a testing situation, but our prior interactions can be a stronghold for a student who is placed in a particular situation, in a particular place and time, alone. I have to hope that the student will "hear" my voice, and his, when he is doing work for someone he may never meet. I have to hope that he can apply the same thinking to that situation that he did when he was reading a self-selected text. I have to think carefully about the learning situations up to that point—the ones that allow independence to happen. My conferences take on a different quality.

I might say:

- If you were reading this for someone you'll never meet, how might your thinking change? (See Figure 3.12.)
- Pretend you're on your own, working to answer questions after reading this text. How would you read this piece differently?
- Tell me about your thinking. What is going through your mind as you read this text?

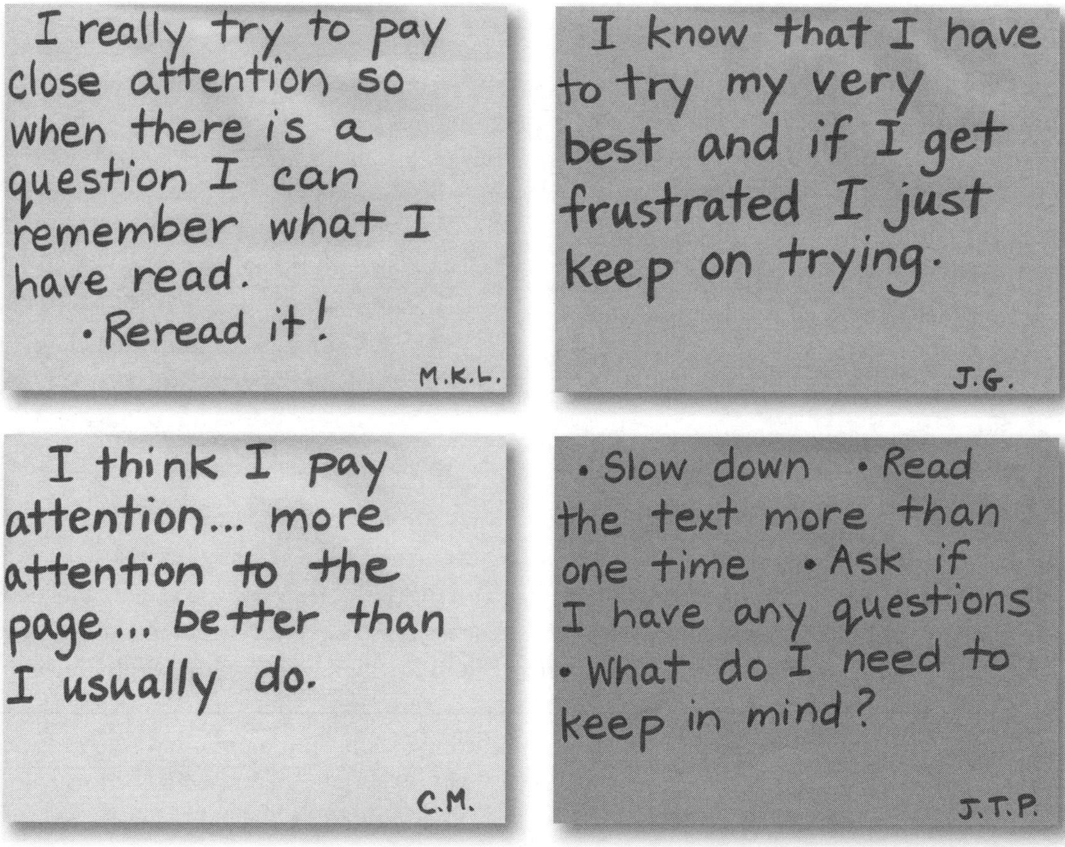

Figure 3.12 Readers record changes in thinking that occur when they read for someone they may never meet.

It seems to me that if we help our students become flexible in this process of metacognition by helping them move flexibly through text for a wide variety of purposes, they will, indeed, become more successful and inspired readers. If we confer with students and help them better navigate text, flexibly noting both purpose and audience, they will become more efficient readers in any situation.

In many classrooms, purpose is decided by the teacher or the publisher. In my classroom, I want my students to develop the understanding of the role purpose plays in their lives as young readers. That is why triangulation takes an active role. I want my students to understand that they are decision makers. Conferring with readers about negotiating purpose enhances flexibility. And, as an added bonus, our conferences become a lot more interesting and focused on the reader.

PONDERING: How much ownership do your students have in terms of purpose and audience? How would they answer the question, Who am I doing this for?

Ashlar 4: Exploring the Gradual Release of Responsibility Model

The gradual release of responsibility is an instructional model that I refine and define as I work with young learners. It has become an important ashlar of my teaching. Over the years, I have developed ways to make it visible to my students.

It was Ellin Keene who introduced me to the gradual release of responsibility model (Gallagher and Pearson 1983). When I began my teaching career, Ellin was working as the language arts TOSA (teacher on special assignment) in our school district. As a new teacher, I took a recommended class Ellin was teaching called the "Language Studio Model." While teaching the course, Ellin introduced us to the specifics of reader's workshop ("studio"). We investigated the structure of the workshop, comprehension strategies, response to literature, and the gradual release of responsibility model. As a first-year teacher, I did not fully grasp the scaffold that the gradual release model establishes for learners. To be honest, I really didn't comprehend its extraordinary role and the model's relationship to the reader's workshop (to learning for that matter), but I was intrigued and willing to learn more. I remember taking my new learnings into the classroom, especially the gradual release model.

Then a few years later along came *Mosaic of Thought*, in which Ellin and Susan illustrated the gradual release of responsibility model, adding a bit more clarity to my understanding (Keene and Zimmerman 1997). The model continued to intrigue me; within its simplicity existed a complexity that deserved further study. All these years later, I have continued to read more, explore more, and play around with the gradual release of responsibility model—as I plan, as I teach, and as I learn.

To develop a backdrop in which authentic conferring can live and breathe, the gradual release of responsibility has become an essential structure in my classroom. To provide more focused individualized instruction, I think it behooves us to develop a clear understanding of how this model works in our classrooms over days, over weeks, or throughout the course of a specific study. In order to make the transition from "all teacher" to having "students assume all of the responsibility" (Duke and Pearson 2002, 210–211), we have to have the gradual release model working as an instructional underpinning; it ensures that wise instruction is alive and well in our reader's workshops (in other content workshops as well). I try to name and illustrate the model for my students and explain to them how working together we are guiding them toward independence. Why not explain to students how my modeling and the shared experiences of working together will, indeed, lead to mindful independence? By establishing a working knowledge of this model, I can help my students develop their own understanding of their unique capabilities as learners. It gives me the opportunity to know when to offer support—in whole group, small groups, and, especially, during conferring situations. If I can add lucidity to my instruction, I must. And how better to add clarity than to talk to students about the gradual release model?

PONDERING: How well do you understand the gradual release of responsibility model? How do you use it in your reader's workshop (or in other areas)?

In *Reading with Meaning*, Debbie Miller describes the gradual release model in this way:

> Chances are that if you think back to a time when you learned how to do something new, the gradual release of responsibility model (Pearson and Gallagher 1983) comes into play. Maybe you learned how to snowboard, canoe, play golf, or drive a car. If you watched somebody do it first, practiced under that person's watchful eye, listened to his or her feedback, and then one fine day went off and did it by yourself, adding your own special twist to it in the process, you know what this model is all about. (2002, 10)

My goal is to let my students in on the secret of how the gradual release model works. Our crafting lessons at the beginning of the year often include discussions moving from think-aloud to collaboration to independence, from my demonstrating to children's doing.

We might begin our discussion with a read of a book like *Little One Step* by Simon James. *Little One Step* is a delightful story of a duck named Little One Step who overcomes his wobbliness and weariness in a perfect parallel to the gradual release of responsibility. The ducks get lost in the woods on their journey to the river and Little One Step just can't walk any farther. His brother tells him to "Watch carefully . . . Just lift one foot like this . . ." and like all good brothers he models how to finish the journey one step at a time. His siblings encourage him to practice and to take things slowly. Side-by-side they continue, and each time Little One Step falters, they remind Little One Step to remember what they have taught him: "One step . . . one step . . ." At the end of the story, Little One Step makes it to the river and shares his sense of pride with his mother, who is waiting for him at the water's edge.

Little One Step can lead to a group discussion of the gradual release model. It is a perfect jumping-off point for a discussion of the model we use for our learning throughout the year. It is the perfect opportunity to talk about the talk that occurred between Little One Step and his brothers; the perfect juxtaposition for the important role conferring plays in reader's workshop.

Laura Benson, a Denver colleague, illustrates the gradual release model as:

◐ ALOUD (Showing How and Telling Why) **Mentors and Models**
◐ ALONG (Practicing Together) **Fellowship**
◐ ALONE (Practicing Independently) **Independence**

Laura's idea of using mentors and models, creating fellowship, and heading toward independence is a simple, thoughtful way to describe the gradual release model to students (Benson 2001). Imagine, thinking of learning side-by-side as fellowship. Conferring during the process helps bring fellow learners to a level playing field as you move through the process, together.

I like to find a variety of texts that illustrate various steps of the gradual release model. I use books like the following:

Amber on the Mountain by T. Johnston

Jeremiah Learns to Read by J. Bogart

Saturdays and Teacakes by L. Laminack

A Story for Bear by D. Haseley

Now One Foot, Now the Other by T. dePaola

City Foxes by S. Tweit

Thank You, Mr. Falker by P. Polacco

The Girl on the High-Diving Horse by L. O. High

How to Catch a Shark and Other Stories About Teaching and Learning by D. Graves

Possum Magic by M. Fox

The Wednesday Surprise by E. Bunting

Any one or more of these books can be used as a think-aloud or as a shared text at the beginning of the school year (or as a reminder throughout the year). Each book can enhance understanding of how we learn because each text imbeds elements of the gradual release model that meander through its pages. My goal is not to "overteach" a text, but when my students and I talk about the gradual release of responsibility model, sharing these texts (along with a graphic to support the visual aspect of the model itself) has lasting impact on student learning. Understanding how the gradual release of responsibility ebbs and flows throughout, say, a strategy study creates a safety net for students. Throughout a study, students know that I will take time to listen as we confer about their burgeoning understandings. Students know that we'll have many opportunities to clarify, modify, and justify thinking as conferrer/conferee as we move through the model.

PONDERING: What texts do you have in your own classroom library that demonstrate the gradual release of responsibility and help make it visible for learners? Take some time to peruse your own collections and see what you can find! How will you use them?

Teaching my students the why behind how we go after a study helps develop their understanding—of a thinking strategy, inquiry into specific content, specific text elements and structures, and so on. And, the beauty is, together we determine how conferring looks along the way—how our responsibilities as both conferrer and conferee change as experiences change. Students learn that the gradual release of responsibility model is recursive. The very nature of the model itself encourages differentiation of student learning that is incremental, collaborative, and ultimately independent.

To better understand the gradual release of responsibility model, I did three things:

1. I created a personal metaphor for the gradual release model based on a recent learning experience that I had (building a fence on our property). Framing my own process as a learner helps mold and clarify my understanding of the gradual release model;
2. I created the following guide, along with my colleagues Missy and Troy, to use when planning a long-term study of a thinking strategy in reader's workshop (I use the same outline to plan a unit of study in writer's workshop). Using this guide helps shape and form my instruction across days and weeks. I have found that outlining crafting lessons across time helps focus the composing time of reader's workshop and often serves as a reference point during reading conferences. It brings purpose and perspicuity to my planning and instruction—it keeps me focused on independence (a sample filled-in version of this guide appears in Figure 3.13, and a blank version is included in the appendix); and
3. With Troy's help, I identified my role (the teacher's role) and the students' role as my students and I move along the gradual release model. Identifying specific roles brings lucidity to the gradual release model and provides a reference point for both teachers and students along the way. (The Defining Teacher and Student Roles chart is included in the appendix.)

Planning a Strategy Study – Reading or Writing
[based on the Gradual Release of Responsibility, Pearson and Gallagher, 1983]

Planning for *Synthesizing New Learnings and Ideas*
(Thinking Strategy or Unit of Study)

Assessment
(Specific evidence gathered to indicate understanding)
- Pre/Post student definitions and Likert scale questionnaire
- Two notebook responses and reflection
- Three examples of coded text
- Drawing of metaphor and reflection
- Major Point Interview and conferring notes

Thinking and Planning
(How will it be taught? How is it used?)
Preliminary instructional considerations...
- Explore "river" metaphor
- Revisit previous anchor charts
- Create "Language of Synthesis" chart
- Revisit previous year's study
- Confer with colleagues and reread professional resources

Think Aloud
(Modeling, demonstrating, sharing personal use of strategy)
Texts and Instructional Strategies
- Define on "pre" definition recording form-share
- Personal – Rick Reilly piece
- All I See - Rylant
- "Peanut Butter Slices" (newspaper article)
- Where the River Begins - Locker

Shared Experience
(Inviting participation via whole group experiences)
Texts and Instructional Strategies
- "Growing Cotton"-website
- The Grannyman - Schachner
- Someday a Tree - Bunting
- The Wednesday Surprise - Bunting
- Collect: "What we know about synthesis..." sticky notes

Guided Experience
(Active participation in clusters or individually with support)
Texts and Instructional Strategies
- An Angel for Soloman Singer - Rylant
- Cactus Poems - Asch
- National Geographic Explorer "Butterflies"
- The House in the Mail - Wells
- Toasting Marshmallows - George

Cooperative Experience
(Participation with peers, supporting growth and gathering evidence of understanding)
Texts and Instructional Strategies
- Falling Down the Page - Heard (poetry)
- "Grandmama's Kitchen Table" - Rylant
- A Drop of Water (excerpts) - Wick
- The Wild Side of Pet Fish - Waters
- Collect "What we know now about synthesis..." sticky notes

Independence
(What learners know and do as a result of study—independently)
Texts and Instructional Strategies
- Create and explain personal metaphors
- Student text - think aloud on Elmo
- Pearl Moscowitz's Last Stand - Levine
- Revisit All I See
- Explain "post" definitions

Considerations
Links to Content or Standards
- Memory Writes / Poetry in Writer's Workshop
- Link to photosynthesis and life cycles
- Multiplication concepts – connecting
- Reading – checkpoints 3.4.1, 3.4.2, 3.4.3
- Art – mosaics with same materials – What happens?
-

Personal Definition of Strategy or Study
Synthesis is about change of thought and recognizing that process. It occurs across a text or several texts. Synthesis thinkers monitor understanding, important ideas, and new learnings. Personal meaning is developed as we synthesize. When we share our thinking with others, we create a synthesis. Recognizing how our thoughts adapt, evolve, or become more clear is part of the process. Creating overall meaning is synthesis. Change!

Questions, Wonderings, Investigations
- Comparing synthesis to summary – recognizing the difference.
- What happens to a reader whose synthesis is disconnected or "way off base"?
- How is "purpose" related to synthesis?
- Review the relationship of synthesis to other strategies – look for connections.
- What language is specific to synthesis? How can it be uncovered in a conference?

Figure 3.13 Planning for instruction with the gradual release of responsibility in mind helps guide and focus our teaching. This planning guide provides a template for recording instructional possibilities during a study.

What do I want my students to gain as a result of having a working knowledge of the gradual release of responsibility? In a nutshell, I have one goal: for students to develop a hunger to learn more—to explore and develop their own thinking, their own insatiable curiosity, their own propensity to become more metacognitive readers. The gradual release of responsibility model provides an overarching structure in which conferring can find a permanent home. Simply stated: Teach. Model. Empower.

Ashlar 5: Focusing on the Structure of Reader's Workshop

There is a brilliant book called *Believing It All: Lessons I Learned from My Children* by Marc Parent. It's a collection of father and son stories written to describe Parent's experiences with raising his two young children. Troy introduced the book to me after checking out a copy on Back-to-School Night at his son's school a few years ago. In the book, Parent writes about, well, being a successful parent—and how he hopes to be the kind of father that creates the best learning environment for his sons on the twelve acres his family owns in rural Pennsylvania. He wants their upbringing to be reminiscent of his own upbringing in the country.

In the first chapter, Parent describes the kind of idyllic setting in which he hoped to raise his sons: where young boys can dig for juicy worms, watch the bright stars shine in the sky, chop down young saplings with shouts of "Tim-ber," and play to their young hearts' content. His hope is that these experiences will help his children learn life's lessons with greater profundity and insight.

Consider Parent's description of where he wanted his boys to grow and learn:

> I hoped for a setting that would broaden their minds like a good classroom. A welcoming and forgiving place. A place where they could let down their guard and make mistakes on the way to getting things right. One overflowing with props to engage the senses and provoke the mind . . . A place that challenged without intimidating. Comforted without pacifying . . . This is that kind of place. (2002, 3–4)

When I read Marc's words, they hit me like a ton of bricks! As I reread Parent's description of the place he wanted real learning to transpire for his own children, I thought about my reader's workshop. Was my reader's workshop the kind of "place" that allowed students to let down their guard? Was our reader's workshop welcoming and forgiving? Were mistakes accepted in the reader's workshop as part of the learning process? I thought so.

But I asked myself, what would my students say about reader's workshop? How would they describe the idiosyncratic elements of reader's workshop? How would they describe the role conferring plays in their budding reading lives?

I strive to be very specific and explicit in the way I structure reader's workshop. I think about its implementation a lot.

In the book *To Understand: New Horizons in Reading Comprehension*, Ellin Keene eloquently describes her exploration of the "literacy studio" and in exquisite detail paints a portrait of the understanding that emerges from students in a workshop setting. As I reread it recently, Ellin's words elbowed me as if she were sitting right next to me (harkening back to those beginning teaching days). Without question the workshop is, and remains, an important underlying support structure for the readers in my care.

Listening plays a big part—listening to connections readers are making and how readers understand and anchor their thinking to the text and their understandings.
Randi Allison,
Elementary Teacher

Teacher Keystone Point

I was reminded that I must revisit, rethink, and revise my own understanding of the workshop structure if I want my students to become the kind of readers who are, in Ellin's words, "driven to understand." The day-to-day structure of the workshop strengthens my teaching. And, if done thoughtfully, it can only fortify and support the valuable time I spend with children each day, especially if we take Ellin's advice:

> I do imagine, however, if we want students to engage in the highest levels of thought related to their reading and writing, if we want them to share the quality of fervent learning with other great thinkers in the world, if we want to give more than lip service to the concept of highest expectations, we must consider ways to reshape, even subtly, our time and our interactions with students. We must propel our teaching forward, from good to great, from effective to artistic. We must do what may be hardest of all—*rethink what we believe is already working*. (Keene 2008, 54, 57)

Over the years, like many of you, I have come to understand that each workshop has three specific components: crafting, composing, and reflecting—every day. A simple "wheel" in which we couch our learning (see Figure 3.14).

I have come to believe that the workshop structure provides a hoop iron, or holdfast, of my daily interactions with children. The consistency of the structure works for me and my students. As the teacher, I find it offers flexibility to differentiate instruction and provide meaningful interventions for all readers, from the most reticent reader to the most skilled reader. More important, I believe that it empowers students with the sense of time, self-authority, decision-making, and intellectual depth they need to foster their independence as nascent readers.

It is the predictability, the rhythm and cadence, of reader's workshop that provides ample time for strong literacy work to occur. It is the predictability that provides the time for conferring to

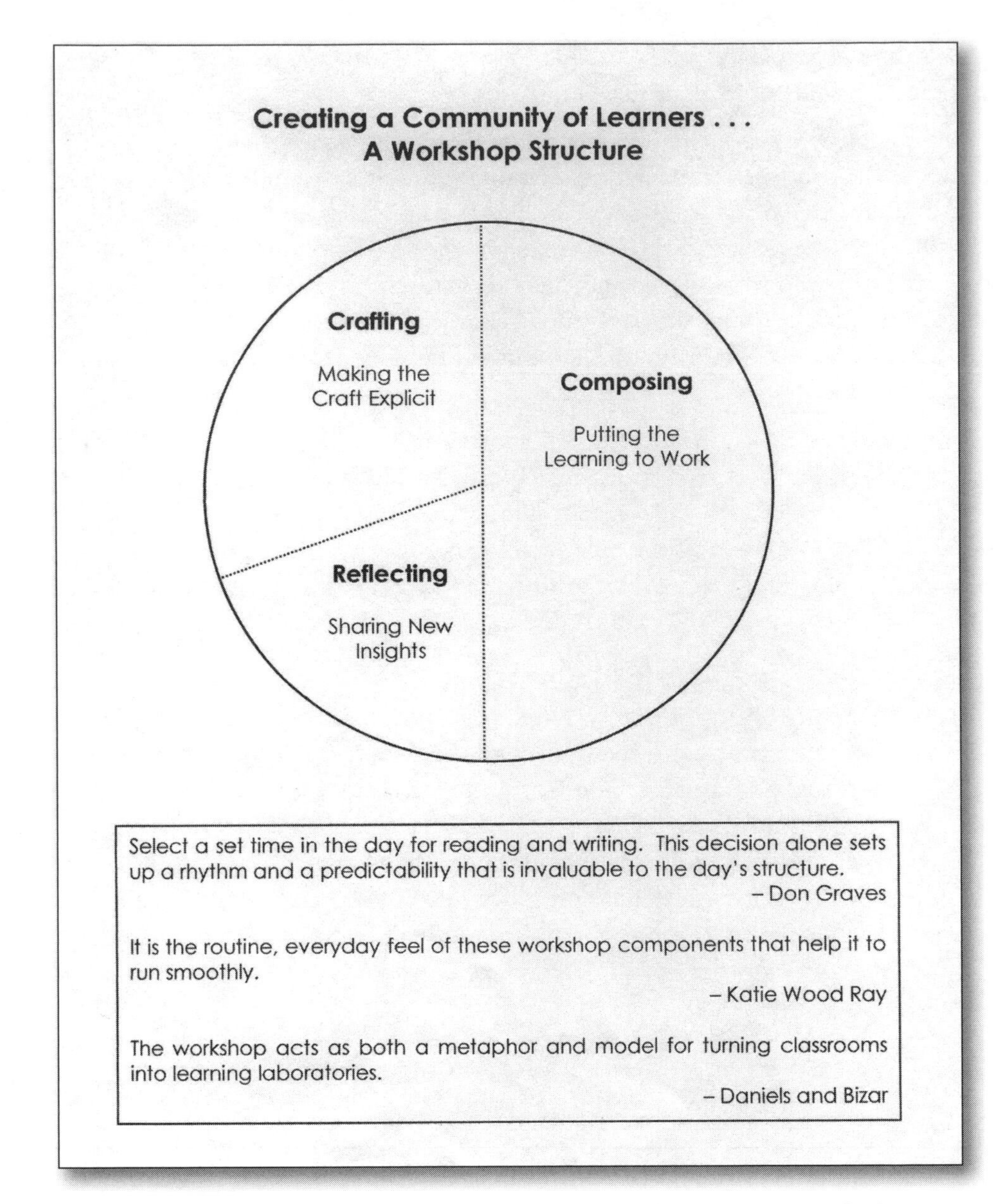

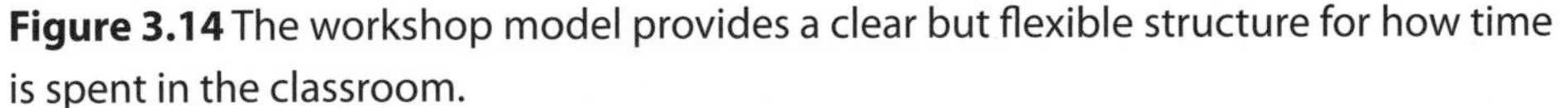

Figure 3.14 The workshop model provides a clear but flexible structure for how time is spent in the classroom.

happen regularly. The very pulse and reliability of reader's workshop allows conferring to become a fundamental, irreplaceable piece of our daily literacy rituals and routines.

Recently I was listening in on a conversation among several of my students that made me realize that reader's workshop is *not* just giving lip service. Providing a structure of support for crafting, composing, and reflecting each day causes language like this to fill the precious airspace of our classrooms:

Devante: Reader's workshop gives us a chance to show our personality. Ya know, like who we are, what we can do, what we can build, and how high we can go.

Haley: Yeah, it helps me to know what other readers do and think.

Devante: Then it combines all the strategies we know and helps us build our stamina. That causes us to be better readers. And then we know what reading is really about.

Cooper: I agree. It helps us become wise readers, not just fake readers.

Cole: And, then we can practice it at home!

Listening in on this conversation reminded me that reader's workshop is inherently:

- Individualized (How else could we show our personality?)
- Strategic (How else could we combine strategies we are learning?)
- Collaborative (How else could we know what others are thinking?)
- Purposeful (How else could we know that we are "wise"?)
- Transferable (How else could we know that we can take our learning outside the classroom?)

PONDERING: Listen in on the conversations your students have during the day. What do they say? What do your students say about your reader's workshop?

The workshop structure (learning through crafting, practicing during composing, and evaluating during reflecting) supports children's continual development by providing a structure that is both predictable and consistent, yet lends itself to flexibility and creativity. The beauty of the workshop structure is that learners come to rely on the rhythm to marshal themselves as they explore their daily literacy experiences. The creation of a workshop provides an edifice for thinking and understanding to be nudged to the forefront of who we are becoming as readers.

Crafting.

Composing.

Reflecting.

In *To Understand,* Ellin is very clear that just renaming the workshop components is not enough. If the components themselves do not nudge students to think more deeply, explicitly, and thoughtfully, it doesn't matter what you call them. I have learned that I have to help my students know and understand their roles (and mine) in the workshop structure. The components, no matter what we call them, must be meaning based, both for teachers and students.

As the year progresses, students must realize that crafting lessons are not "mini" pieces of hodgepodge curriculum (Don Graves once called this the "Cha-cha-cha" curriculum), but rather ardent, connected, meaningful studies of what real readers do (strategies explored deeply over time and skills developed that are needed for independence). Explicit instruction of skills, strategies, concepts, and content occurs in crafting.

Students realize that composing time is not a time to "drop everything and read," but rather a zealous, fruitful time to investigate the real work that readers do, time to go after the craft in meaningful, endurance-driven experiences (independently with conferring support as well as invitational small-group work as needed). Time spent reading independently and reading to and with other readers (when appropriate) takes place during composing.

Students realize that reflecting time is not just sharing time, but rather, a concentrated period set aside each day to publicly say, "Here's what I learned about myself as a reader, and this is what I plan to do with that discovery!" Evaluating strengths and thinking about growth areas, alongside fellow readers, transpires in reflecting. Students reflect in pairs, in small groups, and as a whole class, depending on the purpose and where we are on the gradual release of responsibility model.

The authors of *Beyond Leveled Books* state,

> These common elements are supported by rich conversations that provide a foundation for literacy learning. It is critical that students be engaged in conversations about their reading lives. These interactions with classmates and the teacher support the development of a reader identity. Students engaged in conversations learn about reading strategies that others have found helpful and are able to communicate their own strengths and challenges. A classroom rich in literary conversations opens up a world of books and reading to our students. (Szymusiak, Sibberson, and Koch 2008, 152)

It behooves us to take time to engage our students in conversations about how a workshop structure is an essential part of our day. Students should understand that a similar structure is used in every content area, throughout the day. These meaningful conversations are critical to help students discover and discern the purpose behind their learning identities. As educators, we cannot seriously think that endless isolated drills, fluency graphs, phonics worksheets, spurious response journals, diorama-type projects, and other mundane tasks can live outside of a contextual meaning base. To rephrase Mem Fox's words about writers, "I wish we could change the world by creating powerful writers [readers] for forever instead of just indifferent writers [readers] for school" (1993, 22).

I think we have to ask not only What am I teaching the reader? but also What is the reader teaching me? Am I doing what I need to do to elicit the type of thinking that emulates real-world reading? This kind of thinking begins with students knowing how a workshop actually works. The structure—learning, practicing, and discussing understandings—is the same when working as mathematicians, scientists, spellers, artists, musicians, social scientists, and, in this case, readers. So, spending time learning about its idiosyncratic, recursive, and flexible nature is time well spent. It's a structure that provides the underpinning for all content learning in my classroom.

And, if I want conferring to become a living, breathing, irreplaceable part of my instructional repertoire, kids need to know its purpose and where the bulk of it will occur. Katie Wood Ray calls it the "hope and promise of things to come," when students know that if they do not have the chance to do something today, they will have the same chance tomorrow—it's a given, a promise.

PONDERING: How do you teach your students about how daily work as readers will be structured? How do you invite them into the decision-making process of how your reader's workshop will function?

I reintroduce the workshop model early in the school year. I want students to become even more familiar with this structure than they were in previous grade levels; after all, they are different learners with another year of learning under their belts. I begin our initial crafting about the workshop structure with students gathered at my feet with reader's/writer's notebooks in hand, pencils poised at the ready.

Ben Franklin wisely advised one to read "with a pen in your hand and enter in a little book short hints of what you find that is curious or that might be useful; for this will be the best method of imprinting such particulars in your memory, where they will be ready on some future occasion to adorn and improve your conversation" (Bradfield 2002, 23). So I do. And I want my students to begin to use their reader's/writer's notebooks as a regular part of reader's workshop from day one.

Crafting lessons, especially early in the year, are designed to enhance procedures, routines, rituals, structures as well as thinking behaviors—gradually and explicitly. When I talk about workshop, I begin our initial crafting lessons with two thoughts in mind: (1) What do my students know about the workshop structure? and (2) How will they define their role in each component as well as mine?

It might sound something like this:

"Boys and Girls, I want to talk with you about how we're going to structure our learning time. This year, we're again going to structure our learning using a workshop model." I draw the "wheel" on chart paper and ask, "Does this look familiar?"

There's a collective nod of heads.

Most of my students are familiar with the workshop structure; it is all part of "digging the hole deeper" that I mentioned earlier. My students are older, wiser, more experienced; I do not mind revisiting the structure of the workshop and peppering it with my expectations and any explanations that might differ from their previous experience. Another beautiful part of the workshop is that it allows for teacher flexibility (not in the structure, but in the content).

"Good. I'm glad you've seen it before. And, if you haven't, I'm sure you'll come to understand it as well as the rest of us."

Again nods.

"But before we talk about *this* chart, I want us to take a few minutes to think about the meaning of the word *workshop*." I flip the chart paper and write, "What is a workshop?" and then I say, "Think about where you've seen or heard the word. Think about what a workshop is and what people do in one. Think about that for a minute." I give students some time to contemplate.

"What is a workshop? Turn to your neighbor and talk to him or her for just a minute or two about what you know, or think you might know, about a workshop. Think about a workshop you know in school and maybe one outside of school. See what you can come up with, together. Okay, rotate on your axis and chat with the person next to you for a bit." As my students talk, I listen for any language that emerges; having kids sit close to me gives me a perfect opportunity to eavesdrop. It is important to build in the rehearsal time and time for them to approximate their understanding. And, it gives me a chance to listen in and watch and even jot down a few notes to myself in my notebook.

As the hum of their voices draws to a close, I say, "Okay, now let's try to capture some of our thinking on paper. Here's what I hope to see and hear. I hope to see you writing quickly, thoughtfully, and really trying to get at the bottom of your thinking. Remember the rules you know about a ten-minute write. Everybody writes. If you get stuck, start again with something like, 'A workshop is . . .' or 'A workshop is like . . .'" I set my notebook on the document camera and write down these two prompts.

"What questions do you have?" After I clear up any details or misunderstandings, we all begin to write. Students are getting used to using their notebooks as a tool for recording their thinking. As I write in my notebook, I like to glance up periodically to see who is doing what—who is writing furiously, who is stopping to think, who is doodling, and so on. Early in the year I can see who might need a nudge as a writer, and it gives me an idea of other notebook strategies we might need to learn.

I stick to about ten minutes, no more. I write as well, trying to capture my own thinking about the workshop.

When ten minutes are up, I put down my pen and say, "Finish the word you're on . . . and then we'll chat a bit about some of the things you discovered. First, though, take just a few minutes to look over what you wrote—tweak it a bit if it doesn't make sense, check any key words you think you may know how to spell, add some punctuation you may have forgotten to include." I want to strengthen the process of rereading, and I give them just a minute or two to notice at least one thing that needs to be changed, added, or deleted.

"Now, who'd like to explain their thinking to us?" I wait for a hand or five to go up. I wait. Finally, after about five or six people have volunteered to share their ideas or ponderings with the rest of the group, we chat for a few minutes. As students reflect, I begin to jot down their thinking on the chart.

The charts in Figures 3.15 and 3.16 characterize student thinking about the workshop created by two different groups of children. The charts are similar, but because the readers (thinkers) are different with different experiences, complexities, and understanding, they are not identical. There is also a list that my students compiled about what you should not do in a workshop (Figure 3.17). The thinking on the charts emerged after taking the time to jot down our thinking about workshop in our reader's/writer's notebooks. The student initials on the charts provide a sense of ownership to the students who "make the chart" by sharing the thinking from their notebooks.

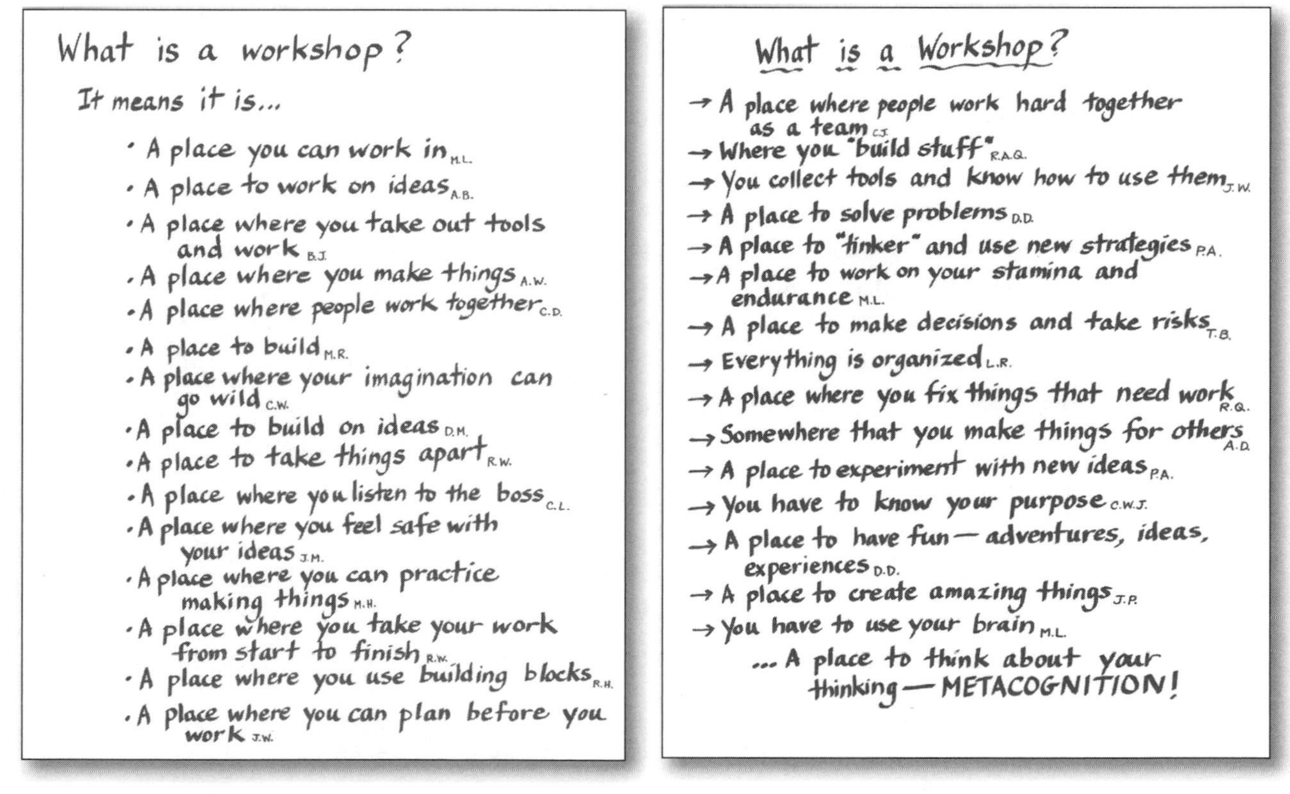

Figure 3.15 Students identify specific characteristics of a workshop.

Figure 3.16 Students answer the question, What is a Workshop?

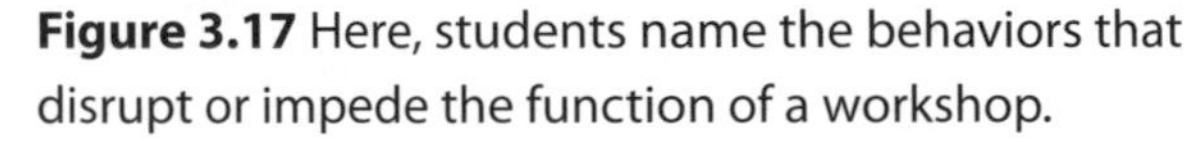

Figure 3.17 Here, students name the behaviors that disrupt or impede the function of a workshop.

So what do these charts tell me? The charts we create during workshop provide a record of our crafting and who has contributed to the community by sharing his or her thinking. They provide documentable information about specific learners' understanding and sincere wonderings. They provide me with possible ideas for future crafting lessons. Three crafting possibilities gleaned: Making sure everyone understands *metacognition*, what it means to be a wise decision maker, how readers take risks and how they record their learning (written response to text). They give me an "in" during individual conferences during composing time ("Devante, remember you talked about a workshop being a place for adventure; what are you doing to bring that sense of adventure to your own reading?" or "Thomas, when we were talking about workshop, you mentioned that it's a great place to make decisions; what decisions are you making today?" or "Rachel, you said earlier today that we fix things in a workshop; what are some of the things you've had to 'fix' today as a reader?"). The seeds we plant during crafting emerge throughout the workshop. The workshop is that important!

After we uncover what we think we know about workshop, we go back to the graphic of the wheel. For the next few days, students think about, talk about, write about, and share their definitions of each component: crafting, composing, and reflecting (Figure 3.18). These are some of the crafting lessons of our beginning reader's workshops. We spent time clarifying the purpose of each of the workshop components.

Together, we then spend several crafting sessions identifying, labeling, and discussing two things:

1. What is the teacher's role during each component of reader's workshop?
2. What is the students' role during each component of reader's workshop?

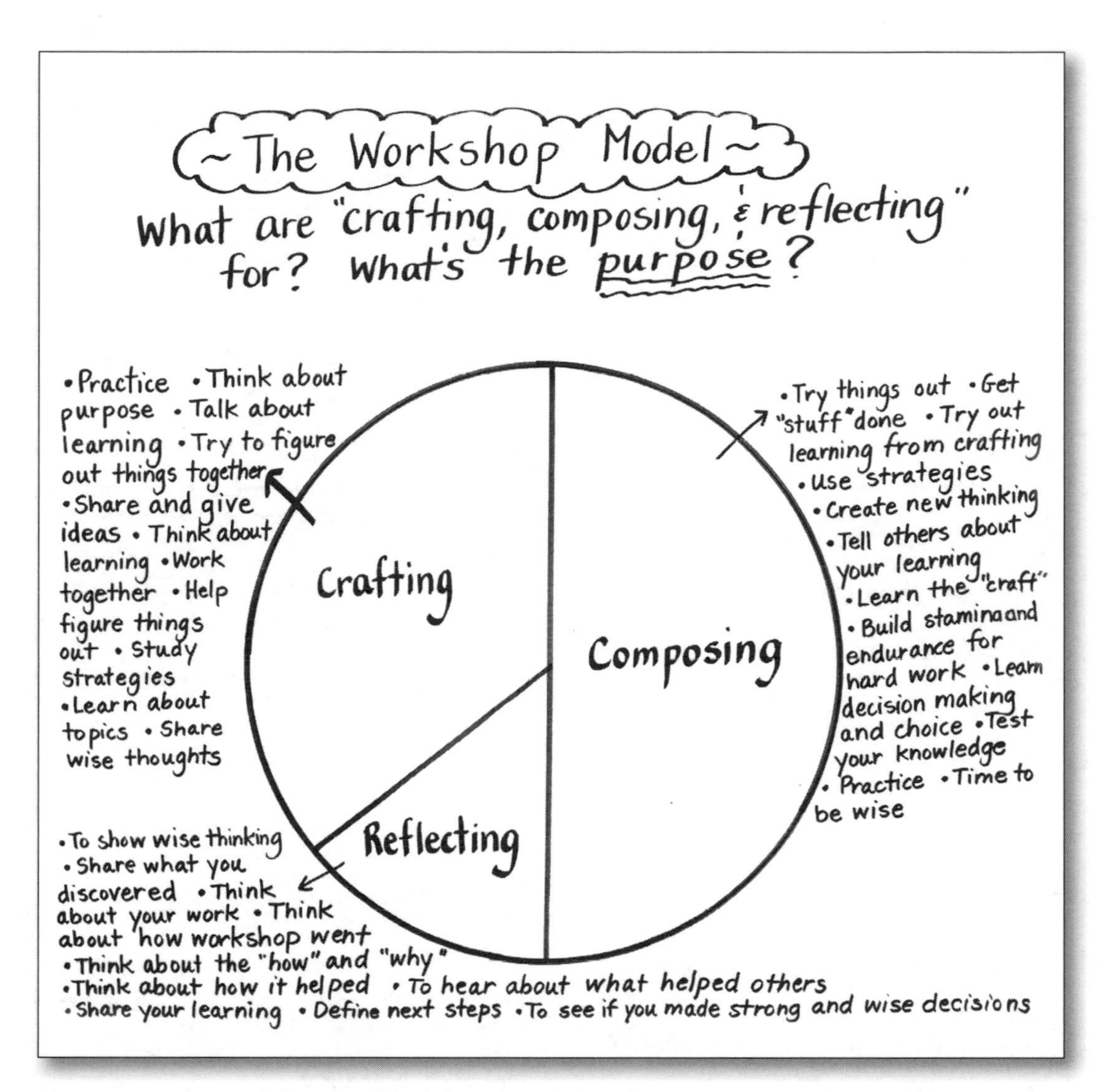

Figure 3.18 The Workshop Model; in this example, students recognize and establish the purpose of each component of the workshop. Identifying teacher and student roles within the workshop (crafting, composing, reflecting) adds specificity to the workshop's function.

The examples in Figure 3.19 show how students describe and define their role and the teacher's in the reader's workshop in Troy's classroom. Three of the charts (Figure 3.20) are from my classroom and explain how students view my role and their role in the reader's workshop. Both Troy and I believe that helping students identify their specific roles creates workshops that function more smoothly and effectively.

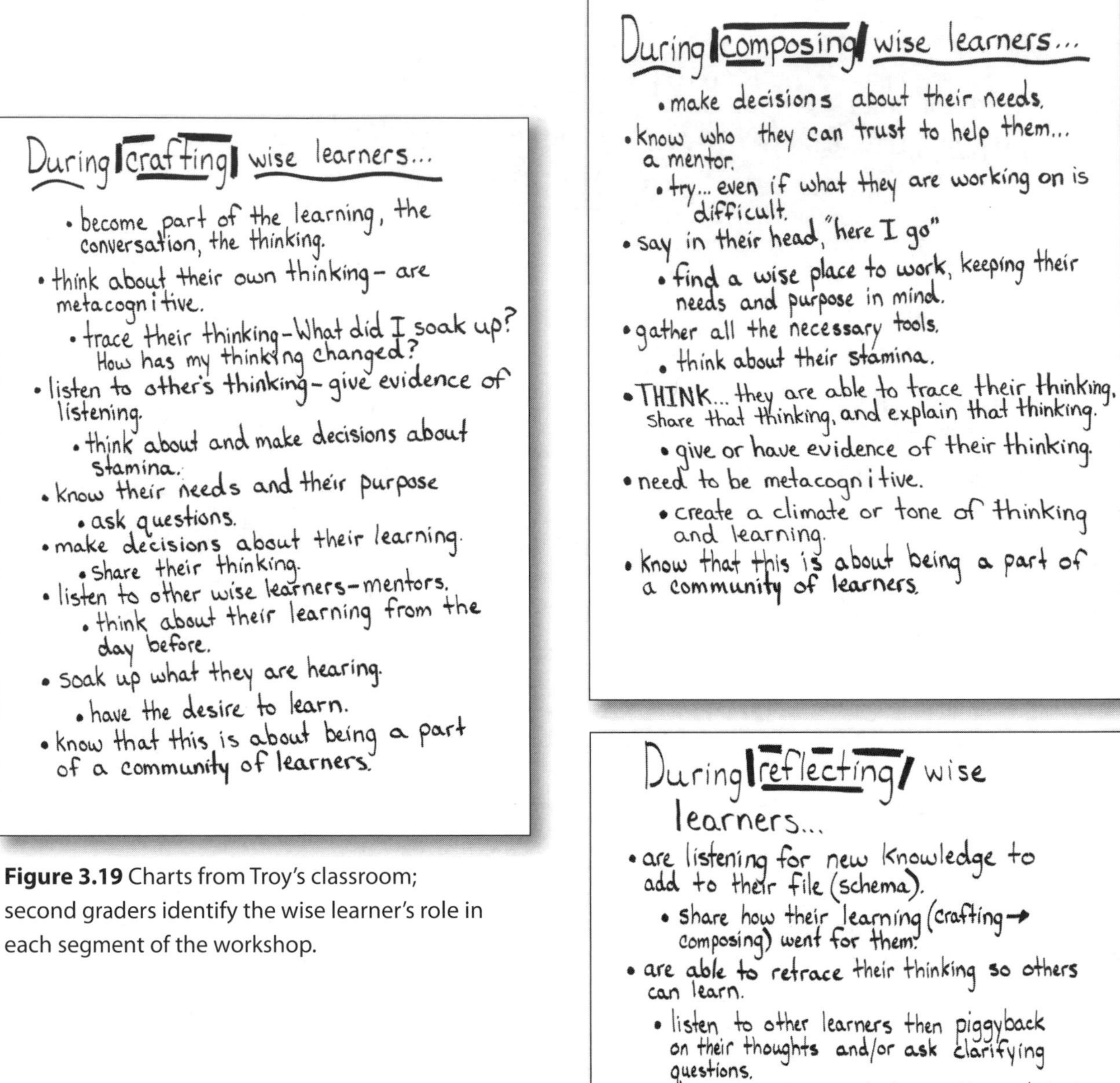

Figure 3.19 Charts from Troy's classroom; second graders identify the wise learner's role in each segment of the workshop.

~ Crafting ~

Teacher

- Plan P.A.
  - Record your thinking on charts and in your notebook H.G.
- Be focused L.R.
  - Share what you know → your schema J.P.
- To help students understand M.H.
  - To help students know how to spend composing time M.L.
- Learn from students K.W.
  - Listen to students T.B.
- Listen to the ideas of others J.W.
  - To make sure you're not lost in your thinking K.W.
- To ask questions H.G.

Students

- To listen A.D.
  - To be thinking about what we try to figure out— to explore S.F.
- To ask questions M.T.
  - To participate L.R.
- To not "check out" C.W.J.
  - To stay focused M.D.
- To stay involved in the conversation A.D.
  - To share your thinking M.T.
- To be part of the community M.H.
  - To learn from each other L.R.
- Be wise K.W.
  - To stay "in the thinking..." J.W.
- To help others think more clearly A.A.
  - To know your purpose M.T.

~ Composing ~

Teacher

- To be flexible A.D.
  - Help you if you get stuck C.J.
- Help you fix your mistakes K.W.
  - To confer M.L.
- Ask questions that are important M.H.
  - Take notes about your thinking (assessment) C.J.
- To check for understanding J.W.
  - To know your purpose and help guide it M.T.
- To help you learn the best way C.W.J.
  - To show examples of how it should work R.A.G.
- To be focused A.D.
  - To check in with individuals or small groups A.D.
- To stay in the community L.R.

Students

- Listening T.B.
  - To answer and ask questions M.H.
- To be able to stick with something K.W.
  - Pay attention to what the rest of the community is doing A.L.
- To have your tools ready M.H.
  - To develop your endurance and stamina M.D.
- To look over your work carefully R.A.G.
  - To make wise learning decisions C.W.J.
- To apply or try out new strategies or skills P.A.
  - Do what you are supposed to do L.R.
- To know your purpose A.D.
  - Follow or explore your thinking J.W.
- Keep track of your learning J.P.

~ Reflecting ~

Teacher

- Ask questions R.A.G.
  - Focus reflection on crafting L.R.
- Listen to students' thoughts... keep track A.D.
  - Ask students "why" and "how" J.W.
- Ask students about their understanding T.B.
  - Ask "how" he or she understands J.P.
- Set up rituals and routines that give students TIME to reflect P.A.
  - To stay organized J.P.
- Record student thinking L.R.
  - To make sure you stick to your purpose T.B.

Students

- To be thinking and sharing what you did S.F.
  - To use time wisely H.G.
- To focus on the speaker J.P.
  - To be flexible M.T.
- To make sure that you prepare during composing T.B.
  - Share your learning and what you did to make it happen R.A.G.
- To share your best thinking M.T.
  - To explain what you "get" and what you "don't get" C.J.
- To talk about how it went M.T.
  - To talk about what you did, why you did it, and how it went J.W.
- To know your purpose C.J.
  - To be positive R.A.G.

Figure 3.20 Charts for Student/Teacher Roles: Crafting; Composing; Reflecting. Third graders determine the responsibilities of both the teacher and students during the three workshop components. Distinguishing specific roles helps strengthen engagement and commitment to learning within the workshop setting.

By defining each component and recognizing specific roles in the workshop, the responsibility of what we do each day as readers is shared. Helping students learn to navigate the components of the workshop and put their own thinking into the representation of the workshop itself creates a system rich in student voice and creativity. D. N. Perkins once stated, "Creative results do not just bubble up from some fecund swamp in the mind. Creative individuals tend to value stated qualities and try straightforwardly to achieve them" (1991, 85).

We want students to take active roles in their reader's workshops so that they can understand, remember, extend meaning, and make their reading experiences memorable. Giving them a voice in defining the structure and the expectations makes the "work" of the workshop theirs. Ownership creates readers who, as one of my students recently said, "Read because we want to, not because we have to . . . it's our time to become thinkers!"

Those are my ashlars. For conferring to be a natural part of my classroom, all five have to be in place:

- A sense of **trust, respect, and tone**
- The strength of **endurance and stamina**
- A clear and defined **purpose and audience**
- Instruction planned along the **gradual release of responsibility model**
- The smoothly running structure of **reader's workshop**

Next time you're walking down Main Street, take a look around. There are two types of ashlar stonework you might see. On buildings that are in disrepair there are broken stones, at one time bonded between mortar, now crumbling, waiting to be replaced by the next new corner drugstore or superstore. But, just down the street stands a monumental, architecturally supreme building in which the ashlar consists of regularly cut blocks, arranged in precise, yet creative ways. This building took a bit more time to build but will endure long after others have turned to rubble, soon to be replaced by something new.

Like Troy, Dana, Cheryl, and Debbie, we must identify our instructional underpinnings, build a strong foundation, add keystones and strong mortar—to build the complex structures in which conferring can thrive. Creating a culture of thinking, in which all members develop by identifying and developing the essential rituals and routines, systems and structures that matter most. I have identified five key instructional ashlars. What are *yours*?

PART 2

WHAT ARE THE ESSENTIAL COMPONENTS OF CONFERRING?

"Once you've established a basic pattern for conferring, then you can develop variations on conference style." But only when you "know and trust each other."

—Adapted from Donald Murray, 1989

A reading conference makes me feel good because I can share what I am thinking and it is important so that I know what I will be looking forward to and what I should be doing for the rest of the time I have the book in my hand.

—Mikayla, Third Grade

Chapter 4

The RIP Model—Bringing Thoughtful Structure to Our Conferring

I once e-mailed Jo Franklin (my daughter's first-grade teacher) three questions about how she handles reading conferences in her first-grade classroom. I asked the following:

1. What is the greatest power of conferring?
2. What do you hope to glean during a reading conference?
3. How has your conferring evolved?

Here are Jo's answers:

The greatest power of conferring is . . .

- Knowing each child as a reader and a thinker.
- Sharing the joy of rich conversations about literature!

During each conference, I hope to glean . . .

- A child's individual strengths to use as building blocks to nudge him or her further.
- How and if a child is applying specific strategies as he or she reads. I can then target confusions and clarify understandings.
- Being able to peer into children's minds as readers and thinkers.

Here is how my conferring has evolved . . .

- I am spending more time listening to children talk about their reading as opposed to having them read to me or answer *my* questions.
- I am just this year focusing on ending each conference with a goal in mind—something the child and I come up with that will help him/her become an even better

reader (and having the child put this on a sticky to keep in his/her lit log as a reminder until our next conference).

- I am doing better (I have found a system that works for me—finally!) at keeping track of each conference—taking notes and being consistent about what I record and when I have met with each child.

PONDERING: How would you answer each of these questions? Jot down your answers in your notebook and refer to them often—especially as you strengthen your own conferring skills.

When I read about Jo and her coming to know conferring more explicitly, I am struck by the fact that she is still thinking about how to hone her skills. As a conferrer, Jo realizes that learning to confer well is a process that is constantly developing—focusing on structure, language, and record-keeping. Jo has done some very specific thinking about how she hopes to improve the reading conferences she has with readers. When I read Jo's thinking, specific words emerge that show the rigor, inquiry, and intimacy she is incorporating into her reflection: *joy*, *rich*, *individual strengths*, *building blocks*, *target*, *peer into*, *focusing*, *goal in mind*, *keeping track*, *consistent*. Jo has come to understand that the ritual of conferring is consistent, but there is a fluidity and flexibility of thought that continues to develop as we confer with children—even first graders. Jo realizes that conferring has become a keystone of her instruction and that it deserves careful thought.

Like Jo, my reading conferences continue to transform and I am always trying to renovate and reevaluate how I confer to make sure conferring is not something I just do, but rather is one of those purposeful conversations that I mentioned in the introduction to this book. One of the things I have done is to try to create a structure to follow in each side-by-side conference:

- A structure that actively involves the reader in decision making, analysis, and documentation of our conversations
- A structure that honors both the reader's voice and the teacher's voice and encourages a shared creation of understanding
- A structure that values a mentoring relationship rich in teaching, modeling, and empowerment
- A structure that encourages building a reader's awareness of how thinking strategies and specific skills can be strengthened through metacognition

In this chapter, I introduce you to the structure in which my reading conferences are embedded. I call it the RIP Model. No, not Read in Peace Model or Rest in Peace Model or Routing Information Protocol (although it could be considered a protocol) or Remove It Permanently Model.

The acronym RIP materialized as I honed my own reading conferences. To provide a predictable pattern to reading conferences, I identified specific outcomes of each portion, or component, of a conference:

R – Review, Read Aloud, Record
I – Instruction, Insights, Intrigue
P – Plan, Progress, Purpose

I realized that, like all good rituals and routines, a predictable structure for reading conferences provides a pattern for me to follow each time I confer with a reader. More important, my students know that each side-by-side conference follows a similar pattern. There is research to suggest that familiar connections and conforming neural networks are key to the formation of meaning and intelligence (Jensen 1998). I have found that a predictable structure makes my conferring more engaging, relevant, and meaningful. And, as Debbie Miller might add, more joyful (2005).

For each element of a conference I will provide an explanation of the components, my intent, and some specific language I might use when I confer (one example of language I might expect to hear from a student and three examples of language I might use to elicit student response). Let's take a closer look at each component of the RIP Model.

R: Review, Read Aloud, Record

The first component of every conference begins with **R**. This element of a reading conference provides an opportunity to review a reader's progress, to take a brief running record or hear the child read aloud for a short time, or to record something the reader chooses to share at the beginning of a conference. I usually start with an open-ended question like, How is your reading going? or What can you tell me about yourself as a reader today?

The following is a sampling of some of what might happen during the **R** component of the conference.

Review

Intent: The reader and I might reconsider learning from a previous conference. Possible language to elicit further discussion or thought:

Student Language

- *I'm still trying to figure out what is going to happen next . . .*

My Language

- *So, tell me, what have you been working on since last time we met?*
- *You said during our last conversation that you were going to try to ____; how is that going?*
- *Tell me a bit about what you have discovered since the last time we conferred . . .*

Intent: The reader and I might review the text she has chosen to read. Possible language to elicit further discussion or thought:

Student Language

- *I started a new book today; it's called ______ and so far ______ . . .*

My Language

- *You've chosen a new book since last time we met; how is that going?*
- *I see you're still reading ______; tell me about how your reading is going . . .*
- *Tell me about what you're reading today . . .*

Read Aloud

Intent: The reader might read a short portion of the text so that I can record a brief running record. Possible language to elicit further discussion or thought:

Student Language

- *Listen to this part, Mr. Allen, I loved it . . .*

My Language

- *I would love to hear you read just a little bit to me. Why don't you read a portion to me that you're thinking about . . . ?*
- *How is this book going? Will you find a short section and read it to me?*
- *Find a part that you especially loved or a part that you're wondering about. Read a bit of that section to me so that we can talk about what you're thinking . . .*

Record

Intent: The reader might share brief answers to a question that I ask or one that he is trying to answer. Possible language to elicit further discussion or thought:

Student Language

- *I am wondering . . . What am I going to do to remember this part ____? It really struck me.*

My Language

- *How is your thinking changing as you've been reading this book?*
- *What have you discovered about yourself as a reader today that seems different from yesterday?*
- *What have you been thinking about today as a reader? What would you like to tell me?*

Intent: The reader might share his use of a specific thinking strategy that we discussed in our crafting session. Possible language to elicit further discussion or thought:

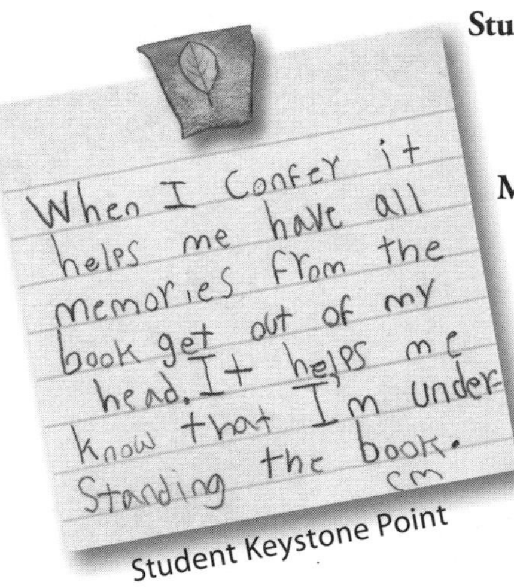

Student Keystone Point

Student Language

- *Mr. Allen, I was thinking about determining importance and here's what I've noticed . . .*

My Language

- *Is there something you understand better today than you did yesterday? (monitoring for meaning)*
- *Tell me a little bit about the pictures this is creating for you . . . What other senses are you noticing? (create mental images)*
- *What is this book reminding you of? (activate, utilize, and build background knowledge)*

Intent: The reader might begin by telling me about a surface structure system he is trying to figure out. Possible language to elicit further discussion or thought:

Student Language

- *I am having a little trouble with this word. Can you help me figure out what it means . . . ?*

My Language

- *Last time we met, you mentioned that you were having some trouble with some of the words in this text. How is that going now?*
- *What parts of the text are sticking in your head today? What new vocabulary have you noticed today?*
- *Is there a sentence in your reading that really made sense to you? Tell me about it . . .*

The first part of the conference, the **R**, is a way of easing into a conversation. It is a means to discover what the reader is thinking, pondering, or discovering. I want to find out what is going on with the reader's process. I also want to get a flavor for how he or she uses a strategy or skill that we have discussed in either a whole-group crafting session, a small-group setting, or during a previous conference.

When I sit down next to a reader, I may have a specific goal in mind based on a previous conference that causes me to take the lead. Of course, I may go in with no preconceived notions about the reader at all. The reader may have something he or she has been mulling over before I sat down, so the student takes the lead. If I have thought about the reader before we confer, I may have several things running through my head:

1. The book he mentioned he is planning to read (I gather a reading status two times a week);
2. Our last one-on-one conversation (I have the notes from our last conference);
3. The strategy or skill we worked on in crafting (How is he reapplying or revising his thinking—the "so what?" of strategy instruction? How is he preserving the strategy to strengthen his reading? How is he applying a new skill?); or
4. Something specific that has nudged me to confer with that particular reader on that particular day. For example, maybe he said something during crafting that struck me and I want to talk with him more about it, or maybe when I was sending students off to read, he asked me for a conference.

The **R** section of the conference gives both the reader and me a chance to focus our conversation. It gives us a chance to ponder and reflect before we move further into a conference. It is a starting point. Almost like the think time we give students after we ask a question, the **R** gives us a chance to build some common language or thinking so that we can move into the conference and formulate a plan.

PONDERING: How do you begin a conference with a reader? What are the specific skills and strategies you hope will emanate when you initially sit down with the reader? How do you uncover them?

I: Instruction, Insights, Intrigue

The second component of every conference begins with **I**. This component of a reading conference is a chance to teach the reader, usually based on discoveries or information gleaned in the first portion of the conference. Remember "teach, model, empower"? I look at the **I** component as an opportunity to go into more depth. It is where the real conversation happens. This is a chance to discuss specific information that came to the forefront during our initial conversation. I look for thinking, strategies, or skills that bubbled to the surface that warrant further dialogue or clarification. An insight might come to light as a teaching point or point of entry into uncovering more about how a reader is understanding or remembering. There might just be something that intrigues me or intrigues the student that we take a few minutes to discuss.

The following is a sampling of some of what might happen in the **I** component of the conference.

Instruction

Intent: The reader and I might discuss his application of the current thinking strategy we are learning during the crafting session of our reader's workshop. Possible language to elicit further discussion or thought:

Student Language

- *At first when I was reading this I was thinking _______, but now I'm thinking that* _______ (synthesizing new learning and ideas)

My Language

- *Talk to me a little bit about the ways you find yourself monitoring your comprehension. What are you doing when you find yourself not understanding something?* (monitor for meaning and problem-solve when meaning breaks down)
- *Let's talk a bit about this word. Tell me about what you did when you came to it . . .* (activate, utilize, and build background knowledge)
- *I notice that you're putting a lot of pieces together. Describe what's happening inside your head as you do that . . .* (draw inferences)

Insights

Intent: The reader and I might discuss specific wonderings the student is contemplating or that I gleaned from the beginning of the conference. Possible language to elicit further discussion or thought:

Student Language

- *I've chosen this book today, and I am wondering if it is a good match for me . . .*

My Language

- *You were able to tell me so much about what you read and what you were wondering. How were you able to do that?*
- *Explain to me why you have _____ as a goal . . .*
- *You stopped for a moment while you were reading to me; what were you thinking when you stopped?*

Intrigue

Intent: The reader or I might be intrigued about something that we noticed in the beginning of the conference. Possible language to elicit further discussion or thought:

Student Language

- *I noticed that I got confused when I read this sentence ______; I'm wondering if you could help me figure it out . . .*

My Language

- *You have been reading this book for a while. How long do you think it will take you to finish it?*
- *I am curious about your book choice. Tell me a little bit about what you were thinking when you chose it . . .*
- *When you read that page to me, you didn't slow down at all. Remember, we talk about "pausing, considering, and reflecting" as we read. What would happen if you read it a little more slowly?*

During the **I** component of the conference, I try to record any learnings that arise. I want to make note of instructional points so that I have a record of what we have talked about as fellow readers, and what I have taught. The middle component of a conference deserves and takes the most time. Once I identify a teaching point, gain some insight into the reader's thinking, or become intrigued as I talk with a student, we have something to guide our conversation. It is important that, together, we talk about book choice, vocabulary, comprehension, text elements, and so on. The revelatory details that come about during the **I** component of the conference lead to the most documentable data. I might say, "Here is what I noticed the reader doing or thinking, and these are the decisions we made about it." The difference between talking and teaching happens in this portion of a conference.

PONDERING: How much do you try to teach in a conference? How do you create rigor without overteaching?

P: Plan, Progress, Purpose

Every conference ends with a review of the student's progress. The **P** portion of the workshop is about what the reader intends to do between conferences, and together we devise a plan that will nudge her further. As collaborative readers, we develop plans that will gradually move the reader forward until our next conference. What is it going to take for her to progress from this point forward? Of course, the plan is intentional, based on a rationale that emerged during our time together. A goal is set. The goal gives the reader an additional purpose; what is it that she will achieve or accomplish as a reader? The goal could be long term or short term, depending on when we'll confer again. The goal can be about a deep structure system or a surface structure system. The goal can be about book choice or reader's response.

For each **P** (plan, progress, or purpose) I have given examples of the language that the reader or I might use to strengthen intellectual intent—one sample a child might start with as conferee and three that I use as the conferrer. The following is a sampling of some of what might happen in the **P** component of the conference.

Plan

Intent: The reader and I, together, might discuss what he hopes to work on before we confer again. Possible language to elicit further discussion or thought:

Student Language

- *I think I am going to spend some time comparing this book with the last book I read and see if I notice a strategy that might improve my writing . . .*

My Language

- *I'm thinking that when you might not be grasping what the text is telling you, you just keep reading without making sure it makes sense. I'd like you to focus on stopping periodically to check on your understanding . . .*
- *Between now and the next time we meet, I'd like you to choose three books that you think fit you as a reader and be able to explain to me why you think they might be wise choices for you.*
- *What would happen if you decided to write a bit more in your reader's notebook each day? Try to see if you can respond to your reading more often, and we'll talk about it next time we meet.*

Progress

Intent: The reader and I might consider the subtleties of a strategy or skill that might stretch the reader to better understand his process. Possible language to elicit further discussion or thought:

Student Language

- *I think I am doing a pretty good job of figuring out unknown words. I'm going to keep track of what strategies I use to help me understand the words I don't know automatically.*

My Language

- *You seem to be having trouble reading the dialogue when two characters are talking. Stop periodically to make sure you know who is saying what . . .*
- *You talked a lot about using your background knowledge. Now see if you can pinpoint those times when it's your background experience that is helping you understand . . .*
- *You've been reading a lot of fiction lately. Perhaps next time we meet, you can share a different genre with me and tell me why you chose it . . .*

Purpose

Intent: We end with a discussion of purpose and leave the conference with the reader thinking about her next steps. Possible language to elicit further discussion or thought:

Student Language

- *I have been responding* ***to*** *the text in my notebook a lot, writing about only my thinking, but for the next few days I'm going to write* ***about*** *what I'm reading and try to summarize a bit more . . .*

My Language

- *You are reading a lot of nonfiction. Try to take note of the text structures that are enhancing your understanding . . .*
- *You had difficulty explaining to me why you chose this book. Next time we meet, be ready to tell me why you're reading it.*
- *I am curious about the questions you are asking as you read. What happens inside your head when you're asking questions? See if you can explain how asking questions is helping you understand the text.*

Every child deserves that moment of an intimate personal conversation that can open and grow his or her worldly understandings and conceptions.
Dana Berg
First-Grade Teacher

Teacher Keystone Point

The **P** section of the conference is the guarantee that readers will be accountable between now and the next time we confer. Often they will choose to share their plan with the rest of the readers in the room when we pull together as a whole group to reflect. Rarely do I push students to share what happened in a side-by-side conference with the rest of the class. I want them to trust that our one-on-one time was just for us (although I know that the three or four kids around us had their ears perked as we talked). I want readers to know that I am not going to force them to bring anything to the whole group without their permission. I want them to share their thinking by their own volition.

The **P** component of my reading conferences has become one of the most critical aspects of conferring. It is the component that leaves the reader saying, "Oh dear, he means business" or "I am ready to tackle this as a reader!" The student might be thinking, "I better think about what I just said because I know next time we meet he's going to ask, and I have a lot of hard work to do!" And, I don't think that is a bad thing.

When I was first learning to confer, I would end a conference by saying something like, "Good job" or "I can tell you're working hard," but I never left feeling like I had taught something, let alone feeling like the student had taught me something. I certainly didn't leave feeling like a student would continue exploring or investigating something scholarly between conferences. Now conferring has taken on new purpose. Now I do leave a conference knowing that, together, the reader and I have made wise decisions about his plan. And, when students know that they are accountable for the plan, for progressing toward a goal, or identifying their purpose for future work, it adds a bit more work ethic to the composing portion of the workshop.

The **P** portion of the conference provides the conferee and me with a walk-away (see Chapter 6, Conferring Walk-Aways). When a student leaves a conference, I want her to have something in mind that may help her remember, understand, extend meaning, or make her reading experience memorable. If both of us have an objective in mind, we leave the conference with a desire to develop and carry on with the learning. The reader's walk-away leaves her changed as a thinker. I walk away with better insight.

RIP. A simple structure (remember Thoreau's words and the prairie ecosystem) forming part of the mortar that holds the keystone in place.

The RIP Model and My Conferring Notebook

Once I found a structure conducive to what I wanted reading conferences to accomplish, I had to figure out a way to keep track of the conferences I was having with readers. And, let me tell you, I tried a plethora of recording methods over the years. I have come to realize that the structure of note taking is a personal decision. Like all problem-solvers, if I wanted my conferring notes to make sense when I explained them to children, parents, or administrators (or when reviewing them myself), I had to make wise decisions about what works best for me and for my students. If I wanted to use my conferring notes to inform instruction, I had to make wise decisions about what works best for readers.

Here is my suggestion: Do not replicate or reproduce someone else's note-taking ideas without first doing some research. See how they work. Attempt a trial run-through for a few weeks. Test them out!

Do not get me wrong; finding a form that looks intriguing is a great starting point—it is part of the process. And, you are welcome to try mine—it just might work for you. I would suggest that you explore several forms, adapt them to fit your style, make them your own (giving credit where credit is due of course). Like Jo mentioned, she has found a system that works for her—finally!

The goal is keeping track of each side-by-side conference and being consistent first in your conferring, then in your note taking.

PONDERING: What are the necessary elements of a reading conference you want to capture as you take notes? What information will best meet the needs of your students?

I remember when I first started taking conferring notes during one-on-one conferences. I decided that I would use computer labels—the self-feeding kind used in dot matrix printers. Each day before reader's workshop, I would tear off a sheet or two or even three (if I was feeling ambitious), I snap them under my clipboard's clip, and head out to confer. I thought it to be the perfect system. I cannot do cute, but I can do functional and purposeful. Computer labels seemed to fulfill a function and meet a purpose.

I had already formulated the RIP model; the conferring structure was in place. My next step was to record student thinking as I conferred.

I used four computer labels per conference. One with the reader's name, the date, and the title of the text he was reading. One label was reserved for the **R**, one reserved for the **I**, one reserved for the **P**. It worked during the conferring. I thought I had the perfect system for record keeping.

I dreamed of each afternoon sitting at my desk, quiet music playing in the background, the afternoon sun shining in the window. I imagined myself, peeling labels, placing them into a three-ring binder, divided into color-coded pages for each reader. As I peeled, I would analyze my jottings, pull together groups if need be, and use information to inform instruction. Utopia.

There was a problem. At the end of the trimester I would have a six-inch stack of anecdotal notes waiting to be transferred to my conferring notebook. I never found the time to sit in quiet reflection. Even though I was gathering lots of great information at the time, it wasn't going beyond the clipboard. It was a disorganized mess. I still find stray notes periodically, still waiting to be placed under a child's name, although those children are probably all in high school by now. For me, this system didn't work as well as I originally thought. What's the old Yiddish saying? "We plan, God laughs"?

There were lots of problems with my Utopian system. I did not keep track with whom I had conferred (how could I, there were computer labels everywhere). I did not have everything in one place, and I did not have what the students and I talked about organized in a central location (but I wrote like a mad man on those labels each day). Like the song says, "It sounds funny, I know . . . but it really is so!" It is likely that I had enough computer labels collected to wallpaper my classroom! Had I wallpapered, at least I would have had them all in one place and may have had the time to reread them. Can you hear my laughter?

So much for that plan. It was a nice thought. But like all Utopias, my record keeping was filled with flaws.

The trouble was, I was just collecting sticky notes. I did not define any real purpose. I was taking notes because someone told me, "When you confer, you should take notes." There was no method to my madness, and my collection tools were primitive to say the least.

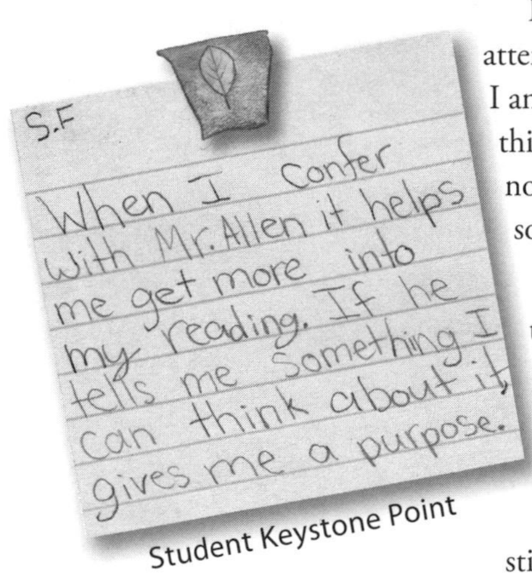

Student Keystone Point

Now, this computer label idea was just one of many note-taking options I attempted to replicate (I picked up the idea at a workshop). And, in all fairness, I am sure that it works for many teachers—maybe even you. If you are reading this and saying to yourself, "Hey, I use computer labels for my conferring notes, and it works beautifully," bless you. That is the point—what works for some may not work for all.

It was not until I created my own conferring form that was congruent to the RIP structure that I found success. It was not until I housed the forms in my conferring notebook that I had them organized in a useful way. It was not until I experimented, refined, and simplified my form that I felt like I was being successful.

Troy Rushmore, my teammate, laughed when I told him about my sticky-note dilemma. He, too, had tried replicating someone else's note-taking system. The system just didn't work and, like Jo and me, he is developing his own. Troy has tried index cards taped to a clipboard, individual notebooks, and is now playing around with the form I am introducing to you here.

What happens if the method we are using to take notes is not a good fit? We give up on taking notes, on gathering the very information we say is critical to the act of conferring. We have no documentation of our conferences. We have no data to serve as a response to intervention, no record of a child's thinking, nothing to back up our instructional practices or belief in conferring. So, someone else decides how you should assess reading.

Be honest. We have all done it. We have all thought, "Ah, this is it!" We have all been to a workshop and said, "That sounds so smart. I am making my notebook tomorrow! This is the answer I've been looking for all these years." At times it feels like a pyramid scheme. (Remember those fancy, quick-fix, dangling carrot ideas I saw at our local reading conference?) So be forewarned, I will be explaining my current note-taking form, and I want you to consider its use and see if you think it fits your needs. (In Chapter 5 you will see the notes I took while conferring with Cole, Haley, and Jaryd.)

But, what if you have not gone through this process of trying, adapting, changing, and creating? You will. I look at it as part of my own journey. Whether you are in your first year of teaching or your twenty-fifth, I think that things as simple as adapting a conferring form can make someone a better teacher. While student teaching, my supervising teacher, Judy Gilkey, said to me, "If you ever get to the point where you think you have it all figured out, it is time for you to quit." Wise words. She taught for more than thirty years. So, whether you are starting to confer, or you have done it for quite some time, it is okay to experiment. Your students are getting one-on-one attention—that's the important part!

Settle into the RIP format first. I believe it is the function of the conference to dictate the types of documentation we gather. Change my form to fit your needs. If you do, please just type a little "adapted from" in the footnote just so you will remember where you saw it for the first time. Please, for goodness' sake, do not photocopy one hundred or more color-coded forms. Acclimatize yourself first. Try the RIP format. The note taking is secondary. Confer, don't collect.

PONDERING: Think about how you go about taking conferring notes. What has worked? What has not worked? How are you currently keeping track of your reading conferences?

Conferring Versus Collecting

On a typical day after school, Troy and I can be found in one of our classrooms reflecting on how our day with our students went. It is good to have a person with whom you can share your frustrations and successes, risk free and without judgment. On this particular day, still thinking about conferring notes, we got into a discussion about taking conferring notes for real reasons versus collecting "stuff" (like my computer labels). We surmised that there is a major difference between collecting and conferring. There are people who collect stuff just to collect it—like a flea market for the *D* word (data). Sometimes teachers collect stuff because someone outside their classroom has told them it's important or necessary (perhaps without questioning the purpose or instructional value). And there are teachers who collect data to support the meaningful learning experiences they provide on a daily basis.

Troy and I decided that if we were going to gather information about the readers in our classrooms we should do so because:

- Conferring notes ought to be a natural outlet and opportunity to help readers and writers create authentic purpose for their literacy endeavors—we can show growth and plan instruction based on what we write down.

- Conferring notes might change from student to student, moment to moment, workshop to workshop—every reader is different.
- Conferring notes may determine the type of relationships that will emerge between literacy colleagues over time—readers see us write down their thinking and know that it is important.
- Conferring notes are a demonstration of recording what matters most—the opportunity to sit side-by-side, eye-to-eye, truth-to-truth.
- Conferring notes are created in an atmosphere of import—richness and depth can be cultivated and harvested.
- Conferring notes provide more than just a glimpse into the readers—they paint a detailed portrait of a learner.

PONDERING: If you were to create your own conferring form, what would you want it to include?

When I designed my Conferring form, I thought about the following criteria. My form had to be:

- Simple and flexible
- Physically comfortable and easy to handle
- Correlated with the RIP structure
- Easy to use to note patterns of growth and progress
- Roomy enough to write on
- Easy to use to record evidence of strategy use
- Functional (so I could write and listen simultaneously)
- Modifiable for conferring in other content areas

A blank version of my Conferring form appears in Figure 4.1.

In my conferring notebook, I use this format, three to a page, double-sided. Simple form. A simple form used to record all the complexities that surface during a conference. I can confer with a child six times per form. For me, having the RIP format along the top helps me stay focused as I confer.

I like having the Plan/Progress/Purpose from our last conference readily available when I sit down with a child. It makes the "Last time we met . . ." language easy to access and remember. It brings our previous purposeful conversation to the forefront of our current conference. The last box on the form becomes the tie that binds one conference to another. Of course, it is

Reading Conferences for ______________________

Date ____________ Title ______________________ Page[s] ________

REVIEW/READ ALOUD/RECORD	INSTRUCTION/INSIGHTS/INTRIGUE	PLAN/PROGRESS/PURPOSE

Additional Comment(s):

Date ____________ Title ______________________ Page[s] ________

REVIEW/READ ALOUD/RECORD	INSTRUCTION/INSIGHTS/INTRIGUE	PLAN/PROGRESS/PURPOSE

Additional Comment(s):

Date ____________ Title ______________________ Page[s] ________

REVIEW/READ ALOUD/RECORD	INSTRUCTION/INSIGHTS/INTRIGUE	PLAN/PROGRESS/PURPOSE

Additional Comment(s):

Figure 4.1 The Conferring form utilizes the RIP format.

flexible—if the reader is not working on the same plan, or has set a new goal for himself, or is reading a different text.

My conferring notebook is simple. It's functional. It is like a good piece of luggage, designed well enough to organize everything I might need on a trip, but easy to carry on the plane. Not too cumbersome. Not too fancy. Not too cute. The contents of my conferring notebook work for me as the conferrer. Its specific characteristics include the following:

- It is a one-inch, three-ring binder. (I try to limit it to one inch. I have a separate file for each child to transfer completed forms to when the notebook starts getting too bulky.)
- It has a separate section for each reader. (I think this brings a nice sense of individualization to my conferring—students know that their section contains their thinking.)
- Each section includes a double-sided Conferring form (see Figure 4.1 and appendix). (I also have forms in each section for other content areas. A side note: Franki Sibberson recommended the dividers I use currently. They have a 45-degree angled pocket. Each pocket holds additional comments from students that I gather throughout the day. On sticky notes, I might jot down student comments not heard during a side-by-side conference [a statement made during crafting, a remark on the way to lunch, thoughts that pop up throughout the day, quotes I overhear during book clubs, comments made when I have a touchstone conference, etc.]. I might also include notes students write to me about their reading, formal assessment data, and so on. I am experimenting with this aspect of documenting important talk that happens outside of a reading conference. Now I always have sticky notes and a pen in my pocket just in case I hear a gem. The pockets provide a grand collection place to tuck random thoughts and ideas that emerge.)
- I track students' current reading with a Current Reads, Current Titles form (see Figure 4.2 for a completed version; a blank form is included in the appendix) in the front of the notebook. (I take a "status" twice a week. Right after our crafting lesson, I ask readers one by one, as I send them off to read independently, how they will be spending time during composing ["Kendall, what will you be reading today? Cooper, are you still reading ____?"]. Twice a week is just enough for me to know what types of reading students are doing. I can also note if I need to confer with a student who is jumping from book to book, whose choice piques my curiosity, who has chosen a book that may sound a bit difficult, and so on. Keeping track of titles helps me know what additional texts I may need to add to the library, or if several children are reading the same series, they might need some time to pull together and chat as a group.)
- I keep a Reading Conference-Check Off form in the front of my notebook (see Figure 4.3 for a completed version; a blank form is included in the appendix). This form is a simple table to keep track of readers with whom I have conferred.

Current Reads, Current Titles

Name	Date: 1/27	Date: 1/29
Thomas	Cowboy Sam	Same
Alexandra	Emma's Journal	Cam Jansen: Carnival Prize
Devante	MTH: Twister on Tuesday	Same
Lauryn	(Absent)	Hungry Caterpillar
Megan	Never Spit on Your Shoes	Same
Sophie	Do Not Open	Santa Paws
Robert	MTH: Revolutionary War	Same
Rachel	Joyful Noise	Dear Mrs. LaRue

Figure 4.2 Current Reads, Current Titles form

Reading Conference–Check Off Form

Name	Date							
Thomas	8/4	8/8	8/12	8/19	8/22	8/26	9/3		
Alexandra	8/6	8/11	8/18	8/25	9/3				
Devante	8/5	8/11	8/19	8/26	9/4				
Lauryn	8/6	8/8	8/20	8/27	9/2				
Megan	8/4	8/12	8/18	8/26	9/5				
Sophie	8/6	8/13	8/21	8/28	9/4				
Robert	8/7	8/12	8/20	8/26	9/4				
Rachel	8/5	8/11	[illegible]	8/26	9/3				

Figure 4.3 Reading Conference–Check Off form

Conferring with students is a deliberate act. The notes I take as I confer have to be just as thoughtful, ruminative, and solicitous. The attention given to detail when talking to a reader should be reflected in the assessment data we gather during our conferences. That is why developing our own note-taking system is so important. As Peter Johnston reminds us, the word *assessment* derives from the Latin word *assidere*, meaning "to sit alongside," and the word *evaluation* comes from the Latin root *e* meaning "from" and *valere* meaning "strength" or "worth" (Johnston 1997, 2). Learning that *assessment* means to sit alongside helped me realize that conferring notes must take a more prominent role in our evaluation of student learning. Our conferring notes are documentation of what the reader knows, what she is thinking, and what she'll do as a result of learning. I would argue that conferring notes are as useful and powerful as more formal assessments in documenting specific growth in reading. If we use conferring notes wisely, we have strong and worthy evidence of how a reader changes over time and becomes more proficient. Sitting alongside a reader invites both of us to consider how she is applying skills, strategies, and thinking in the context of her own reading. (See Lexee's conference notes in Figure 4.4 for an example.)

I cannot have an "If I make it, they will read" attitude. If my conference notes lack purpose, I need to reconsider my note-taking structure (remember, don't make a year's worth of someone else's form until you've tried it for yourself). Starting out slowly is better than not starting. Your conference notes are meant to inform your instruction or cause you to reflect on a student's individual needs or strengths. Your conference notes are solid testaments to the kind of formative assessment that can inform reading instruction.

Of course, I rely on other assessment information to monitor readers' development as well. My conferring notes are just one piece of something much larger.

Troy described it best during one of our after-school rap sessions. We were talking about gathering a body of evidence to assess and evaluate our students. We got into a discussion of the types of assessments we do with children. Our discussion went something like this:

Troy: This whole dependence on narrow, program-driven data about learners is getting out of hand. We're trying to plot children on graphs. It's like all of a sudden something like fluency outweighs comprehension and levels outweigh the decisions readers make while they are reading. Tests outweigh thinking. The small pieces outweigh the whole child. We have to do a better job of documenting growth in a wise way.

Patrick: You're exactly right. We have to look at students respectfully and sensibly by building a body of evidence that focuses on the instruction we're providing on a daily basis. That's why I think conferring is such an important part of what we do as teachers of reading.

Troy: And, I get it. We need both, but think about this for a minute . . . I bring you a picture I just took of, let's say, Graham. He's bending over near the water fountain in the picture. What would you think?

Patrick: That he's thirsty? That he was just getting ready to get a drink? That he's in the hall, not doing what he's supposed to be doing. (We chuckle.)

Troy: Well . . . that's not *quite* where I was headed. Think about this: at that moment you're only getting a snapshot. That's the only part I could fit in the frame and you're basing your

Reading Conferences for: Lexee

Date 10/30 Title The Chalkbox Kid Page(s)

Review/Read Aloud/Record	Instruction/Insights/Intrigue	Plan/Progress/Purpose
·finished Magic School Bus at the Waterworks ·retell ✓+ T/ Why? S/ I read this in first grade "I could read the words, but now I understand..."	S/ "When I was little our teacher didn't teach me to understand the words, she just wanted us to know the words..." T/ What caused you to understand rather than just know...? S/ My B.K. and B.E. T/ How? (Pause..)	S/ "... I didn't know about the book, now I do..." T/ "Spend some time thinking about what is helping you understand instead of just know..."

Additional Comment(s): beginning to use schema language, work on "the how" – detailed retell –

Date 11/4 Title Ramona and Her Mother Page(s) p.17

Review/Read Aloud/Record	Instruction/Insights/Intrigue	Plan/Progress/Purpose
Ving in T/ What have you been thinking? S/ "... Not sure, I'm still thinking about it... but I'm having lots of B.K. and B.E. from this book... I'm noticing a lot..."	T/ "You just started – What's helping you understand?" ... Pause – Quiet – Thinking... S/ "Need more time to think about it some more..."	·Meet on Thursday or early next week... T/ "Be ready to tell me..."

Additional Comment(s): noticing schema, needs time to reflect, new read –

Date 11/11 Title Ramona and Her Mother Page(s) n/a

Review/Read Aloud/Record	Instruction/Insights/Intrigue	Plan/Progress/Purpose
Ving in ·read aloud ✓+ T/ "Tell me what you've been thinking..." S/ "When I didn't know about understanding words, I didn't know what they meant... but I knew how to say them... Now I'm using my schema..."	T/ "What made the change?" S/ "If I never understood that, I'd never know how well I could understand the book... Now I can read more, read harder books, and know a lot more than ever before... my schema kicks in..."	Next time... T/ "Begin to think about the questions you're starting to ask..." (new strategy)

Additional Comment(s): explains how schema helps, explicit, using B.K./B.E. to "get" the text

Figure 4.4 Conference notes for Lexee provide a record of her thinking and understanding over time. Specific details from three of Lexee's conferences help pinpoint specific reading skills and behaviors she is using. Conferring notes serve as a clear representation of Lexee as a reader.

decision on what he's doing in that one small frame. There's more to the picture though, what you can't see . . . You can't see that Graham was, indeed, starting to get a drink of water. But, as he leaned over, he noticed his shoe was untied or he was picking up a piece of trash. You don't see the rest of the picture.

Patrick: Oh, I get it. I need to step back. Talk to you about what you saw, not just what was happening at that exact moment in that frame. Maybe you could have snapped several shots to show a more detailed picture . . .

Troy: And, it's even more than that, I think. It's like taking a picture versus recording a video. A picture can be so canned: "Okay, smile. No, no, a little to the left, that's it . . . Look at me. Good. Good." But a video gives you every detail; it's active. A picture is so subjective. It's so still. So permanent. You either like it or you don't; it's so minute.

Patrick: Yeah. The great thing about watching a video is that you can slow it down, rewind it, step away for a moment. Talk about it with someone else. Watch it in slow motion. See how it unfolds over time.

Troy: You can't do that with a snapshot, really. I look at a picture and immediately make a judgment: "Oh, he's not smiling; he must be sad" or "Oh, he's getting a drink." I make a decision based on that one single moment. It's different when I watch a whole video. I get to experience more, think about more . . .

Patrick: We watch something develop. It's like you get to see the process. You get to be more objective and form an opinion about something bigger. And, you can freeze it on one frame if you want to take a closer look at a particular scene.

Troy: Right. That's why when we look at a reader, we have to use a wider lens, gather more information. Pull out our video cameras! Use what we see kids doing every day to support their growth and development. Then we can focus on the small details or look at it in broader terms. I'd want you to have the whole picture of what Graham was really doing in order to understand why I took that picture. Compare that one picture to the whole video.

Patrick: That's what happens when we confer. We get to see a child over time. If we're taking notes consistently, meeting regularly . . . we get to know a reader's strengths and growth areas, over time.

Troy: And we can stop, clarify, ask questions, slow things down, speed them up. Our goal isn't to take that quick snapshot and be done with it. We don't lead the child to the outcome we want. Snap! It's done. Conferring is like video, it's ongoing. And the results might not be as stiff, or posed, as that single snapshot we took on one particular day.

Troy's right. I want to gather other evidence in order to document growth throughout the school year: formative and summative assessments, readers' responses, book club evaluations, strategy study work, progress toward district and state standards, and so on. All are important.

Conferring allows me to gather written evidence as my students move along the gradual release model; conferring happens in the moment and so does assessment. My conferring notebook gives me a place to hold that evidence, building a frame-by-frame, long-term, live-action movie. I want children to recognize their accomplishments and celebrate their journey of becoming proficient readers. When I pull up beside a child, I know I will leave knowing her better as a reader. My conferring notebook is meaningful to me; its contents help assist my teaching. I do not need special features that are not necessary; no bells and whistles for me.

PONDERING: What will your conferring notebook look like? What will you include? How will you go about getting started?

So, what would I recommend?

Start conferring.

Create a structure for your conferences.

Think of a way to gather information about the reader.

Find a way to keep your notes organized and usable.

Use that information to inform your instruction.

Reflect on your success.

And, if need be . . . start again.

I end this chapter with a poem by William Stafford (2003). When I read it, I think about those times when I sit down with a child to confer: To *review* what he is doing as a reader, to have him *read aloud*, to *record* my noticings. To provide *instruction*, to gather *insights*, to be *intrigued*. To *plan* together, to *progress* further, to set a *purpose*. I have to be ready. Are you?

You Reading This, Be Ready

Starting here, what do you want to remember?
How sunlight creeps along a shining floor?
What scent of old wood hovers, what softened
sound from outside fills the air?

Will you ever bring a better gift for the world
than the breathing respect that you carry
wherever you go right now? Are you waiting
for time to show you some better thoughts?

When you turn around, starting here, lift this
new glimpse that you found; carry into evening
all that you want from this day. This interval you spent
reading or hearing this, keep it for life—

What can anyone give you greater than now,
starting here, right in this room, when you turn around?

Grandma was pleased when I learned to read, but when I fell head over heels in love with the magic of words, a bond formed between the two of us unlike anything the rest of the family shared. Nothing pleased her more than finding me reading a book, and I must've made her plenty happy because I read 'em as fast as I could get 'em checked out of the bookmobile that lumbered down our country roads once a month.

I was just a little thing when Grandma surprised me with a very special gift. I'll never forget opening up the box that held a brand-new typewriter and hearing her tell me to write down my own words. In the ensuing months and years, Grandma eagerly read every word I pecked out with my two skinny forefingers. Grandma Rushing went to her grave at ninety-four, still believing I'd be a famous writer. Our dream—hers and mine—remains unrealized, but it's okay. Her gift to me was her belief in me. I wish every child could be given such a priceless treasure.

—Shellie Rushing Tomlinson, 2008

Chapter 5

Cultivating Rigor, Nurturing Inquiry, and Developing Intimacy

Defining the instructional ashlars that strengthen the environment in which conferring thrives gave it a natural role in my reader's workshop. With the environmental ashlars soundly in place (trust, respect, and tone; endurance and stamina; purpose and audience; the gradual release of responsibility model; and the structure of reader's workshop), I looked closer at the specific elements of conferring.

The ashlars themselves strengthened a culture of thinking founded on rigor, inquiry, and intimacy, but these elements must live and breathe within the context of conferring. But how?

I turned to my colleague Lori Conrad to hammer out how we might bind these elements specifically to reading conferences. We realized that connecting these elements to each reading conference would, as Ellin Keene says, "Create an unseen culture of rigor, inquiry, and intimacy by continually expecting more, probing ideas further, and pressing students to explore their intellect" (Keene 2008, 32). Our work with colleagues at the Public Education and Business Coalition taught us that each element was essential to creating a classroom culture where thinking and learning could thrive. Together, Lori and I defined each element and asked three questions demonstrating how each element thrives in a reading conference. We knew that cultivating a sense of rigor, nurturing a sense of inquiry, and developing a sense of intimacy were significant to strengthening reading conferences.

In this chapter, I present our definitions and questions, demonstrating how each component brings scholarly and thought-filled discourse to a conference. You will meet three students, Haley, Cole, and Jaryd, whose reading conferences illustrate the value of connecting rigor, inquiry, and intimacy to conferring. There is no better place to grapple with all the complexities, challenges, triumphs, and surprises that "thinking about your thinking" can bring than during a reading conference. The elements of rigor, inquiry, and intimacy help readers "fall head over heels in love" with reading.

PONDERING: How do you define rigor, inquiry, and intimacy within the context of a reading conference?

Cultivating Rigor: The Cognitive Context of Conferring

A good school for anyone is a little like kindergarten and a little like a good post-graduate program—the two ends of the educational spectrum, at which we understand that we cannot treat any two human beings identically, but must take into account their special interests and styles even as we hold all to high and rigorous standards.

—Deborah Meier, 1995

Haley is a social reader and loves to talk about the text she is reading—in whole-class discussions, small-group chats, and during one-on-one conferences. She reads a wide variety of texts and is always trying to improve the strategies she is using. Haley is a "think out loud" reader, meaning she is always willing to share her ideas with those who show an interest in what she has to say. She says, "When Mr. Allen confers with me I learn things like words or what sentences mean and things I never knew and that makes me smart."

Recently, Haley was reading *The Whale* by Cynthia Rylant. I had just purchased a small collection of books to add to our classroom library, and this was in the stack (I let kids peruse new books before putting them out into the classroom library). If you haven't read *The*

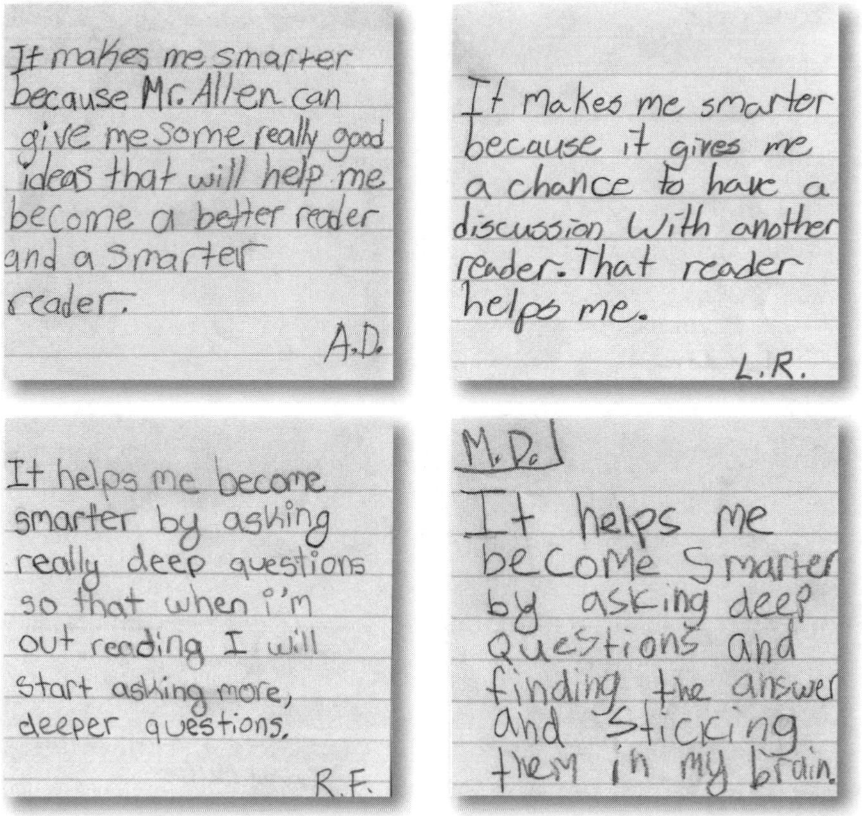

It makes me smarter because Mr. Allen can give me some really good ideas that will help me become a better reader and a smarter reader.
A.D.

It makes me smarter because it gives me a chance to have a discussion with another reader. That reader helps me.
L.R.

It helps me become smarter by asking really deep questions so that when i'm out reading I will start asking more, deeper questions.
R.F.

M.D.
It helps me become smarter by asking deep questions and finding the answer and sticking them in my brain.

Figure 5.1 Students identify rigor's role within the context of their own experience with conferring. Each student explains how conferring helps him or her become "smarter" as a reader. Rigor is about the thinker and the thinking.

Whale, it is a quaint story about Pandora the cat, Seabold the dog, and Whistler, Lila, and Tiny, the three mouse children. The "family" lives in a lighthouse, and in the story they come to know a baby beluga named Sebastian. In our classroom Cynthia Rylant is one of our favorite writing mentors, so even *Mr. Putter and Tabby* and *Henry and Mudge* find a spot in our library. Good books are good books, and although Haley reads well above the norm, she often chooses to read from Rylant's "ready for chapter books." Haley is delightful, and as a conferrer, I always know I will be challenged by Haley's passion for reading and writing and leave our conference just a little wiser.

Pulling up a chair beside Haley, I was glad to see she was reading *The Whale*. I knew she had just chosen the book, and I was curious about her choice. Sometimes conferring with a reader right after she makes her book choice sets the tone for your conference. "So, Haley, how are you doing today?"

"Good," she replied.

"Tell me about what you're reading."

"*The Whale*. It's one of the new books."

"How's that going?" I asked. I knew Haley would tell me.

"Well, I'm at the beginning, and at the end of that first paragraph, I stopped and asked myself what was important. But I think I read too fast because I didn't understand it. I didn't really. I didn't figure out what was important. So I went all the way back to the beginning and I read it slower . . ." Our crafting lesson that day was a continued look at how wise readers are able to determine what's most essential in text as they read.

"Um," I muttered.

Haley continued, ". . . just to slow my thinking down and then, um, what I did was when I heard something important, I jotted it down in my notebook and that helped me because I could just tell you or someone what I just read." She looked at me.

"Hmmm . . . what was it that you discovered was most important?" In my mind I was curious about why she had stopped after the first paragraph to jot something in her notebook. I was wondering if there was something she was struggling with that caused her to reread so soon into the text.

"Well, I discovered that they had a family. It was a family that lived in a lighthouse, but some of them weren't lonely at all. I wrote that down, and then it said right here, 'The lighthouse stood on top of a cliff of sharp rocks beside the sea. And it looked as if it were the most *for-lone* [forlorn]. . . '

"I didn't understand that word, so um, and at the end of the paragraph I was going to write, 'What does this word mean?' and then I was going to try to figure it out."

"Hmmm, what did you decide?"

"Well, I didn't really get to it yet because I just read the end of the paragraph and wrote down what I thought was important, and um, well, I think *for-lone* means [Haley reread the passage quietly] . . . I'm just trying to figure out a word that might fit in there." Haley points to the word *forlorn* and looks up at me. Waiting for me to give her the meaning, perhaps?

"Yeah, what do you think?" I wanted Haley to tell me what she thought might work. I knew Haley was an expert at figuring out word meanings. In crafting sessions, Haley is always willing to play around with synonyms, new vocabulary, and word meanings. And, we have conferred often about how to determine importance at the word level. (We were in the middle of a study of determining importance in text when this conference took place, about halfway through the gradual release of responsibility model in our study of this thinking strategy.)

Haley continued reading, "'And it looked as if it were the most' . . . lonely . . . and empty place in the world?" She substituted *lonely* for *forlorn.*

I reassured her, "Yeah. Forlorn could be lonely, sad. I mean, Cynthia Rylant did such a good job because earlier she gave you the words *lonely* and *empty* to fit with the rest of that sentence."

"Hmmm . . ." Haley pondered. I could see that she was thinking about the rest of the paragraph that she had just read.

I continued, "So it looked sad, or lonely, yeah, perfect. It is exactly what that word means. How did you figure that out?"

"Well, I, 'cause at the beginning it said it was a lonely lighthouse, there lived a family of animals, like just 'in a lonely lighthouse.' I just thought that word might fit in there because it says, 'it's empty' so I was thinking of words that would like fit with empty . . ."

"Right, right . . . ," I encouraged.

"Like not a *happy* and empty place, but sad and lonely."

"Haley, that's the perfect thing to do as a reader, to think about words that fit with an unknown word, words that fit in that space. Because not only do you have to determine what's important as you read and slow down your thinking like you said you did, but you also have to determine what's important about words. And you ask yourself, 'Is it an important enough word to spend precious time to figure out?'"

"Well, I thought it was pretty important. Because that word might be coming up during here," she pointed to the next chunk of text.

Then she added, "And, I didn't understand this part 'cause I think I need to read it slower. It said, 'And it looked as if it were the most lonely or sad and empty place in the world, standing there all alone. But if one drew closer to this lighthouse everything about it changed.'"

"Hmmm . . ." I was curious about Haley's thinking. A "simple" text, but she was spending the time to make sure she understood the meaning behind it. And, I loved how she said "lonely or sad or empty" in place of "forlorn and empty." She really made sure she understood the text.

"But if *what* drew closer to the lighthouse, like . . ." She paused.

I said, "But if *one* . . . if somebody . . . if a person, like sometimes we say, 'Well, if one would just be quiet' and we're really talking about a person. It's another way to say *somebody*."

"Oh," she responded.

I sensed she had never noticed this language before now. "It's a schnancy, fancy way to say that. Does that make sense?" She nodded.

"Haley, do you know what I love that you're doing? I love that you're slowing down your thinking to try to figure out words that you don't know and really making an effort to do that. Now, you have to balance that, right? And decide when it is that I'm going to jot down my thinking and when I'm not." We paused. "So what are you going to do after I let you go?"

"I'm going to do what I just did with you by slowing down as I read and thinking about what I just read, writing it down and at least trying to remember, to understand, to extend meaning, and make it memorable . . ."

"Yeah, and then what?" I asked.

"If I see a word that I don't understand or I don't know what it means or I can't pronounce it, I think I'll write it down in my notebook, just to write it down if I just don't know it. To the side, I'll think of words that might fit with it. Like if the word is in a sentence, I'll write, 'And it looked as if it were the most forlorn . . .' and that's what I would write, and I'd draw arrows pointing to what that might mean or something . . ." I could see that for Haley, jotting down her thoughts in her reader's/writer's notebook was a strategy she was trying out during reader's workshop, trying to create a synonym web of sorts.

"Just don't spend too much time on that because the goal is to get some reading done. So don't make the *notebook* the focus, make the *reading* the focus. I mean, if you get it, you don't need to take the time to do that every time, do you?"

Haley nodded in agreement. She was anxious to get back to her reading.

"All right, I'll let you go at it."

I left my conference with Haley wondering about this idea of rigor. Haley is a reader who reads fluently and at an appropriate level. Yet, she is tussling, engaging in a struggle about words—especially in a book that is supposedly well below her "reading level." It is important

Date 3/24 Title The Whale Page(s) ______

Review/Read Aloud/Record	Instruction/Insights/Intrigue	Plan/Progress/Purpose
S/ "Stopped and asked myself what was imp.- didn't know. Went back to beginning, read slower." "Just to slow down my thinking - I jotted it down..." T/ "What did you discover?" (retell ✓+)	S/ "Didn't understand 'forlorn'... reread. Trying to figure out what fit..." (reread) S/ "Lonely?" T/ "Could mean that..." How? S/ "...related it to empty..."	T/ "D.W.I. in text and with words... Ask, 'Is it important enough to figure out?'" S/ "I'm going to slow down, write it down... think of words that might fit..."

Additional Comment(s): D.W.I word level, uses schema, moves slowly (power of reflection)

Figure 5.2 Conferring notes for Haley

that Haley is trying to strike a balance between what she records in her notebook and what she is trying to figure out for herself as a reader. I could have just said, "Haley, the word is *forlorn*—it means 'sad,'" but with her it is about her own metacognition, her own playing around with determining importance in text. I loved that she recognized *forlorn* right away as a word she wanted to understand. And, you can bet she remembers it!

The conferring notes I took during this conference (see Figure 5.2) show how I recorded it.

There was a sense of rigor that developed when we conferred:

Haley was uncovering a genuine struggle and wondering.

Haley knew I was listening.

Haley knew I was trying to teach.

I began this section on rigor with a quote by Deborah Meier; if you can, get your hands on a copy of *The Power of Their Ideas*, and turn to page 48. Read her perspective of kindergarten as she believes it should compare to learning at all levels. She describes kindergarten as "the one place—maybe the last place—where teachers are expected to know children well" (Meier 1995, 48). She explains (in grander, more explicit detail) that kindergarten teachers:

- Know children by "listening and looking"
- Realize that children are "incorrigibly idiosyncratic" and that learning must be "personalized"
- Understand that building self-reliance is essential
- Cater to "children's growing independence" by providing choice and allowing them to "move on their own steam"
- Organize their rooms for "real work, no passive learning"
- "Put things in the room that will appeal to children, grab their interests, and engage their minds and hearts" (48)

When I read her description, I thought to myself, "Now this is the perfect definition of *rigor*!" Educators use the word *rigor* (from Latin, *rigorem* meaning "numbness, stiffness") to describe the work we do with children (which is quite ironic since *rigor mortis* has its roots in the word *rigor*). But, I am going to toss etymologies aside and define *rigor* as the explicit, multidimensional, complex, individualized, and cognitive instructional practices we use in our classrooms (that's better than the phrase *stiff and unyielding*). The kinds of things that Meier espouses in her brilliant description—those should be the definition of *rigor*.

Conferring help's me Understand what's going on in the text because we are talking about it out loud.

R.A.Q

Student Keystone Point

There is something intriguing about listening to a reader like Haley explain her thinking. She was only one paragraph in, and yet she was so inquisitive about gaining a sense of understanding. She was so inquisitive that she was willing to put aside reading for a bit to try out determining what's important at the word level. Haley was aware of meaning all along; she just needed to talk through it a bit.

In a recent e-mail, Cheryl Zimmerman wrote, "So much of conferring is about connecting—throughout the year, but especially early on. Making that all important eye contact and making it clear that individual thinking is valued. Also establishing the stance of a listener—showing that it's not all about the teacher talking." For Haley, it was important to have someone sitting nearby for a few minutes so that she could ferret out her thinking—not in a group, but with an individual who was sincere in his curiosity about what she was doing as a reader.

I think it was important for Haley to have a place to jot down her thinking. In my classroom, students know that their reader's/writer's notebooks are tools they can use to record their fierce wonderings or notes to themselves as a reader. Haley may have overgeneralized that purpose a bit, and because I noticed that, it may be something we need to talk about as a whole group. If not, it is a balance that Haley is trying to figure out—how to make the most of her composing time as a reader (knowing that we have discussed the fact that composing time during reader's workshop is for that purpose, to read).

So, too, bringing rigor into a reading conference is striking a balance—finding that state of stability where a reader is able to make rational decisions and judgments about her process as well as reading the text. You'll notice that I did very little of the talking in my conference with Haley. I was trying to guide her to make her own decisions about figuring out unknown words and the amount of writing about her reading she chooses to do. I wanted her to clarify her thinking.

Let me take some liberty and adapt some of Linda Rief's words by switching the focus from writing to reading:

> When conference questions turn the decisions back to the writers [readers] they are forced to make evaluative judgments. These decisions made in progress help them better the writing [reading]. If kids can be taught how to detect and diagnose strengths and weaknesses and how to come up with the strategies for dealing with those problems through conference questions and suggestions, then we have taught them not only how to become better writers [readers], but how to be independent writers [readers] along the way. (1992, 125)

When I think about cultivating rigor, having a chance to teach the thinker and the thinking, I consider three questions:

- How do we uncover students' strengths, struggles, and genuine wonderings?
- How much do we listen?
- How much do we teach?

How Do We Uncover Students' Strengths, Struggles, and Genuine Wonderings?

Every reader is different. Sometimes during a conference, I am more willing to say, "That word is *forlorn*; it means something is sad. Does that make sense to you?" But, with Haley, I was able to let her engage and be somewhat perplexed about the beginning paragraphs of *The Whale*. I mean, really, it is not a text that is as easy as it looks. First of all, the family is obviously blended (a cat, a dog, mice . . . all living together in a lighthouse). They live right on the edge of a rocky cliff. They befriend not only a beluga but also a cormorant (who even knows what a cormorant is unless you are an ornithologist?). And, Rylant's descriptive language does require one (ah, that word again) to stop and think. That's the beauty of Rylant's writing; she challenges us to think deeply even in the simplest texts. I believe Haley realized that this was a book that deserved some thought.

So, when we sit down to confer with a student, we are really attempting to understand something that happens inside the reader's head. And, like my colleague Jim said about his running, it is not always easy to explain what goes on inside your head as you run a marathon. As we know, "Mature reading is generally done silently in the privacy of one's own head. This is not a problem for self-evaluation, but it poses a bit of a problem for teachers who wish to assess their students' reading" (Johnston 1997, 192). But I think it behooves us to try to uncover a reader's strengths, struggles, and genuine wonderings.

As students read texts independently, I believe it's my job to meet with them individually, as often as possible. I try to touch base with each student on a daily basis. I do this with two different styles of conferences:

1. A side-by-side conference: This is a conference in which I sit down with the reader and spend four to six minutes (during composing time) conferring with him or her (like the conference I had with Haley). I usually try to do *at least* five of these conferences daily.
2. A touchstone conference: For this style of conference, I walk around the room in between my side-by-side conferences. I touch base with at least three other readers in the room (often a simple hand on the shoulder and asking, "How are you doing?") between each side-by-side conference.

I uncover strengths, struggles, and genuine wonderings by conferring often and regularly. Conferring allows me to monitor a reader more efficiently. It helps reinforce her application of a specific strategy of study (e.g., a thinking strategy we discussed during crafting). It helps me see what reading responses she is recording in her notebook (e.g., how is she keeping accurate records of her daily reading experiences?). I can make note of the skills and strategies she is acquiring, applying, and transferring to her reading (e.g., a brief running record, the questions she is asking, her choice of text). I can notice the language she is using to articulate her metacognition (e.g., is she transferring the language of schema used during crafting and using it herself?). I can see if she is making a connection to her writing (e.g., is she noticing specific writer's tools in her reading that she hopes to transfer to her own writing?). That's rigor.

To cultivate means to foster growth, to encourage growth. If I hope to uncover a reader's strengths, growth areas, or wonderings, I strive to make each conference a living, viable, and visible interaction. I foster growth by asking sincere questions. When I ask a child, "How is it going?" or "Can you tell me a bit about your reading?" I do so sincerely. As the year progresses, I find myself using my voice less and less. Once students know the basic pattern of our conferences they are more aware of expectations. Conferences become a time for students to naturally discuss themselves and their reading.

But, at the beginning of the year, conferences might include a scaled-down version of a think-aloud. A think-aloud is a strategy we use often during crafting lessons to demonstrate our own use of a strategy or skill. The same can be done while we are sitting by a child. If a child is just learning to talk about her thinking, we can say, "Listen to me as I try this strategy out. Your job right now is to watch and listen to what I'm doing. I'm going to think aloud a bit, and then I'm going to ask you to tell me what you noticed . . ." Bringing the think-aloud into a conference is a technique to use when you first start conferring. It teaches readers how to be explicit while unveiling their thinking as readers—at the word level, the sentence level, and the whole-text level. A conference think-aloud can focus on deep structure or surface structure systems and is an easy way to have a student begin to navigate her conference, with a little practice. Lev Vygotsky's infamous words "What the child can do in cooperation today, he can do alone tomorrow" hold true as we consider conferring as an instructional keystone (1962, 188).

When I asked Jessie, a third grader, how conferring helps her think about text, she said, "I think it helps me understand the text better. It makes me more interested in the text. It makes me want to ask more questions. It makes me be more metacognitive . . . and I want to be!"

How Much Do We Listen?

Rigor is cultivated the more we listen. "In order to listen, we must first be quiet" (Kenison 2000, 104). This is one of my wife's favorite lines from a book I gave her for Mother's Day a few years back. Isn't it the truth? We must first be quiet. The book goes on to say,

> Sometimes we must listen in order to discern the truth of a moment . . . and we may discover that it takes great courage and determination to listen and to wait for truth to emerge. . . . Listening involves making a choice—right now, just for a moment—to stop dead in your tracks. To stop moving, to stop talking, to stop making noise. As Madeleine L'Engle has said, "When I am constantly running, there is not time for being. When there is no time for being, there is no time for listening." (Kenison 2000, 104–105)

What would happen if we took these same words into our reading conferences? Might our readers be better served if we find the courage and determination to listen? Might our readers feel less stressed if we wait for truth to emerge? Are we allowing time for our readers just to *be*; just to be readers? It sounds pretty esoteric and enigmatic, but I'm certain it is something we can all take on as a goal as we confer.

Often visitors to my classroom comment on the amount of time I give children to think. But it wasn't always that way. When I was student teaching, Judy Gilkey (my cooperating teacher and now one of my dearest friends), used to say, "Patrick, when I come around the corner, I can hear your voice. You need to give kids time to think!" I took her words to heart. Now it's my goal to fill the empty spaces of my instruction not with another question, but with think time. I try to emulate this in my one-on-one conferences with children.

In Haley's conference, it was about giving her time to tackle the complexities of the text (e.g., the word *forlorn*, the idea of "one must," etc.). Did I respond to Haley's concerns? Sure. But briefly and only after plenty of time for her to delve into her own concerns as a reader. It takes practice. People who watch me confer say, "Oh, conferring is so easy for you, you know exactly what to say and when to say it. You must have always been a good listener." Seriously? Ask my wife. After she wipes the tears of laughter from her cheeks, she will tell you that listening does not come easy to me. I have learned that if I want readers to tell me about their book choice, talk to me about their word hurdles, explain their use of a strategy, reflect on their own metacognition, or do any of the multifarious things a reader must do to understand, remember, extend meaning, or make reading memorable, I have to listen. Cheryl says, "Like I observed in your room long ago, I think it's the eye contact, the proximity, the one-on-one experience. I think the power comes from devoting undivided attention to the student and *listening*!"

Over the past few months, I have recorded more than forty reading conferences. I replay them on my iPod (sick, I know), but it is so interesting to try validating, reasoning, and coming to grips with the balance of power in each and every conference. I find myself saying, "Oofda, I shouldn't have said that!" or "Yikes, I talked right over her!" It's a good learning experience. Being a good listener means we do have to "shut up and listen" or how else will we know what we need to teach?

A fellow teacher, Leslie Leyden, related a story to me about a reader in her first-grade classroom. She said, "A student was reading a Henry and Mudge story with me. She was reading with the *most* delightful expression I've yet to hear from a first grader. I asked her why she found it necessary to use her voice like she was (loudly with increased intonation, etc.). She said, 'Well, the author wants me to! That's why she writes in these [pointing to the exclamation marks] and she made the word SPLASH! with big capitals! She wants me to read the book with *excite-ah-mint!*'"

Leslie said, "I loved how this student personalized Cynthia Rylant and said, 'She wants me to . . .' This proves her connection to books!" I think it proves that Leslie took the time to listen and let rigor take its course. Think of all the things Leslie learned about that student in that short amount of time (e.g., fluency, mentor text, schema, punctuation—all rigorous concepts for a six-year-old). This child was an informant for Leslie. She told her exactly what she needed to hear.

In *Mosaic of Thought*, the authors tell us,

> Thinking about one's thinking is a central piece in the mosaic of reading, vital to people who read deeply. Metacognition is a turning inward, purposely at first and automatically thereafter, to reexamine our processes of comprehending, changing interpretations of the text and our reflections in order to elaborate and deepen our own understanding of a text. (Keene and Zimmerman 1997, 43)

I am thinking that if we want this "turning inward" to show its face in our reading conferences, we have to rethink the purpose of our conferring and what our goal in each conference really should be. We enter each conference with an open mind and a listening ear. Listening will lead us to purposeful next steps instructionally and will help us better meet the needs of the reader—at that time and in that moment.

PONDERING: How would your students describe you as a listener? In your reading conferences who does most of the talking?

How Much Do We Teach?

This is the eternal question for anyone who has tried to confer on a regular basis, no matter the content (reading, writing, mathematics, art). Since the main function of a conference is to teach, after all it is the root word of our job title, it is also something we have to think very clearly about each time we confer. We are the most proficient model of a reader in the classroom (one hopes), and we have to bring our knowledge and experience with us to each and every conference. And, if we add the work of "reader" to the mix, we are coming to each conference as reader and teacher.

And then there is that blasted word *rigor* again. I used to be a *question bombardier* (remember my original conferring list?). I certainly thought I was bringing a sense of rigor to those conferences, but in actuality I was probably trying to teach way too much in one sitting. I was forgetting to (1) keep the conference and the teaching short enough to accomplish something important, meaningful, and applicable, and (2) know when to say just enough, stop, and move on to the next reader waiting in the wings.

Rigor must be thought of as a measure of quality, not perseverating on hardship or difficulty. It's not about moving the reader into more difficult text or trying to play "stump the reader" by asking a thousand and one questions. If we can sit down with a first grader, a third grader, or a fifth grader and ask one high-quality, thoughtful question, then we've succeeded at bringing a sense of rigor to the conference. That is how much we teach.

Our best teaching should provide a certain amount of ambiguity, be slightly provocative, and provide a realistic challenge. In our reading conferences the teaching can most certainly center on a curricular goal; interesting, age-appropriate text; or a sense of complexity of thought. How much do we teach? It depends on the individual reader at the time we sit down beside her. That is the challenge for us, as teachers, because a conference changes reader to reader, moment by moment, and we have to be at the ready.

What is going to provide the reader with the right amount of instructional thrust? Perhaps it is the language we use to elicit the thinking as we confer that dictates the amount of teaching necessary. Reading is an active process of seeking and making meaning, and you have to have language to make that happen. I now pay particularly close attention to the language I use when I confer, which is something I did not necessarily do when I was first learning.

In *To Understand*, Ellin states, "People learn best when a *few important concepts* are taught *in great depth over a long period of time* and when they have opportunities to apply those concepts in *a wide variety of texts and contexts*" (Keene 2008, 109). Might we not then use conferring as one of those contexts? I think our language must befit the occasion and should commingle with the language we used during our crafting lessons.

Familiarizing ourselves with the six cueing systems, both the surface structure systems (graphophonic, lexical, syntactic) and the deep structure systems (semantic, schematic, and pragmatic) is one place to start. Developing a clear understanding of the thinking strategies and how they work in our own reading might be another means to strengthen the rigorous language we might use as we confer. Reading and discussing *Choice Words* by Peter Johnston with another colleague not only helped me improve the kinds of conversations I have with readers, but also clarified the purpose behind the language used in each conversation. Teaching in response to what the reader is saying and using meaningful language during our conferences keeps the conferring both individualized and connected, one conference to another.

What do we teach? We teach something that might move the reader forward, might nudge her to take a risk, might extend her learning, might encourage her to strengthen her endurance, might meet a curricular goal, might challenge her intellect, might bring about lasting change, might provide insight she can share with others—the prospects are immeasurable. Rigor will emerge. Just ask Haley.

Nurturing Inquiry: The Analytical Context of Conferring

Reading is a gift.

Read, and wait.

Curiosity can't be forced. It must be awakened.

Read, and trust the eyes that open slowly, the faces that light up, the questions that will begin to form and give way to other questions.

—Daniel Pennac, 1999

Cole is a quiet boy, good-natured and always willing to work hard. If he has the right book in his hand, he will read for extended periods of time, especially because he thinks carefully about choice. If you nudge him to think about a strategy or skill, either during crafting or while he is reading independently, he will accept the challenge. When I confer with Cole, I know I will leave the conference more enriched as a thinker myself. He is both thoughtful and reflective.

Recently he has been reading Mike Lupica's "Comeback Kids" series. Another student brought one book from home, and he and Cole have been trading off each time they find a new one. I get excited when students bring in new texts that I have never seen. It defies the myth (oh, I did not mention this one earlier) that you have to have read every book in the classroom library to confer with a reader. Hogwash! When students are reading new or challenging text, a "let's figure this out together" conference is often the most inquiry based. These conferences might aim to strengthen background knowledge, solve a problem, or help resolve an issue into which the reader might be delving. These conferences lead both conferrer and conferee on a mental journey. The analytical nature makes for interesting talk. When you confer with Cole about a sports book, he takes the lead—sports are his passion.

Cole recently chose *Ida B . . . and Her Plans to Maximize Fun, Avoid Disaster, and (Possibly) Save the World* by Katherine Hannigan from a basket of "gift" books I have in my room (a collection from visitors, observers, and friends that has accumulated over the years). In this

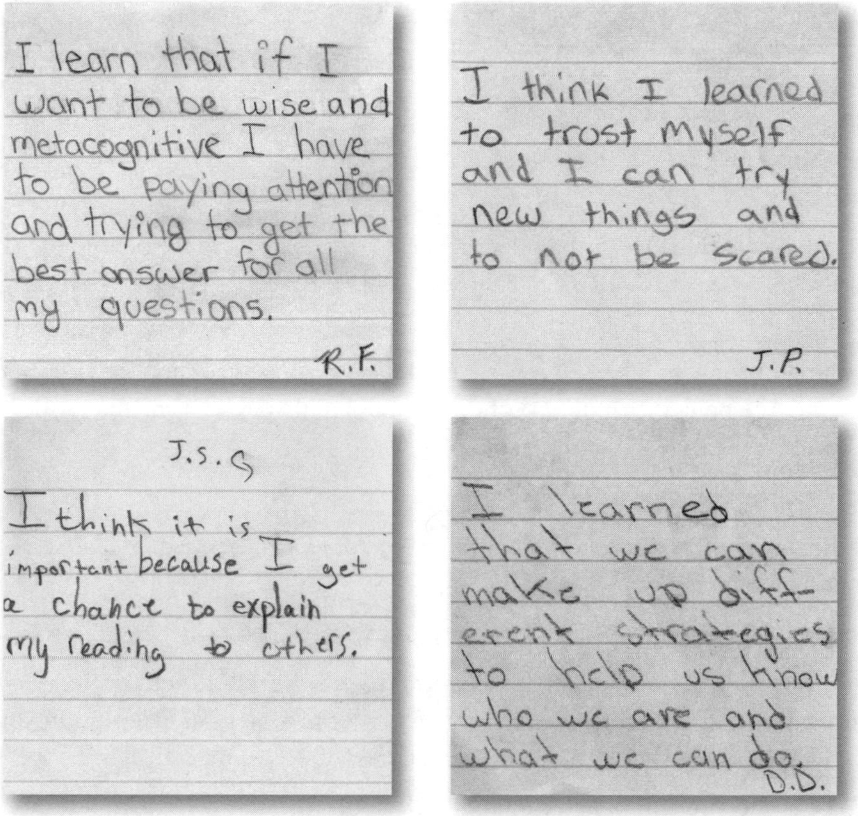

Figure 5.3 Students describe the function of inquiry and its role in conferring. Each student defines how conferring enhances his or her learning. Inquiry in this case is about conversations that lead to meaningful, documentable data.

book, Ida B looks at life as "one of those days that start and just keep heading toward perfect until you go to sleep" (Hannigan 2004, 1). She is an only child living on a small family farm and spends her time "talking and listening" (conferring, perhaps?) to the mountain, the brook, and the apple trees in their orchard. Nature becomes her friend and confidant while she's being homeschooled. But that all changes when her parents make the decision for her to go to the local school (due to her mom's illness). This is a quiet, poignant, lyrical, and somewhat idyllic book; not your typical Cole choice. When I sat down next to Cole, I was curious. I wanted to see why he chose this book and what he was thinking about so far:

"So Cole, you're reading *Ida B.* How's that going for you?" I asked.

"Pretty well," he answered.

"Yeah, what do you mean, pretty well?"

"Well, I'm liking it and it's kind of been getting me to really, well, she's [Ida] in a place kind of like where I live . . . Well, I don't live on a farm, but there's a big open space behind my house. And I'm kind of, over break, wanting to do what she kind of does," Cole replied.

"What does she do that you're interested in doing over break?" I asked.

"After lunch she goes out into the apple orchard or to the creek and she hangs out there until dinnertime . . ."

"Hmmm, lots of freedom she has, doesn't she?" I interjected. "I love the title: *Ida B . . . and Her Plans to Maximize Fun, Avoid Disaster, and (Possibly) Save the World.* What do you think that's about?"

Cole thought for a moment. "Um, it's kind of like what the whole book is about. And what I found in the book is that on one of the pages it has that exact same line"—he looked up at me and back at the book—"in the book."

"So what do you think that means?"

"It's kind of what the whole story is going to be about." Cole paused. He looked at me with an *I just told you that!* look.

I went on, "So what have you discovered about yourself as a reader right now?"

"That I can really determine what's important with this book because I can sometimes experience what she experiences." Cole was trying to use the strategy of determining importance with this text, which was the strategy we were talking about during crafting.

"Um . . . So do you think there's a link between determining what's important and using our schema? Hmmm. That's interesting. How do you think that's helping you as a reader?" I was sincerely curious about how Cole was weaving two thinking strategies together. I am always curious when students start really thinking about how the thinking strategies are helping them as readers.

"Um. Because then I'm really interested in the book and want to keep reading it. I maybe . . . I might . . . want to read another book by this author."

"Yeah, Cole, I'm not sure she has another book. I can't remember if she has another one. She might. This is her very first book," I said, turning the focus back to this book.

"She's going to school, and I am kind of confused because I'm wondering if it's back when she was a kid or if it was right now. Because she was homeschooled, and then she was going to school, and she didn't like the school, and she came back to homeschooling." Cole hadn't yet gotten to the part where she finally felt comfortable at school because of the relationship with her teacher.

"What's going on with her mom in this book? Do you remember?" I asked.

"Nothing's really going on with her mom yet," Cole answered.

"Oh, because I think that's one of the things you're going to discover is a big part of it, and you're going to have to let me know when it happens . . . with her mom. Just keep that in mind. It's been a while since I read it. Anyway, how do you think people would describe Ida?" (I realized that I overstepped a bit there and wanted to pull Cole back to what he understood.)

He went on, "Um, creative, um, imaginative, she uses her imagination a lot because the trees talk to her and the river talks to her a lot. And, she's kind of . . . she has the freedom to go out and just be alone with herself on the farm."

"That freedom to be alone with herself, that's an interesting thing to think about. I wonder if people would think she was kind of odd," I interjected.

Cole chuckled. "A little maybe . . . because she talks to the trees and they talk back. And when she was in school the creek was talking to her: 'Come on. Come on. Come play . . .'" (Cole said this in a quiet, singing tone, like he was repeating the sound of the creek in Ida B's mind.)

"Yeah. Like her imagination. I think it's so smart that you figured that out. And that's exactly what I would say, creative, imaginative, and she has the freedom to be by herself. Well, I'm eager to see what you do as a reader with this. What do you think your plan is going to be?" I asked.

"I read about a page and then I write something important. Then I read another page and I write. Then at the end I see what the whole big idea is, and I try to figure that out," Cole explained.

"And do you think that's helping you?"

Cole nodded.

"How?"

"Because then, I can, if I only read like a chapter I can get the big idea of that chapter and then I can infer what the next chapter is going to be about . . ."

"Good. All right. It sounds like you're learning a lot about yourself as a reader," I said.

"Yep!" Cole added.

"You'll have to let me know what you think when you get to that part about, um, you know, about her mom . . . It's a great book . . . it's tough . . . it's not easy. All right, anything else?" I knew it was time to move on to the next student.

"Nope," Cole said as he turned back to his book.

I left my conference with Cole feeling as though he was developing a sense of inquiry—of trying to figure things out. I was impressed that Cole was utilizing several strategies—determining what's important in text, drawing inferences, and activating background knowledge—he was trying to figure out how those three strategies were interacting and how they were helping him as a reader.

I loved that Cole was pulling himself inside the text. "I want to do the same thing she is doing . . ." I can picture Cole, going out onto the greenbelt, finding a quiet spot, and taking time to listen. He recognizes the importance of understanding the character's point of view. He was getting to know Ida B well. He understood she was imaginative. She was creative. She was given a freedom that Cole longed to explore for himself as a reader. That's extending meaning—that's inquiry.

The conferring notes I took during this conference (see Figure 5.4) show how I recorded it.

Date 3/23 Title Ida B. Page(s)

Review/Read Aloud/Record	Instruction/Insights/Intrigue	Plan/Progress/Purpose
S/ "going pretty well..." "It's getting me to think- over break I'm going to hang out like she does..." T/ "Why's that?" S/ "It's what the whole story is about mostly..." T/ "What have you discovered?"	S/ "I can really D.W.I. - sometimes experience what she does..." T/ "Tie between schema and D.W.I.?" S/ "Really interested in author..." (retell-vague...) S/ "Ida is creative, imaginative, freedom to be alone..."	T/ Plan? S/ "Read a page – write what is important... see whole big idea... then infer about the next chapter..." T/ Talked about how difficult text is...

Additional Comment(s): multiple strategies, pulling self into text, point of view –

Figure 5.4 Conferring notes for Cole

There was a delightful sense of inquiry that developed when we conferred:

Cole knew he was growing as a reader and charting a path for his own growth.

Cole knew I noticed what he was doing and tried to name it for him.

Cole knew that Katherine Hannigan was a mentor from whom he could learn.

Daniel Pennac's writing strikes me. I reread *Better than Life* at least once a year. I love the ambiguity and mistiness of reading a book that is translated from the French—the subtle changes in language, trying to figure out how meaning impacts my reading and the reading of the children I teach. In one section Pennac writes about a child discovering the meaning of the word *mommy*, the first time a word made sense for him. He leaves the experience feeling "lead turn into gold" (1999, 47). The inquiry into that discovery clarifies, for me, the analytical context of conferring. Pennac then writes:

> You never get over that transformation. You don't return from a voyage like that unchanged. No matter how inhibited, the *pleasure of reading* presides over every act of reading. By its nature, its alchemical sensuality, the pleasure of reading has no fear of visual media, not even the daily avalanche of pictures on the TV screen.
>
> Even if the pleasure of reading has been lost (which is what we mean when we say that my son, my daughter, young people today, don't like reading), it hasn't gone very far.
>
> It's just under the surface.
>
> Easily found.
>
> We simply need to know where to look. To focus our search, we should state a few home truths that have nothing to do with the effect of the modern world on today's youth. A few truths that concern only us. We who say we love reading and who claim we want to share that love. (1999, 48–49)

Pennac's words remind me of Cole. I know that when he leaves after reading *Ida B*, he leaves changed. Our conversation struck a chord with me; the way he was trying to blend the strategy work he was doing—comparing Ida to himself. It was a natural form of inquiry for Cole. He was imagining what it would be like to be Ida and brought a little bit of her world into his. Talking and listening to Cole, I understand the challenge of looking for growth as readers mature throughout the year—trading in their sports books for a different read, a different text, a different kind of thinking. It takes time. Conferring with Cole gave me the sense that he was sincerely interested in Ida's fate and was trying to understand it while mulling through his own experiences. Cole was doing what Debbie Miller urges us to do when we confer, helping readers get to know themselves so we can get to know them. It is about experience.

I ran across an article about collaboration and teacher education and read an interesting definition of *becoming experienced* using inquiry as a model. The authors quoted Hans-Georg Gadamer:

> "Being experienced" does not consist in the fact that someone already knows everything and knows better than anyone else. Rather, the experienced person proves to be, on the contrary, someone who . . . because of the many experiences he has had and the knowledge he has drawn from them, is particularly well-equipped to have new experiences and to learn from them. The dialectic of experience has its proper fulfillment not in definitive knowledge but in the openness to experience that is made possible by experience itself. (1983, 355)

This reminded me of the kinds of conferences I've seen in which teachers serve as *keepers of the knowledge* (be it strategy, content, or specific skill knowledge) and assume they are conferring to "fix" the reader. If we believe that a sense of inquiry can live in our classrooms, albeit in this case during reading conferences, we have to come to each conference assuming a level playing field.

We are, of course, the teacher, and we do come to each conference well equipped as such. But, nurturing inquiry comes by sharing our experiences as readers and helping children uncover their own growth and needs and insights. Looking for patterns (like Cole combining several thinking strategies to strengthen his understanding) and helping students think through their own processes is paramount. One defining moment during our conference was when Cole looked up at me and chuckled about Ida B's quirkiness; that struck me. Had I not sat down with him for those three or four minutes, I would not have heard him laugh, and I certainly would not have known how seriously he was taking Ida B and her world. Moments like these do not happen until we sit next to a child and listen.

In terms of writers, Katie Wood Ray says, "I believe in the efficacy of an inquiry stance in the teaching of writing. *Efficacy*. My Webster's has only one definition for this word: the power to produce an effect" (2006a, 246). Efficacy is the very reason I strive to nurture inquiry in reading conferences. I want readers to be active in thought, effectual in understanding, powerful in opinion, and competent in describing themselves as readers. Had Cole not taken the time to tinker with his thinking, consider his own experiences and compare them to the character's, try to figure out the character's homeschooling situation, think about Ida talking to trees and brooks and such, I am not sure he would have continued reading. Without efficacy, the capacity of creating a desired effect, the opposite would occur—we might well create unsuccessful and incapable readers. A sense of inquiry must live in our reading conferences as well as in our workshops themselves.

When I think about nurturing inquiry, creating conversations that lead to meaningful, documentable data, I consider three questions:

- How can we find specific patterns of growth and need, including elements of strong literacy craft?
- How might we make note of what we see and what we learn?
- How might we match students with mentors they can learn with and/or from?

How Can We Find Specific Patterns of Growth and Need, Including Elements of Strong Literacy Craft?

My goal is to confer often enough with a reader to see a pattern emerge over time. Of course, it is important to remember that like all good inquiry, patterns emerge when the conference is focused on a thoughtful question. Open-ended questions like, "What are you noticing about yourself as a reader?" or "What have you discovered about yourself as a reader since last time we met?" or "Last time we met, you said you were going to focus on evoking sensory images. How is that going for you?" lead to a natural sense of inquiry during a conference. It makes sense that for a pattern to emerge, we want to think carefully about the language we use with readers from the moment we sit down beside them. And we also have to remember that often that language comes from the student.

Conferring helps me take what I know and tell it to someone to see if we can make it into a strategy. D.D.D.

Student Keystone Point

While nurturing long-term inquiry, making discoveries about a reader over time, we do not always follow a clear-cut, organized inquiry model. However, over time, we might think about the same elements of inquiry that writers consider when studying a particular craft. Writers often notice something about a craft, talk about the craft, make a theory about its use, give a name to the craft, think of other places it is used, and envision themselves using the craft. In other words, "learning to read like writers" (Ray 1999, 120).

Cole was reading like a reader. He noticed that he was using background knowledge to relate his experiences to those of Ida B. He talked about how "I can really determine what's important with this book because I can sometimes experience what she experiences." Together we named it: combining determining what is important in text with our background experience. Cole will spend time trying to see if those strategy connections continue as he reads. The information I gathered from Cole during our conference about Ida B gave me specific information about his understanding of the text. And, he will internalize the new learning. A conference is a perfect place to develop inquiry.

We also have to remember the wise words of Gordon Wells:

> Constructing stories in the mind—or storying, as it has been called—is one of the most fundamental means of making meaning. Whether at home or at work, in the playground or in the club, it is very largely through such impromptu exchanges of stories that each of us is inducted into our culture and comes to take on its beliefs and values as our own. (Calkins and Bellino 1997, 18)

There is a sense of impromptu conversation that leads to meaning making—about words, sentences, or whole chunks of text—that can result from a conference. These spur-of-the-moment discussions will often lead the reader with whom we are conferring to delve into further study of a reading skill or strategy. We have to be prepared to let the conference take a spontaneous route of thought.

To create a sense of spontaneity and to nurture inquiry we must think about the following:

- Focusing the majority of our questions on divergent thinking that might help students uncover something about themselves as a reader (and make note of their thinking).
- Responding by paraphrasing whenever possible so that students do not look for our validation, but rather understand that we are interested in what they are learning as a reader.
- Providing ample think time, for both the reader and the conferrer. A mutual understanding of when to talk and when to listen helps shape the success of a conference.
- Knowing about reading instruction itself—what do we know (and what do we need to learn more about) and what are the authentic skills and strategies we utilize as readers that we might share with our students during a conference?
- Avoid discouraging the reader and reserving judgment when possible (unless, of course, during a conference the reader is developing a misconception about a skill or strategy).
- Refrain from telling the reader exactly what to do.

During a conference, I look for examples of the student applying the thinking strategy we are investigating and learning. I look for students who can read fluently and change their cadence and rate appropriately. I look for students who, over time, are able to explain the specific skills they are using and, more important, how these skills are helping them to understand, to remember, to extend meaning, or to make the text memorable.

If we confer often enough, we will see patterns beginning to emerge (the good and the bad). And, we know that it is our job to document what we are seeing. Ultimately we look for ways that readers are enhancing understanding of their own practice and development as readers. Like Cole knowing that somehow schema and determining importance are related . . . and figuring out how.

PONDERING: Think about a reader in your classroom. What patterns do you see emerging for him or her as a reader? How do you know?

How Might We Make Note of What We See and What We Learn?

More and more we hear the *D* word, *data*, being tossed around educational circles. Schools spend thousands of dollars on programs that aim arrows at learners, trying to hit the bull's-eye of their learning targets. The data points look fancy and organized when we plot them on a graph, and some might be beneficial if used wisely. But it seems that we sometimes forget the *C* word, *children*. At times, folks are more interested in a target number or a plot point than they are in a child. Maybe that was not the goal originally, but gathering data (often out of context) sure is becoming more and more prevalent.

When I sit down with my child's teacher, I do not want to see a number on a piece of paper about her being in the ninety-eighth percentile for this or that, unless the teacher can explain how that affects my daughter's interactions with text. I do not want to see a graph showing me that my child reads a passage quickly and moves along a continuum, unless the teacher can explain how she varies her rate and prosody when she is reading aloud and how the miscues she is making may be interfering with her comprehension. I do not want to hear about the latest program that my child is using to test her comprehension on a computer screen unless the teacher can tell me some of the books my child has independently chosen to read during reader's workshop. Isn't her time in school more important than that?

I want my child's teacher to tell me what strategy she is working on in reading or what writer's craft she is studying. I want to know what she is thinking about when she's doing it, and how she is sharing that learning with her teacher and the rest of her classmates. I want her teacher to tell me that she cried at the end of *Charlotte's Web* or *Greetings from Nowhere* or wrote a piece of poetry in her reader's notebook in response to *Love That Dog* or *Falling Down the Page: A Book of List Poems*. I want her teacher to tell me that she wrote an article for the classroom blog about a book she and her friend discovered in one of the classroom book baskets. I want her teacher to say to me, "Recently, I sat down beside Lauryn and discovered that . . ." *That* is the data I want.

Of course, that is my parent voice talking. As a teacher, I understand that we have to show growth over time using standard measures to identify reading achievement, but we must do it wisely. I understand we have to evaluate the effectiveness of our instruction, document progress, and show specific patterns of achievement, but we must do it with the child in mind. I understand we can use measures like the Developmental Reading Assessment (DRA2) to focus on specific points of intervention in word analysis, fluency, and comprehension, but we must do it individually. I understand that we have to make note of how readers who need an extra boost respond to interventions, but we must do it purposefully.

As a teacher I tailor instruction and make note of student success. I strengthen a student's use of both surface structure and deep structure systems. I would like to propose that conferring can enhance, and often exceed, the types of interventions we offer our students. But we must (1) become more proficient at conferring, (2) document what we notice during our conferences, and (3) know what makes a proficient reader tick.

Recently, Troy shared a quote by Bev Bos with me. I have it hanging by the door of my classroom: "What your children take home in their hearts is far more important than what they take home in their hands." When parents come into my classroom, I want them to read this quote and know that my focus is not on "stuff" but on their child. I want parents to understand that what we carry in our hearts, and in our heads, is more important than tangible stuff.

Bos's quote hangs near the door alongside the Jeff Moss poem "On the Other Side of the Door" (2003). The poem reads:

On the other side of the door
I can be a different me,
As smart and as brave and as funny or strong
As a person could want to be.
There's nothing too hard for me to do,
There's no place I can't explore
Because everything can happen
On the other side of the door.

On the other side of the door
I don't have to go alone.
If you come, too, we can sail tall ships
And fly where the wind has flown.
And wherever we go, it is almost sure
We'll find what we're looking for
Because everything can happen
On the other side of the door.

When I think about both the quote and the poem, I realize the importance of noting what I see and hear during conferences and what I learn about individual readers as I confer. As we delve into the analytical nature of conferring, we must keep the *D* word as well as the *C* word in mind. Our goal is to collect *data* about *children*. About readers.

In Chapter 4, I introduced a specific structure I use during my reading conferences—the RIP Model. I also reviewed record keeping and how I organized conferring notes in my conferring notebook. Conferences, although conversational in nature, must have a structure to them. The notes we take during a side-by-side conference can, and should, be used to document a child's strengths and growth areas. Ron Ritchhart and David Perkins state,

> Thinking happens mostly in our heads, invisible to others and even ourselves. Effective thinkers make their thinking visible, meaning they externalize their thoughts through speaking, writing, drawing, or some other method. They can then direct and improve these thoughts. Visible thinking also emphasizes documentary thinking for later reflection. (2008, 58)

We help make the invisible visible for children, parents, and ourselves when we talk through our inquiries and make note of them.

As teachers, if we want a child to walk away from a conference with something in his head or in his heart, we should keep records of our conferences (otherwise how will we remember?). As teachers, when a child walks through our classroom door, we should remember that conferring is one way for us to document what happens during our interactions with readers. If I had not written it down, I would never have remembered what Cole was thinking or what he understood.

PONDERING: What do you learn in your reading conferences? What are some of the ways you note your findings and how do you use those findings to inform your instruction or better understand the reader with whom you are conferring?

How Might We Match Students with Mentors They Can Learn With or From?

When I think about matching students with mentors they can learn from, I think about this passage describing how Bronson Alcott, the father of Louisa May Alcott, would talk to others throughout his travels:

> Bronson Alcott was always a singularly good talker, a stimulating talker, who seemed to make other people have better thoughts than they ever had in their own company. The invitation to stay, if accepted, led to his spending long hours in those libraries, rich with the treasures of three generations, which were enchanted ground to him, for never before had he been within reach of a real supply of books of this sort. History, philosophy, poetry—he plunged deep into them all, trying to absorb as much as was humanly possible before he shouldered his pack and went on again. After this feast of learning, he had what is another priceless necessity—long, quiet hours in which to think over and appraise what he had read. He tramped the roads alone, sat under the hedgerows and ate his solitary lunch, exchanged brief greetings with the travelers he passed, but always went on thinking, thinking. Very few are the courses in education which allow time to think; but this education of Bronson's was complete, even to that final need. (Meigs 1995, 9–10)

Reading conferences should encourage students to engage in similar invitations to discuss, dwell, and think deeply about themselves as readers. When we are studying a particular writer's craft, for example, writing memoir, one of the first things we do is to invite writers to study a wide variety of memoir, to see what they notice about the craft. We want them to familiarize themselves with the specifics of the text so that eventually they can envision themselves writing one of their own.

The same can be said for an inquiry into a particular skill or strategy as a reader. Through our conversations, I should be noting the kinds of decisions readers are making about their reading process and the types of materials they are choosing to read. Whenever possible, I want to put the responsibility on the student. After several conferences, over time, I might encourage a student to:

- Choose a particular author or series of text to better meet the reader's instructional needs—"I know you're interested in sports. You might want to consider reading a book by Matt Christopher . . ."
- Form a book club with another reader with similar interests—"Alice is reading this same book. I'll bet she would enjoy talking to you about it . . ."
- Apply a specific thinking strategy to a broader range of text from a wider variety of genre—"Sometimes when I am trying to infer, I like to read Jean Little's poetry. Perhaps you should try reading . . ."
- Respond to text in his reader's or writer's notebook—"I can see that you are thinking a lot about what you are doing to solve the mystery; maybe you should try to write down some of the clues you're gathering along the way . . ."
- Reread a particular piece of text—"I sense that you're still having a lot of questions as you are reading this book. Maybe you should reread the last few pages and think carefully about . . ."
- Focus on what is happening at the word level—"As you read to me, I noticed that there were several words you tripped over; what are you planning . . ."

Conferences that encourage students to envision themselves practicing a particular behavior or strategy are one way we provide students with mentorship. In many cases, their mentoring relationship correlates with their own metacognitive behavior (e.g., "I know that last time I read a book by Cynthia Rylant, I really had to pay close attention to the mental images I was getting; this time I need to remember to . . .").

Sometimes that mentor is the teacher. I have to share my own thinking with a student during a conference to help nudge him to apply a particular skill or strategy (e.g., "You know, when I am drawing inferences in text, I try to pay close attention to specific words; listen to me as I read this section and tell me what you see and hear me doing as a reader . . ."). Sometimes that mentor is a familiar author (e.g., "I notice that you read a lot of books by Barbara Park. Have you ever thought about . . .").

When we encourage readers to form a mentor relationship, we have to remember that mentorship involves a tremendous amount of trust. Conversations whose sole purpose is to nurture a sense of wonder (with a text or another person) also involve trust. The trust involved in moving readers into mentorship comes from what Lori calls "Creating a daily opportunity for students to answer the question, 'What do I know about reading and about myself as a reader that I didn't know before?' It is a time for examining the ways in which their thinking has evolved and clarified." We might ask ourselves, "What does this reader know about himself as a reader?" and "What am I learning during this conference that I didn't know before?" as a means to encourage students to take more risks in other types of text.

Cole made his own choice when he chose to read *Ida B.* But many readers need specific encouragement and corroboration in finding ways to support their thinking. If we do not help them, it might take longer for them to "shoulder their pack." I am thinking in particular of those reluctant or reticent readers (Donalyn Miller [2009, 28] calls them "dormant" readers) who often need us to bring a sense of mentorship to our conferences. They are the readers who need more experience with revisiting book choice, need to hear us share our metacognition, or need us to demonstrate an unknown word strategy more often. A reading conference is a perfect venue for us to serve as this type of mentor.

For all readers, we best nurture an inquiry stance by supporting intellectual engagement. It was my conversation with Cole about his growing understanding of who Ida B is that led to meaningful, documentable data. Cole's journey, his inquiry into the text and into his thinking, was nurtured during the few minutes we shared, reader to reader. Our conversation gave me some of the *D* word, but the most rewarding and long-lasting consequence of our conference was the focus on the *C* word. Cole's inquisitiveness led to his own inquiry, his own efficacy. A child and his thinking.

Developing Intimacy: The Social Context of Conferring

Words do not make meaning themselves: they provide a vehicle for making meaning. Language is full of gaps and ambiguities that we must resolve through connections with our experience. Different readers will make more or less different meanings. Consequently, when we assess their understanding we will want to know "how" they understood what they read rather than "whether" they understood it. I mean this both strategically (how they went about it) and experientially (what kind of meaning they made).

—Peter Johnston, 1997

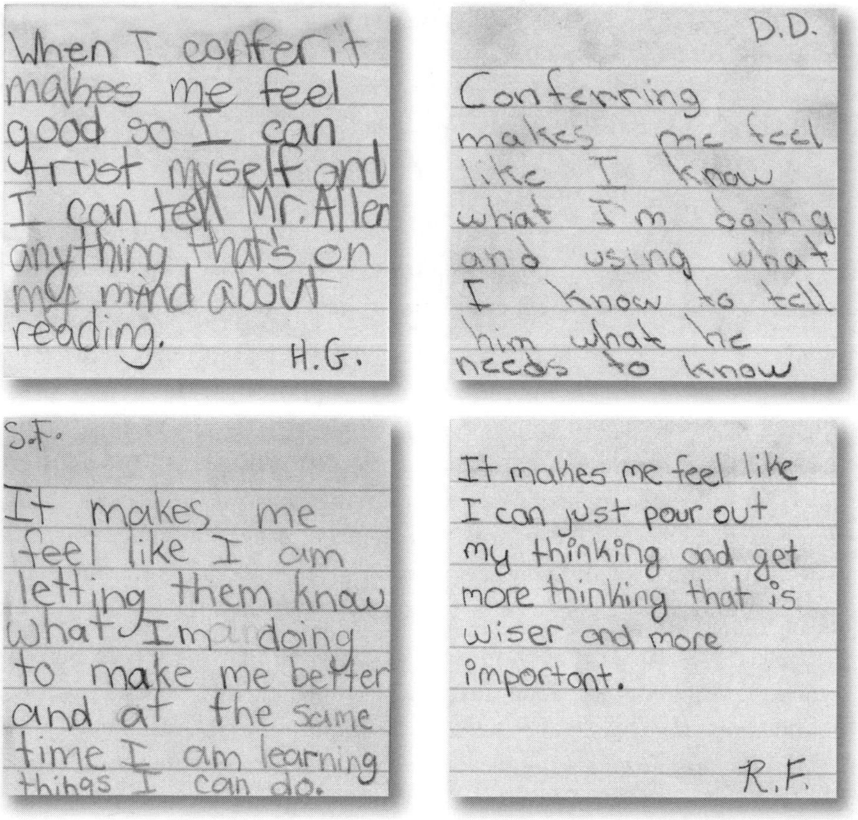

When I confer it makes me feel good so I can trust myself and I can tell Mr. Allen anything that's on my mind about reading. H.G.

D.D. Conferring makes me feel like I know what I'm doing and using what I know to tell him what he needs to know

S.F. It makes me feel like I am letting them know what I'm doing to make me better and at the same time I am learning things I can do.

It makes me feel like I can just pour out my thinking and get more thinking that is wiser and more important. R.F.

Figure 5.5 Students clarify the need for intimacy during a reading conference. Each student maintains that conferring plays an important role in his or her reading life. Intimacy is about fitting into a larger community of readers and writers.

Jaryd had been reading *Farmer Boy* by Laura Ingalls Wilder for several days. Jaryd is a wise thinker, strategic and curious. He has a knack for developing new metaphors to describe his thinking. When working one-on-one or when sharing his reading with the whole class, Jaryd is always the boy who says, "It's like . . ." and fills in the blank with an amazing analogy or comparison. Jaryd talks about books "getting more questions outta me" and how he is often searching for answers. He says that being a metacognitive reader means "getting what's in your head out!"

During one of his *Farmer Boy* conferences, Jaryd was telling me about some of the decisions he was making as a reader. He had been reading this book for a week or so, and in my mind I was thinking, "I know this book is tough. Probably too tough. I wonder what Jaryd is thinking about it. I wonder how he's bringing his own background knowledge to the text. What's he doing to figure out the things he doesn't quite understand?" Had I not conferred with Jaryd, I would have never known what was in store!

As I pulled up a chair next to Jaryd, I asked him how it was going (secretly hoping he would say he was about to make a new book choice). We had conferred about *Farmer Boy* before, but Jaryd was sure he had made just the right book choice and his plan was to stick with it.

"Hey, Jaryd, how's *Farmer Boy* going?" I asked.

"Pretty good," he responded, looking at me. Then I waited. (Since early in the year, students know I'm going to say, "What does *pretty good* mean?" or "Tell me more about *pretty good*." So now, they usually jump right in with their thinking. I looked in his eyes until he was ready to share.

Jaryd started by reading just a little chunk of the book to me and was stumbling on several of the words, including *Almanzo*, the main character's name. He was pronouncing the words fairly accurately, but I could tell he was perplexed. "You know, there's something about this book. It just lets something out I don't understand." I loved his language, and I was dying to know what the book "lets out" that was getting in the way of his comprehension.

I looked him directly in the eyes. "Tell me about that, Jaryd." I waited.

"Well. I've tried the five-finger rule, and that didn't work out so well. That was tellin' me it was hard, but I just kept on reading. Then I finally realized the book just kept getting harder and harder and harder for me to get. It just lets out a lot of hard words that I don't understand."

"You're right, Jaryd, this is a really tough book. Maybe because it takes place such a long time ago and maybe because you haven't developed your schema about being like Almanzo. So what are you going to do?"

"Well, I'm not sure, but I think I've decided it might be good if I drop it for now."

"That might be a good choice, Jaryd," I added. I looked at him and offered up an alternative. "What would happen if you decided to have someone else read it to you? Maybe you can read it with your dad. You can borrow the book if you want to and take it home to read with him."

"I could, but I'm not sure. I may just decide to make a better choice for now."

"Great. Write down the title in your notebook. Maybe you'll decide to take it home later. You might also want to spend some time writing a bit about what you're thinking about as a reader." I waited for a moment and then asked, "So Jaryd, what *did* you learn during your time in *Farmer Boy*?" I waited again.

"Well, I learned to trust myself." I almost jumped out of my chair; I couldn't wait to hear how he was going to explain this idea.

"Really, how?" I calmly asked.

"I guess I just had to trust myself to do what was best. I knew I wasn't getting it, but I wanted to keep trying, but maybe I kept going for the wrong reasons. I was faking it a lot. But now I know I have to trust myself."

"Hey, Jaryd, that's a great discovery. Trusting yourself as a reader. Wow! I've never heard anyone say that before; you've really got me thinking about that idea. How can I trust myself as a reader? Hmmm . . . that's a good question."

"Yeah, I need to think more about it though," he said.

"That's a perfect plan, Jaryd; I can't wait to find out what you discover."

As I left my conference with Jaryd, I was energized. Jaryd had learned something about himself. He learned a big lesson about what it means to be a reader. He learned to trust himself and to make decisions based on that trust. I didn't have to say, "Well, Jaryd, this book isn't at your Lexile level, and I think it's too hard for you," or "Jaryd, I think you need to make another book choice. Here, read this instead; it's a level 34," or "Jaryd, you should be reading books from this basket." That would have been the easy way out for him, and the choice would have been mine.

There are times I nudge children toward appropriate book choices, certainly. But, because I knew Jaryd well and our conference was slow, thoughtful, kind, and intimate—like all conferences we had had before—he was able to take some time to make the decision for himself. See Figure 5.6 for how I recorded this conference in my conferring notebook.

Date 2/11 Title Farmer Boy Page(s)

Review/Read Aloud/Record	Instruction/Insights/Intrigue	Plan/Progress/Purpose
S/ "Just lets out something I don't understand..." (struggling w/ some words) S/ "Tried 5-finger rule—but it's getting harder..." T/ "Do?" S/ "...I might drop it for now..."	T/ "Might be a good choice..." S/ "Yeah..." (quiet) T/ "Might read with someone else or dad..." S/ "I may just make a better choice..." T/ "Write down title... what did you learn about yourself?"	S/ "I learned to trust myself... I guess I just had to trust myself to do what I know was best..." T/ "Great discovery..." S/ "Yeah—I need to think more though..."

Additional Comment(s): trust (huge), decision making, book choice

Figure 5.6 Conferring notes for Jaryd

There was a sense of intimacy that developed when I conferred:

Jaryd did the talking.

Jaryd owned the text.

Jaryd and I sat side-by-side as we talked.

There is something uniquely social about sitting down next to a reader like Jaryd. I love sitting side-by-side with a child, encouraging him to negotiate his understanding of his process as a reader and his comprehension of the text he is reading. Sitting with a reader, helping him explore the ambiguities and resolving *how* he understood, not *whether* he understood: that is intimacy. Like in the course of my conference with Jaryd, it is always a goal to delve into a reader's understanding—of words, sentences, or whole chunks of text—but more important, it is finding out how he went about coming to know.

When I pull up my chair next to a reader, I am most interested in his thinking. I want to find out how the "cogs" in metacognition are working. Understanding of content or finer details of the text or word level struggles are important, but I love the explicit knowledge that results from those few short minutes where we spend some time figuring out how to be a wiser reader . . . together. Then I have a better handle on what I might teach the reader in the conference.

Striving for a sense of camaraderie in a reading conference is essential. To be able to "see" the intricacies of an interaction with the reader—what he is thinking, what he is remembering, what he is discovering. When a sense of genuineness and sincerity in a conference emerges, important things can happen. A reader is more willing to share the decisions he has made, the risks he has taken, and the insecurities about what he is grappling to understand and how he is problem solving. A sense of camaraderie leads to a kind of goodwill and fellowship in a conference that allows both the conferee and the conferrer to discuss ideas, pose questions, encourage enthusiasm, pause when challenges arise, and gain insights . . . together.

Lisa Olsen, a fellow teacher, once told me, "I think the reading conference is shrouded in mystery largely because we think some sort of divine intervention needs to, or is going to, take place. By viewing conferences in this light, we neglect to see and hear the simple truths; truths that tend to be more evident when we take a step back and observe someone else conferring. Every conference will without a doubt build trust and strengthen the relationship we have with our students, allowing teachable moments to occur. If we could just focus on the beauty of a child, sharing his or her thinking and being able to have a readerly discussion with a captive audience, perhaps, then we could hear those simple truths."

Simple truths.

Lisa understands the importance of knowing children. And, how can we possibly focus on the beauty of a reader if we do not recognize the social aspect of conferring as an essential element of a conference?

I have learned that a give-and-take relationship with a reader makes for a better conference. It makes for a more individualized conference. Don't get me wrong. I am not advocating that a conference be a feel-good session. But there is something to be said for the ingredients that promote intimacy between two readers. My daughter Lauryn says, "I don't want someone to hover over me like a basketball defender when they're talking to me about my reading. I want them to sit down and ask me what I'm thinking about and what I'm learning." If I want a reader to share his process with me, I cannot hover, but I can pull a chair up next to him, reader to reader, and initiate a conversation.

We have a responsibility in each and every interaction. We are accountable to ensure that the student meets district reading standards, that he develops appropriate surface-level skills, that he is fluent, that he makes wise book choices, and that he applies thoughtful deep-level strategies when going after a piece of text. All of these things will happen if we do our best to develop sagacity and prudence when working with him regularly in one-on-one situations. If a reader knows that we are harboring each reading conference in safety and trust, we can better get at the heart of what he is doing as a reader—both his strengths and growth areas.

The social aspect of a reading conference, of any conference, will eventually blend into the greater good—of the child's readerly life, as Lisa suggests, or by catapulting a child into the "literacy club" that Frank Smith describes in his work (1987, 2). There is a necessary sense of comfort and security and relevance that pervades part of each reading conference. When it does, we can get to the nitty-gritty, instructional aspect of helping a reader make sense of his or her reading. There's a mutual respect that comes from working closely, reader to reader, mentor to mentor.

Developing a sense of intimacy means we have to "declare ourselves committed to the idea that all children can think at high levels" (Keene 2008, 77). I believe that one way to show that commitment is to confer regularly with individuals. When I think about developing intimacy, that close scholarly relationship with the readers in my room, I consider three questions that Lori and I developed:

- Who does the talking?
- Who owns the text?
- Where do I sit?

Who Does the Talking?

In a reading conference, I strive to have the child do most of the talking. Of course, the "talk" varies from reading conference to reading conference, depending upon the purpose of the conference. But I have learned that the reader is better served if his voice, his thinking, fills the airspace during a conference. But, that wasn't always the case. Recently I watched an old videotape of myself conferring during reader's workshop. I dusted off the VCR, popped the tape in, and watched.

After spending the first few minutes shuddering and lamenting about the guy on the tape with dark hair and a mustache, pounds lighter and with far fewer wrinkles, I got to the heart of what I saw. I was like that question bombardier, posing question upon question like artillery, expecting brilliant thinking but not providing time for brilliance to manifest itself.

There I was sitting at a private table in the corner of the room, near the sunny window, rather than moving through the room, conferring notebook in hand. The reader was across from me, not sitting next to me. I was taking control of almost every conference, doing most of the talking, and although there was a sense of intimacy, it felt somewhat forced and unnatural. Don't get me wrong, I *was* conferring: I was digging deep, I was trying to get a glimpse of each child's process as a reader . . . *but*, I was doing most of the work! A lot has changed since I first started conferring with individuals. Thank goodness it has—it should; we all have to start someplace. What I saw on that videotape wasn't horrible, but it was proof that my conferences today are much more engaging and certainly much more intimate than they were in the past. Students probably left those reading conferences wondering, "Okay, what am I supposed to do now?" Now, when I leave one reader to meet with another reader, the reader has a more clearly defined plan and purpose.

Don Graves writes:

> Listening to children is more a deliberate act than a natural one. It isn't easy to put aside personal preferences, anxieties about helping more children, or the glaring, mechanical errors [miscues] that stare up from the page. I mumble to myself, "Shut up, listen, and learn!"
>
> Through our active listening, children become our informants. Unless children speak about what they know, we lose out on what they know and how they know it. Through our eyes and ears we learn from them: their stories, how they solve problems, what their wishes and dreams are, what works/doesn't work, their vision of a better classroom, and what they think they need to succeed. (1994, 16)

The line "through our active listening, children become our informants" is exactly what we need to think about to reshape the effectiveness of our reading conferences; we do need to be quiet and listen. I have taken Don's words to heart. I have learned to live with that awkward silent space, think time, if you will, that sometimes occurs during a reading conference. The time between when a question or wondering is posed and the student's response is something I have learned to cherish. It gives the conference breathing room, or what Ellin might call a chance to "dwell."

Too often, when I was first learning to confer, I would fill up that space with my voice, but I have had to learn to let time stand still for a moment; let the reader decide how he will fill the space (and, of course, be ready for another nudge just in case he doesn't know where to take his thinking).

Laura Benson says, "Whether reader or writer, one has to be in control, in the pilot's seat so to speak, in order to understand or be understood. The devotion of all our efforts as literacy teachers is toward giving our students the potential to be independent, joyful, and purposeful readers" (2001, 40). Laura is wise to put the reader in the pilot's seat. That's where he belongs; in control, ready to seize the moment—whether sharing his understanding of the current strategy of study, a perplexing inference, a word that he recognizes and just cannot put his mind around, or while reading a chunk of text aloud with fluidity and inflection. If teachers take control of the conference with their voice at the helm, will the child choose to take any control in his learning? If we are the question bombardier, asking nonstop questions (Tell me about your reading. What is happening? Have you made a text-to-text connection? What happened when you read that word? Is this the right book choice for you?) without recognizing that sense of intimacy, our conferences are all for naught.

PONDERING: Listen to your own conferring. Record several days of conferences on an iPod or video camera. Take some time to listen, to watch, to reflect. Is there a sense of intimacy emerging?

Who Owns the Text?

In the book Cole was reading, *Ida B . . . and Her Plans to Maximize Fun, Avoid Disaster, and (Possibly) Save the World* by Katherine Hannigan, Ida has just started to attend school at Earnest B. Lawson Elementary School, her first experience with public school. Ida isn't all too happy about the idea of no longer being homeschooled. There's a wonderful section where Ms. Washington (her teacher) invites Ida to read aloud to her for the first time. Ida has the book in her hand, and Ms. W. pulls up a chair next to her. The teacher puts her head back and closes her eyes in anticipation of Ida reading, ending with "Whenever you're ready, Ida."

The author goes on to describe Ida's apprehension: "I got tingly in my fingers thinking about opening up the book and reading those words out loud, making my voice go high and low, rough and smooth, like I did in my room . . ." and later Ida adds, "I closed my eyes, put my right hand on top of the book and passed it lightly across the cover. It was cool and smooth like a stone from the bottom of the brook, and it stilled me. A whole other world is inside there, I thought to myself, and that's where I want to be" (Hannigan 2004, 149).

Although her teacher nudged Ida's choice, Ms. W. was listening. When Ida glanced over at her teacher, she saw her smiling and heard her whisper, "Thank you very much, Ida. That was lovely," and Ida was changed. That's intimacy.

In Ida's situation there was a magical moment when the book Ida's teacher had chosen for her suddenly became her choice. She owned it. She owned the way she read it aloud. She owned the words as she got lost in the text. She owned the feelings she had when she closed the book and felt the "full-blown happiness" of a reader.

Ownership is a huge factor in creating intimacy in a reading conference. Are there times when we nudge children to make a better book choice? Sure. Are there times when, as the teacher, we narrow choice to ensure success? Sure. Are there times when we let readers grapple a bit, reading books that are just a tad bit out of their reach (like Jaryd's *Farmer Boy*)? Of course. If Jaryd had not taken ownership in his decision to put *Farmer Boy* away for a while, he would never have realized how to trust himself as a reader.

In *Beyond Leveled Books*, the authors say that without ownership in the experience of choosing text, students cannot "be expected to move into the real world prepared to make choices for reading, to recognize authors and characters, and to love to read" (Szymusiak, Sibberson, and Koch 2008, 23). There will be times when, as their teacher, I have to jump in and help my students make wiser choices. They know that during reading conferences, I will be there to guide them to make wise choices, should they need a nudge. And, of course, throughout the year we will revisit the idea of "How does a wise reader make an appropriate book choice?" in whole-class crafting sessions.

In *Developing Minds*, Arthur Costa states:

> Students demonstrate growth in thinking abilities by increasing their use of alternative strategies of problem solving. They collect evidence to indicate their problem-solving strategy is working, and if one strategy doesn't work, they know how to back up and try another. They realize that they must reject their theory or idea and employ another. They have systematic methods of analyzing a problem, knowing ways to begin, knowing what steps must be performed, and what data need to be generated or collected. (1991, 101)

When students are given ownership of the text they are reading, these characteristics of persistence will emerge in a reading conference. When students "own" the thinking (as well as the text), they can analyze, contemplate ideas, and collect evidence. Jaryd knew that he owned *Farmer Boy*, and through our conferences, he reached the point of having enough data to know it was time to move on to another text. But, the decision to do so was his (in this case).

When I sit down to confer with a child, nine times out of ten, it will be with a book of his own choosing. Conferring regularly with readers gives me the opportunity to see how my students' reading diets change throughout the year. Our ongoing whole-class discussions about book choice help shape them into readers who read from a variety of genres throughout the school year, but often it is a conference that determines whether or not a reader is in an appropriate text.

Will children remember the magnificent words I spoke over them in a lesson on questioning or will they remember me sitting beside them and listening to their questions?

Janice Gibson
First-Grade Teacher

Teacher Keystone Point

When I pull up a chair beside a reader to find out what he's thinking, how his reading is going, I need to remember the words of Daniels and Bizar, "If a student wasn't thinking *before* he started reading, and he wasn't thinking *while* he was reading, why would he be able to think *after* reading? . . . Since reading is thinking, we must provide young readers with rich text worth thinking about, strategies to help them think, and others with whom to think" (2005, 37).

PONDERING: How do you instill a sense of ownership in your readers? During a conference, who would they say owns the text?

Sitting with a reader during a conference helps uncover what he is doing *during* reading, giving him a chance to muck about in his reading as an individual before he perhaps shares it with the whole community. The book is his and so is the thinking that emerges in the conference. In *Reworking the Workshop*, Daniel Heuser states that conferring "is a private moment between adult and child, a powerful teaching and assessment technique rolled into one" (2002, 95). The time we spend in a reading conference strengthens the pragmatic relationship between the reader and the classroom community.

Where Do I Sit?

Remember the videotape I mentioned? Something else happened when I watched that tape. I had invited Ashley to meet me at the conferring table for a reading conference. Before I sent her back to work, I asked, "So, is there anything else you're wondering about?"

"Yeah, Mr. Allen. Sometimes when I'm out reading, I look over here and wonder, 'What is he telling them that I should be hearing too?'"

I looked at Ashley at that moment (with much the same dumbfounded look I gave Randi when she asked me about my beliefs), and for a moment I didn't know what to say. "Ashley, you're right. I'm probably saying a lot of things that you should hear, that's why I try to confer with you as often as possible." I sent Ashley off to work, but her words still rumbled through my mind.

It was at that moment that I decided I would never call kids over to a table to confer again. The table in the corner became another place for students to work during composing time. Since then, my conferences take place out among readers. If I'm conferring with someone like Ashley, other readers sitting nearby can eavesdrop on our conversation if they choose to do so. If I am conferring with someone like Ashley, out among the masses, I will have a better sense of the pulse of the composing time itself. The intimacy of reader's workshop changed that day, thanks to Ashley's comment. Now, I confer wherever I find the reader—at a table, at his desk, on the floor, in a comfy chair.

Sitting close to the reader, shoulder-to-shoulder, gives each conference a warmer feeling. No table sitting between me and the reader, off in the corner of the classroom. This brings conferring into the heart of the workshop—where the actual "work" is happening.

"A successful conference begins and ends with the child. Teachers who find out what the child is doing and thinking can then use that knowledge to motivate and challenge" (Heuser 2002, 106). Sitting next to a child while you confer guarantees that those few minutes together will begin and end with the child. Sitting next to Jaryd, on his level, brought about a conference that changed his course as a reader.

Where do we sit? We sit side-by-side, carefully listening. The way we look at the student, a spark of intent in our eyes, leaning in naturally, gives the student the sense that for the next few minutes he has our undivided attention. It says to the reader that we have only one purpose—to listen. It is a stunning act, sitting next to a young reader, waiting to be amazed! It's like Anne Sullivan writing, "My heart is singing for joy this morning. A miracle has happened! The light of understanding has shone upon my little pupil's mind, and behold, all things are changed!" (Keller 2003, 226). And, who knows, a reader might just trust himself a bit more if we choose to move in and listen—at just the right time. Just ask Jaryd.

This poem, "When Someone Deeply Listens to You" by John Fox (1997), sums up the concept of rigor, inquiry, and intimacy. When I read this poem, I realize that all three concepts come back to listening and listening well:

When someone deeply listens to you
it is like holding out a dented cup
you've had since childhood
and watching it fill up with
cold, fresh water.
When it balances on top of the brim,
you are understood.
When it overflows and touches your skin,
you are loved.

When someone deeply listens to you
the room where you stay
starts a new life
and the place where you wrote
your first poem
begins to glow in your mind's eye.
It is as if gold has been discovered!

When someone deeply listens to you
your barefeet are on the earth
and a beloved land that seemed distant
is now at home within you.

PART 3

WHAT EMERGES FROM OUR READING CONFERENCES?

The urge to make and build seems to be an almost universal human characteristic. It goes way beyond meeting our need for survival and seems to be the expression of some deep-rooted part of being human. It isn't surprising then that these acts of creation should be such a large part of children's play. But we don't have to understand all of someone else's creative efforts. What's important is that we communicate our respect for their attempts to express what's inside themselves.

—Fred Rogers, 2003

Today I met with Mr. Allen. I think this was the first time he announced a little bit of our conversation out loud . . . I'm glad I met with Mr. Allen because he helped me find the answers, but they were the ones I already had. Maybe I just needed to talk about them. Hmm . . . Maybe I should investigate.

—Ashley, Third Grade

Chapter 6

Conferring Walk-Aways

The urge to build is somewhat innate. My father had the trait. My son Graham has the trait (if it's genetic, I think it skipped a generation). When he was in kindergarten, Graham came home each day and told us about the block structures he and his buddies were building in the empty classroom next door. Mrs. Miller let them keep their ever-changing structures up all week. Each day during choice time, Graham and Marco would build elaborate structures out of the blocks, move them around, adapt them, and ultimately stand back and survey their work. They would get their teacher, pull her into the structure laboratory, and say, "Hey, Mrs. Miller, look what we built!" And Mrs. Miller would smile and say, "Tell me about it." And they would. They would walk away satisfied with their accomplishments and begin planning for next week's structure.

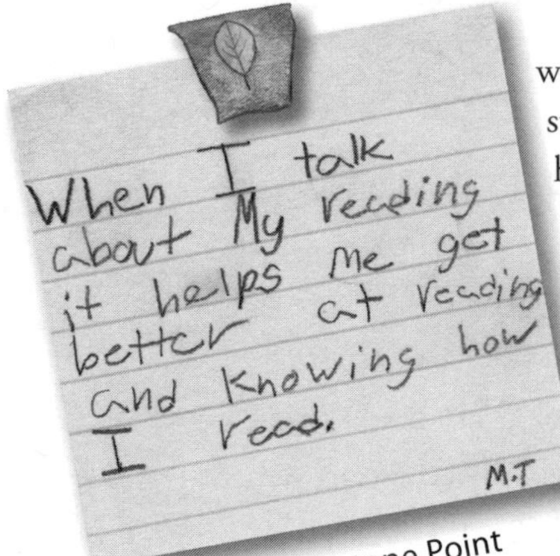

Student Keystone Point

In 1914, after Charles Pajeau, a stonemason by trade, spent months in his workshop "tinkering" with the idea of creating a set of soundly engineered sticks and wheels designed to interconnect and challenge children's minds, he knew he was on to something. As a child, there is something pleasing and engaging about Tinker Toys, and they have endured to this day (my wife's childhood set is still remarkably intact). Pajeau's idea for these toys came from observing children playing with pencils and empty wooden sewing-thread spools (Caney 2006). From observing children. When I discovered this, I was astounded.

I started thinking about the central role observation plays when conferring with readers. If we could sideline some of our counterfeit beliefs, refocus some of the emphasis on the *D* word (data), and sit down side-by-side with young readers, imagine the results. We should observe children tinkering with words, sentences, and whole text. We should listen to children think while they explore as readers (each of us with a notebook and pencil nearby) and ask them to explain their thinking and reasoning to us. Perhaps we could build something grand and long lasting—independent and engaged readers who walk away from conferences with strategies and tools to help them become confident, effective, and deeper readers.

To support independence, one of our goals is to develop metacognitive readers—readers who think about their thinking. If this is a goal, how can we make sure readers walk away from reading conferences more aware of their reading process?

Using the RIP Model, we are metacognitive as conferrers, thinking about a specific structure as we engage children in conversations about their reading. Metacognition consists of three basic elements (Kujawa and Huske 1995):

1. *Developing* a plan of action,
2. *Maintaining* and *monitoring* the plan, and
3. *Evaluating* the plan.

PONDERING: Listen to and transcribe one of your conferences. What do you notice about your own conferring metacognition?

Aren't these the exact elements we want readers to engage in before, during, and after a conference? We want them to walk away from each conference with a plan of action in mind and know how to implement it.

As I confer, I certainly hope that I am building the capacity for my students to think independently without me there guiding them. I want students to walk away with *something* after we confer.

To define that *something* I came up with the term *walk-away*. A walk-away is a tool or strategy used or discovered as students negotiate text and develop the capacity for independence, so that next time we meet and I ask, "How's your reading going?" they can tell me.

So what specifically do children walk away with after a conference? What do I walk away with as their teacher?

Remember the original web you created, "What emerges in a conference?" Many of the ideas you listed on your web could be considered walk-aways, assuming the idea emerges as you confer throughout the year.

Early on, as I began to think more about the idea of walk-aways, Cheryl Zimmerman visited my classroom and observed my conferences with video camera in hand. She observed what students and I were taking away from the reading conferences she watched, and she transcribed some of the language she noticed. Cheryl and I created a table that lists the following:

1. A specific walk-away that Cheryl noted,
2. A synthesis of Cheryl's observations (language and other specific noticings) that led to each walk-away, and
3. The implications I contemplated about each walk-away (both for me and for students).

In one reader's workshop, during approximately six reading conferences, Cheryl made the observations listed in Figure 6.1.

Figure 6.1 Conferring Walk-Aways

Walk-Away	Cheryl's Noticings	Implications
Sincere questions	"So what are you thinking?" "How did you know?" "Can you explain that more clearly?"	**For me:** The language I use with my students is critical. I have to think carefully about the types of questions I ask students during a conference. **For students:** Sincere questions encourage a student to explain his thinking. If I model divergent questions, he can better question himself as he reads independently.
Assessment of surface structure systems/fix-up strategies	As the reader reads aloud, miscues, word strategies, etc., are noted in anecdotal records.	**For me:** I cannot ignore the surface structure cueing systems. They are especially important with emergent readers and readers who are reading more sophisticated text. Surface structure cueing systems include Graphophonic, Lexical, and Syntactic. **For students:** A reader learns to negotiate text and apply surface structure strategies discussed in conferences to his own reading. His ability to fix up is strengthened. He can understand word-level, problem-solving strategies.
Instruction	"When readers ask questions, they need to decide to either stop and think then and there, or to stick the question in the back of their mind and continue reading. I noticed you . . ."	**For me:** Instruction is what bridges the gap between conferring and conversing. Every conference has an instructional component—be it new learning or reinforcement of previous instruction. **For students:** A reader is expected to apply what he learns in a conference. A student is encouraged to monitor application of the instruction he receives after he leaves a conference.

Goal setting	"Today as you read, I would like you to pay special attention to the dialogue. Ask yourself if you know who is saying what. I'll check in with you tomorrow to see how it's going . . ."	**For me:** The plan is key. It lets readers know that thinking is never finished. Readers leave a conference with something in mind that will provide ongoing work and depth of thinking. **For students:** The student leaves a conference with a goal in mind. I often write the plan on a sticky note or encourage the student to write the plan down so that he can remember what he has promised to work on between conferences.
Moments of silence	Both Patrick and the reader allow themselves a little "think time" in order to question/respond thoughtfully.	**For me:** Time to think is imperative. It makes or breaks a conference. It gives both teacher and student the opportunity to ponder. It also helps strengthen the sense of rigor, inquiry, and intimacy. **For students:** Some students are long thinkers. They need time to think. Each student comes to realize that think time is something we do not only during the conference, but anytime we are talking with another learner.
Underlying messages are sent	Patrick allows kids to interrupt a conference only when they need to check spelling on their "How Do I Spell It?" sheet. The message is that spelling is important. The interruption is minimal—usually no words are spoken.	**For me:** I must limit interruptions during conferring. The time is valuable for the reader, and I teach students about expectations. As a community, we must decide what might warrant interrupting a conference. **For students:** A student learns to be a problem-solver. He learns how to negotiate his time and respect others' learning. He learns that conferring time is sacred and that he must solve his problem himself or ask someone else to help him.

Book choice is assessed in two ways	Is the book at an appropriate reading level? (No numbers or letters are assigned to levels. Children have been taught how to assess levels on their own.) Or Is there a need to nudge the reader into a new genre? New author?	**For me:** The conference is the perfect venue to discuss book choice. Book choice is a personal decision, and readers know that a conference may deal with the text the reader is choosing. It may also be a time that I nudge a reader to make a more appropriate choice of text. **For students:** Book choice is an important skill to learn. Knowing his purpose and his own abilities leads to independence. A reader knows that book choice is his responsibility. He leaves a conference knowing whether or not he has made a wise choice and what he plans to do about it.
Test tips are revealed	"You know how this author used bold print and big capital letters to begin the chapter? You will see that on the CSAP sometimes . . ."	**For me:** I try to mention the things that will infiltrate our community, like testing. Revealing these tips during a conference helps learners know that what's coming is something they already know a lot about; it alleviates some of the fear. **For students:** If a student learns that tests are not something to fear, it makes test-taking season less stressful. He leaves a conference with a natural, nonthreatening reminder.
Previous goals are revisited	The reader is aware of his/her history. "Remember in September your goal was to slow down as you read . . . Guess what, you're doing it!"	**For me:** The P portion of the conference is worth revisiting. They know that I monitor their growth and refer to their previous goals often. I think the plan speaks to accountability on the student's part. **For students:** A student knows that from conference to conference, across the year, the plans he focuses on are important. He knows that we will revisit goals.

Deep structure systems and comprehension is assessed	"What are you thinking? What are your questions? What do you think is important in this chapter? Tell me about how you're using sensory images."	**For me:** The deep structure cueing systems are critical. A conference provides time to recognize and clarify individual understanding of thinking strategies and their implementation in a reader's in-the-moment reading. It builds congruency between our comprehension work and our conferring work. Deep structure cueing systems include Semantic, Schematic, and Pragmatic. **For students:** A student can apply and discuss his application of a specific thinking strategy. He can probe ideas and discuss his comprehension more deeply.
Vocabulary is developed	"What does *good* mean? Can you describe how your reading is going using another word?"	**For me:** A conference is the perfect setting to build meaningful, contextual-based vocabulary—either the reader's oral vocabulary or written vocabulary from the text. **For students:** A reader learns new vocabulary in context. He develops and strengthens his understanding of words and their usage within the context of his reading.
Crafting lesson content is assessed	"How will determining importance help you as you read this mystery? What sensory images were you creating in your mind as you read?"	**For me:** If students are being held accountable for strategy or skill usage, what better way is there to assess it? The side-by-side opportunity to see how a reader is using a new or previously learned strategy or skill is imperative to evaluating a reader's application of a thinking strategy. **For students:** A student takes information from crafting lessons and applies skills and strategies to his reading. He makes the connection between crafting lessons and his reading.

Learners self-assess and self-evaluate	Patrick asks, "How's it going?" The reader is expected to be specific.	**For me:** Readers are held accountable. Self-reflection puts judgment into the learner's corner. The reader is the one explaining his strengths and growth areas. I can listen and look for a means to provide essential next steps. **For students:** A student is a problem-solver. He is able to verbalize and justify his reading role. He can better describe his reading process when he has the responsibility to do so.
Attention is fully devoted to the learner	Eye contact, knee-to-knee, distractions are ignored, and quotes from the reader are captured in Patrick's notes.	**For me:** This strengthens intimacy and documentation. The conference is exclusively for the reader. It should be a peaceful, almost reverent time. The implementation of a workshop is vital to ensure that readers get my full attention during a conference. I have to set expectations for specific rituals and routines. **For students:** The conferring time is for him. He knows that his conference is for him to develop as a reader.

When she originally gave me her list, I was flabbergasted. I knew conferring was essential, but I had no idea that after six conferences I would be leaving with such rich, complex, and explicit information about what emerged as I conferred. I was able to walk away with valuable information and better identify my purpose as a conferrer.

PONDERING: What do you think readers take with them, instructionally, as a conferring walk-away? What will students leave your conferences knowing? What will you leave knowing about the reader?

What Cheryl's observations taught me is that children were leaving each conference with specifics about themselves as readers. They were leaving each conference with specific language that would nudge them as readers. As a result, conferring took on a new look, a more unwavering level of import, after Cheryl and I talked about her observations. If teachers are able to identify walk-aways, notice the language they are using during conferences, and think about classroom implications for themselves and their students, they can better understand that conferring is indeed a keystone of instruction.

The following are transcripts of reading conferences I had with two students. Listen in and see what you might add to your last pondering.

A Conference with Jacob

Jacob was reading David Williams's *Walking to the Creek*, a picture book about two boys—twins—who were spending time on their grandparents' farm. I sat down next to Jacob, and I was curious about his book choice. Jacob is a reader who likes to ponder. Reading conferences with Jacob usually take on a reflective tone. They are slow moving, but purposeful. Jacob is quiet and thinks carefully before he jumps into a conversation. I love his cautious optimism. We were in the middle of a study of Determining What's Most Important (Determine the Most Important Ideas or Themes). In the transcript, Jacob's dialogue is in bold print. The think bubbles are a record of what I am thinking, my own metacognition, as I listen to Jacob's conference (trying to determine the walk-aways). Our conference sounded something like this:

The R portion begins...

I am curious about Jacob's book choice. It's a title I haven't seen in a while.

How's it going, Jacob? What are you reading?

Walking to the Creek.

Walking to the Creek. Tell me about it.

It's about these two boys, twins, who go down to their grandparents' a lot. They always, well mostly, go down to a creek to look for fish and . . . (long pause)

Jacob is pausing. I don't jump in. I give him lots of thinking time. And he uses it.

And . . .

And every time they leave, their grandparents always say, like, "Be careful."

Uh-huh.

Jacob is retelling. I sense he's thinking about something else. It's time to ask him a question.

And then their grandpa thinks he's too old to have, like, fun, so, he just says, like, "Go have fun while you can."

So, what are you thinking about as you read this book?

Now I see that Jacob is really thinking about the big idea, which was part of our crafting session.

Um . . . (Pause)

I think that, um, it might be about like trust and stuff or something. If the grandparents trust the kids, *they* might be able to trust them too.

Jacob has identified trust as the theme of this story. He's gone beyond just a retell. I want to see how he drew that conclusion.

What are some of the things that made you think this book is about trust?

The grandparents let the two boys go a mile or two down the road by themselves, um, so that made me think of trust . . .

I wanted to reteach the concept of determining the big idea. Trying to get Jacob to explain more of his reasoning.

Interesting . . . So that might be that big idea.

So, tell me Jacob, when you're reading, how are you making those decisions that it might be about trust?

Here I think Jacob is relating schema to the notion of trust. His pause lets me know that he was trying to really sum up his point—synthesize, if you will.

Um, 'cause, um . . . (pause) **that if somebody can trust you with a few things, they can trust you with a lot of things.**

Are there specifics in the text besides "walking a mile down the creek"? Are there other things that have given you that idea of trust?

I'm giving him a nudge to look back in the text.

Um . . .

Look back and see. (Jacob looks back).

Good. Jacob has gone back to the text twice to support his idea about trust.

Maybe that the grandparents let them go roam the farm by themselves 'cause they have to be careful of all the animals.

And, um, maybe (turns pages) **. . . Maybe they** (the grandparents) **trust them more because they're with their two dogs, and if anything goes wrong they can guard them.**

I'm letting him know it was so smart to return to the text, to reread.

P . . . Starting to move into the plan...

Yeah, I'm wondering if when you go back and do some rereading maybe that will help. I think that's an interesting thing to have picked up as a theme or a big idea.

But what are the signs of trust? I think that this would be a really interesting thing for you to take notice of as a reader and notice what's going on in your head when you're identifying the signs of trust.

Maybe when we confer next time, we could talk about that. What do you think? Could you stick with this book for a couple of days and we can talk about that?

Yes.

I make a note so I remember to come back.

I'm going to jot down here that I'll meet with you on Thursday, and we'll see how that goes.

Now that he has a plan, he'll work independently. He knows I'll be back to talk on Thursday.

Spend a couple days in this book and see what happens. Jacob, that is really wise thinking . . .

The walk-aways Jacob and I left this conference with:

- Jacob is able to retell.
- Jacob needs time to think and ponder.
- Jacob knows that he can return to the text for support.
- Jacob is trying to apply the thinking strategy of determining what's most important.

PONDERING: What were some of the things you noticed in this conference transcript? What are the walk-aways?

- Jacob is identifying the theme.
- Jacob understands the idea of trust.
- Jacob is trying to intersperse his own schema and synthesis.
- Jacob is strengthening his ability to understand.

My notes for this conference appear in Figure 6.2.

Reading Conferences for: Jacob

Date 3/23 Title Walking to the Creek Page(s)

Review/Read Aloud/Record	Instruction/Insights/Intrigue	Plan/Progress/Purpose
S/ Two boys, twins, go to their grandparent's a lot, they always say "be careful"; Grandpa thinks he's too old to have fun... tells them to "have fun while you can." — Might be about trust (identifying theme?) T/ Why? retell ✓	S/ Grandparents let them explore... two miles... I thought of trust T/ How are you making decisions? S/ "If you trust someone with a few things—they trust you with a lot of things" T/ Text? S/ "Grandparents trust them..."	T/ Go back and do some rereading? Signs of trust? Notice what's going on in your head... Next time... talk about that, spend some time in text. Confer: (two days?)

Additional Comment(s): retelling, returns to text, determining what's imp., schema

Figure 6.2 Conference notes for Jacob

A Conference with Mikayla

Mikayla was reading Harley Jessup's *Grandma Summer*, a picture book about Ben and his slightly eccentric grandmother. Ben spends the summer with Grandma and isn't really happy about the prospect of spending time alone with her. Mikayla is a voracious reader; she reads a wide variety of text. She is conscientious and makes wise choices for specific purposes. She responds to her reading in her reader's/writer's notebook almost daily, usually writing about her thinking. Reading conferences with Mikayla are thought-provoking and deliberate. She really tries to apply thinking strategies to her reading. Mikayla and I conferred during a study of Monitoring Comprehension (Monitor for Meaning and Problem-Solve When Meaning Breaks Down). Mikayla's dialogue is in bold print. My thinking is bubbled on the side of the transcript (trying to determine the walk-aways). Our conferring time sounded something like this:

R . . . she jumps right in, she's used to the format.

Mikayla points out her purpose right away. I know we'll have to come back to the great-grandma connection.

So, how's it going?

Good. I'm reading *Grandma Summer* because a couple weeks ago when I was in California my great-grandma passed away, so . . .

She jumps right into a retell without me posing questions.

And at the beginning his grandma brings him to this little house, and it's by a beach. And at first he didn't like his grandma and he didn't like opening the shutters and helping his grandmother open up the door with the rusty old key.

And, um, and then since his grandma kept calling him Darling, he's like, "My name isn't Darling; my name is Ben."

(We both laugh.)

Laughter is a natural sign of inferring. We both did it, adds to intimacy.

I thought that was pretty funny because he's like . . . I think he thought he was worried, I think he thought she was calling Ben, Darling, like for his name.

I . . . moving into the second part of the conference.

Returned to text. Reading like a writer. Picking up the description. Mikayla understands that our reading informs our writing.

And when I was reading back here (goes back in the text), **I think it was really descriptive because it said, "Together, they unhooked the heavy storm door. Grandma turned the key in the rusty lock. The dark house looked spooky to Ben, but Grandma said, "Oh, I do love this old place. It smells just like summer. Let's open up the rest of these shutters."**

What do you think she meant by "it smells just like summer"?

Interesting. Could be? I really didn't have an answer I was looking for, just curious.

Um, probably because the last time she's been there it was summer and then she left.

Hmmm . . . So, how's it going in terms of keeping track of your thinking as you're reading?

I knew she would start to talk about comprehension.

Um, kind of good because I'm able to remember what's been happening in the book.

Why is that?

Finally . . . a question. Mikayla has been doing most of the talking.

Probably because when I come to words I don't get, I keep rereading them until it makes sense.

Yeah, where has that happened for you?

Trying to get her to support her thinking a bit more.

Right here . . . (points to text)

Right here it says, "'Do you think Japanese Glass Floats still wash up on the beach?' Ben asked." And I didn't really get that . . . (rereads)

Able to pinpoint the exact place in the text where she got stuck.

"'Do you think Japanese glass, floats still up on the beach?'"

A miscue. She read "Japanese Glass Floats" . . . as "Japanese glass, floats" . . . not in her schemata.

Then I kept reading it and then I thought back in the book. And it said there's this green ball of glass and, uh, it's called glass float. And I didn't get when it said that, so I had to think back in the book.

Mikayla understands the necessity of rereading.

That's a perfect thing . . . you know when we think of that idea of remembering. Like connecting it to something we've already read *in* the book. Because usually authors might throw in the same kind of ideas maybe later on, so we've really got to do some thinking back. That's a good strategy.

Adding some of my thinking to her repertoire.

Did you write that down when you were thinking about how to remember the other day?

I don't think I did.

Nudging Mikayla to use this as an opportunity for authentic response.

P . . . moving into the planning portion

That's a really good strategy though. What else are you thinking?

I'm thinking that this author has written another book before because of the way it's written and how it's put together.

Reading like a writer. Thinking about her writing work later in the day. Natural connection for Mikayla.

Right. So what's your plan after I leave?

Um. That I . . . I want to get some good information out of this book like, that he comes to like his grandma.

Hmmm . . . So are you kind of expecting that to happen?

Yeah.

Have you gotten some clues about that in the text?

Yeah, um, right here, in fact. (returns to the text) **And, up here.** (points to a specific section)

So you've made this prediction that he's going to end up liking his grandma. Am I right?

Yeah.

Nudging Mikayla to think about the process of inferring.

And you've picked up some clues, right? You know what we call that?

No.

Don't you remember from Mr. Rushmore's room? Starts with an *I* . . . Here, I'll write it down . . . I-n-f . . .

Name inferring for her. She understands strategy work, so it is good to give her a bit of a reminder here. I know she's learned about inferring previously.

INFERRING!

Yep. That's it. That's exactly what you're doing, so that's a really good plan . . . see if the inferences you're drawing about him coming to like his grandmother actually play out at the end . . . Thanks for sharing with me.

You're welcome.

Such politeness.

I love this book . . . (pause) . . . makes you want to go to the beach, doesn't it?

Yes.

I thought it was important to bring up her grandmother again. Planting the seeds of writing.

All right . . . You know at the beginning of our conference you said you chose it because it reminds you of your own great-grandmother—is that still happening?

Yeah, kind of.

Bringing back the idea of extending meaning.

That's a perfect way to extend meaning. You know, tying that into your writing somehow. Just a thought . . .

The walk-aways Mikayla and I left this conference with were:

- Mikayla takes a leadership role.
- Mikayla is understanding the text.
- Mikayla is rereading for a variety of purposes.
- Mikayla understands book choice.
- Mikayla reads a wide variety of text.
- Mikayla monitors for meaning.
- Mikayla rereads.
- Mikayla understands how to read like a writer.

PONDERING: What were some things you noticed in this conference transcript? What are the walk-aways?

My conference notes appear in Figure 6.3.

Reading Conferences for: Mikayla

Date 3/20 Title Grandma Summer Page(s) ______

Review/Read Aloud/Record	Instruction/Insights/Intrigue	Plan/Progress/Purpose
S/ Couple weeks ago in Calif. great-grandma passed away – retell ✓+ grandma takes him to little house by beach- didn't like her or the house.. Grandma called him Darling- he said his name was Ben (thought this was funny) – reread descriptive "Together, they unhooked..." T/ "Smells like summer?"	S/ Probably summer last time T/ Keeping track of thinking? S/ Remember what's happening Keep rereading words that don't make sense... (points to text)... Do you think Japanese Glass Floats... reread, thought back in book – made sense T/ Write that down? Reviewed idea of remembering...	S/ "Thinking about another book she's written... but I want to find out if he comes to like his grandmother..." T/ Text clues? (inferring) "Still remind you of your grandmother?" ... extend meaning (writing nudge)

Additional Comment(s): leadership, rereads for purpose, reads like writer, book choice

Figure 6.3 Conference notes for Mikayla

Jacob and Mikayla are two different readers. The walk-aways were different. But what was similar? Both conferences included the following:

- A sense of rigor, inquiry, and intimacy
- The RIP Model
- A sense of purpose
- Time to ponder and reflect
- A focus on understanding, remembering, extending meaning, and making reading memorable
- A mix of surface-level and deep-level strategies
- Evidence of specific thinking strategies

"Conferences are an elegant example of how assessment can actually become one with instruction" (Daniels and Bizar 2005, 230). Both Jacob and Mikayla gave me a better understanding of who they are as readers. They were eloquent in their coming to know themselves as readers in such different ways. My role in each conference was slightly different—a bit more coaching with Jacob, a bit more listening with Mikayla. Each conference provided us with the opportunity to think more deeply and consider what it means to become a wiser reader, together.

PONDERING: Who will you find to help you think about and analyze your reading conferences?

When I was conferring with both Jacob and Mikayla, they chose the path the conference would take. My initial question became part of the process, but much of the time I was quietly observing and noticing the types of thinking they were doing and the decisions they were making as readers. Our discussion focused on their processes, paying close attention to any patterns that emerged, holes that needed to be spackled, and the skills and strategies they were using to better understand the texts they were reading (notice both students were reading picture books).

My conferences with both Mikayla and Jacob were unrehearsed, yet predictable. I provided instructional support when I felt it necessary to jump into the conversation (more so with Jacob, since Mikayla took the leadership role during her conference). The notes I took during each of their conferences created a record of their thinking and they are also available for me to provide purposeful feedback to both Jacob and Mikayla either at that moment or sometime in the future. We were able to focus on the behaviors that both Mikayla and Jacob were using as readers. They both walked away a different reader, and I walked away a different teacher.

My wife, Susan, has a degree in early childhood education. I was perusing her bookshelf and picked up *Miseducation*. It's by one of her heroes, David Elkind. In it, I read:

> Education is not a race. A child who learns to read at age three has in no way "won" over a child who learns to read at age six or seven. A true race has a well-marked finish line that all participants must cross to determine the winner. In contrast, "learning to read" is a lifelong process. For example, I did not really learn how to read Freud until I was a postdoctoral fellow, when my teacher, David Rapaport, painstakingly guided me through one of Freud's books page by page. . . . Learning does not stop after we have learned a skill or left school or college; learning and education are lifelong processes that come to an end only when we do. (1987, 83)

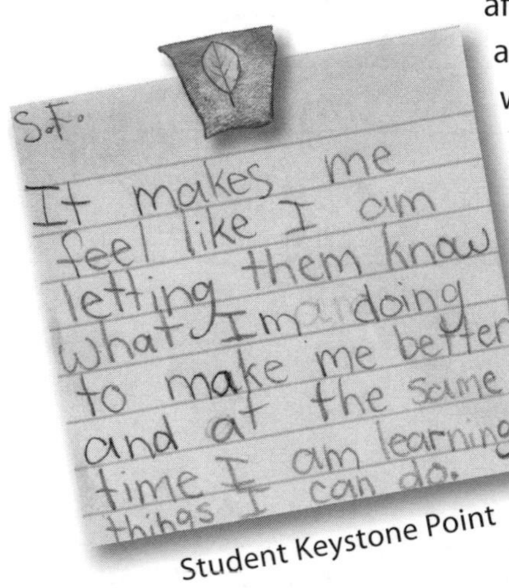

Student Keystone Point

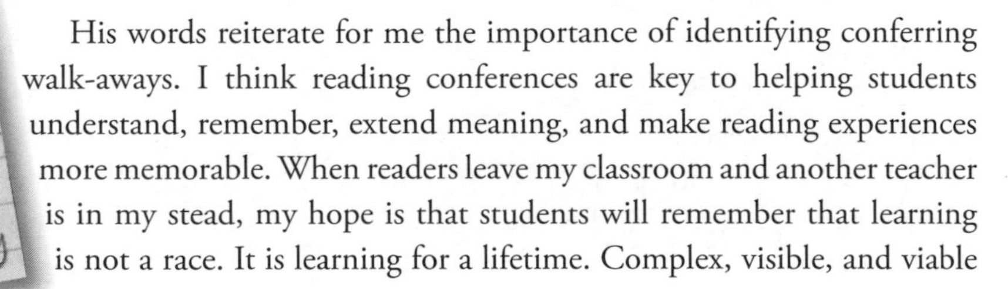

His words reiterate for me the importance of identifying conferring walk-aways. I think reading conferences are key to helping students understand, remember, extend meaning, and make reading experiences more memorable. When readers leave my classroom and another teacher is in my stead, my hope is that students will remember that learning is not a race. It is learning for a lifetime. Complex, visible, and viable thinking doesn't happen quickly. But, if we can think more clearly about the walk-aways of each conference, will not our students be all the richer for it?

In my notebook, I wrote the following entry after a conversation with my colleague Troy Rushmore. We were talking about *having* understanding and what *having* that understanding means in terms of reading. *Having* is not a "he's got it and he doesn't" attitude, it is an awareness of the process, of the individual, over the long haul. I wrote:

It's not just the final understanding, but the process of seeking what understanding is throughout the process that's important—there is a synthesis that causes you to revise and change during the process—in the end you come up with something bigger than you thought. This can only happen when there's a sense of independence alive and growing in our classrooms.

What I know now I never thought I'd know—that's what gaining understanding is, it's the changing in thinking that occurs by naming it along the way, not at the end—especially if I can wrap it around the context and content of thinking.

Having is when I've wrapped my thinking around some new learning; something has changed. Having happens in the process. Sometimes the having can only occur when we have had the chance to talk one-on-one with a colleague, a peer, another learner . . .

I want my students to value what they are learning, knowing that understanding is vital, and appreciating that their work must carry on... I want their experience, their history, to be far different from mine.
Troy Rushmore
Second-Grade Teacher

Teacher Keystone Point

I know that Jacob and Mikayla left their conferences *having* a better grasp, a better discernment, of themselves as readers. I left each conference with a better awareness of who they are as readers. They left each conference knowing they will have many more opportunities to engage in side-by-side, eye-to-eye conferences. They know I will fully devote myself to each of them, individually, in future composing sessions of workshop. There's a sense of trust that is strengthened workshop to workshop, teacher to student.

I walked away knowing more about Jacob and Mikayla. Each of them walked away knowing more about themselves as readers.

It is a conscious decision we make, as teachers, to tinker in thinking—to, with, and by students. Our interaction with individual readers as we confer helps us walk away from each conference having added to our knowledge of the individual readers in our classroom. Conferring gives us a chance to evaluate a student's thinking behaviors and comprehension, fluency, word-level skills and problem-solving strategies, and engagement and motivation. Students walk away satisfied with their accomplishments. Students walk away knowing that it is the process of becoming proficient, independent, mindful readers that matters most.

But one day, quite unexpectedly, Hush said,
"Grandma, I want to know what I look like.
Please could you make me visible again?"
"Of course I can," said Grandma Poss,
and she began to look through her magic books.

She looked into this book and she looked into that.
There was magic for thin and magic for fat,
Magic for tall and magic for small,
but the magic she was looking for wasn't there at all.

Grandma Poss looked miserable.
"Don't worry, Grandma," said Hush.
"I don't mind."

But in her heart of hearts she did.

—Mem Fox, 1983

When I confer with Mr. Allen I always learn something new . . . like this one conference we talked about how when I put my background knowledge and my thinking together, it turned into something new. And that's where it helps me because if we didn't confer, then I wouldn't have had that knowledge.

—Jackie, Third Grade

Chapter 7

Conferring Ain't Easy

I chose to call this chapter "Conferring Ain't Easy" because, well, it isn't. You'll excuse the bad grammar, because I just think conferring, well, *ain't* easy. The phrase *conferring ain't easy* came about as I was talking to a colleague about conferring and she looked at me and jokingly said, "You know, conferring ain't easy!" We both laughed. I said, "You're right; it ain't!" The idea that conferring isn't easy (what is?) became a running joke in our conversations.

When I began working with the Public Education and Business Coalition (PEBC), I was involved in staff development training with Ellin Keene and Colleen Buddy as the group's cofacilitators. In one of our gatherings, Colleen shared a list of guiding principles she had developed for staff developers. They had names like "The Dick and Jane Principle" and "The Monet Principle" (a brilliantly crafted list of the pitfalls and successes we might run into when working with adults). Colleen has the unique gift of using metaphor and analogy to bring thinking to the forefront of her work as a staff developer and literacy specialist. (Colleen's complete list is in *Learning Along the Way* [Sweeney 2003] on pages 8–9.)

Katie Wood Ray suggests that, as a writer, one of the most important questions I can ask myself is, "What have you read that is like what you are trying to write?" (Ray 2006b, 36). With Katie's words and Colleen's commentary in mind, I have created a list of Conferring Premises. Premises that I thought about as I tried to understand the notion of conferring more explicitly.

I share this list with you because

1. it makes me laugh,
2. it makes me think, and
3. I think we need to again be reminded of some of the nitty-gritty details of conferring.

I have wrestled with each idea on the list as I have tackled the notion of conferring. In the following section I present my list of assertions.

Conferring Ain't Easy

To confer effectively, I must acknowledge the following premises:

Expect the Unexpected

I have to be flexible; I never know what a learner might say—I have to be prepared to listen. I have to be open to each reader's thoughts and actions, and I have to think about how to respond wisely.

It's Fun, But It's Not a Picnic

Sitting side-by-side with a student talking about thinking is amazing, but we must remember that it's also hard work on both our parts. Both conferrer and conferee play an important role in making a conference worth the time and effort.

Conferring Is Teaching, Not Fault Finding

My goal in every conference is for the student to leave with something he can muck around with until next time we confer. Sometimes that decision is up to the student, sometimes I make the decision. Either way, my focus in a reading conference, like a writing conference, is to find favor not fault.

You're Darned Write

I want students to use their reader's/writer's notebooks effectively and personally. In many conferences I'll say, "You should write that in your notebook," or "Make sure you include that in your response today." I want conferring to blend itself into other aspects of the workshop, including the work students do when they reflect about their reading in their notebooks.

Shut Up and Listen

One of my favorite singers, Mary Chapin Carpenter, sings, "Shut up and Kiss Me." I literally sing it in my head to remind myself that I have to remember to shut up and listen. Who should do most of the talking? The conferee. (By the way, *shut up* is on my list of ten things not to say; I cringe when I hear it, but in this case it reminds me that I have to be quiet—and "be quiet and listen" just isn't as powerful.)

Get a Grip

One goal is to get to the nitty-gritty of researching and assessing a learner's strengths—focus on the learner. I have to know the student well, *get a grip* on his or her reading strengths and growth areas, and bring that to our conference.

Think and Search

I listen to what the reader is saying, think about a teaching point, and go for it. Let the reader lead the thinking. It is like asking questions as we read—sometimes we have to *think and search* for answers. With practice, I have gotten better at identifying teaching points during a conference.

Nudge Thinking Deeper

It's important to note attempts at strategy usage and encourage learners to take their thinking deeper—not only to name the strategies they employ but also to think about how they are helping. It's important to note their work at the word level too. Both can happen in a conference. Knowing each reader well helps me focus my conferring either on a surface structure cueing system or a deep structure cueing system.

Yes, I Do It Too

Learners need to see that I use the same skills and strategies as a learner that they do: I have to practice what I preach and share my thinking as a fellow reader. A think-aloud is sometimes a critical part of a conference, especially with emergent readers.

Find the Key to Success

Even our most reticent learners need something they can find success with right away; I have to nudge them to continue to practice a skill or strategy that emerged during a conference. Readers that are more seasoned also need to know they are being successful; I can't forget that even sophisticated readers need to confer.

Stick to the Plan

I have to leave learners with a nudge to apply the learning from the conference once I've left their side. The plan can be theirs or mine, but they need to know that endurance matters and that once we leave the conference, we both have hard work to do until next time we meet.

My Knees Are Killing Me

I have to be comfortable when I am conferring and make the reader feel comfortable too. Proximity is important. Being comfortable might mean learning to ignore the little distractions going on around the room. I have to pull up a chair or sit on the floor next to a reader rather than pull him away from his independent reading.

You're Being Condescending Again

All learners deserve trusting opportunities to stretch themselves, no matter their abilities or needs. Children can spot a fake a mile away. I have learned that the best conferences are steeped in sincere language and sincere questions. I sometimes take a second or two to develop my question, so the reader knows it is one I truly care about knowing the answer to and that I believe he should be able to answer, or at least think about for a bit. One note: conferences are not a place to be sarcastic, even with students with an urbane sense of humor.

What Did We Talk About?

Take notes. Decide how to use them. If I am just touching base with a student, I may choose to jot myself a quick note (to add to my notebook). If I am sitting down for a side-by-side conference, I always try to take notes; sometimes right after I confer I scoot to the side and jot down the thinking. I am continually practicing this, trying to get better.

Help, I'm Drowning!

It is important to find a colleague with whom you'll study conferring. I talk a lot about conferring with others; even if we don't agree, I am a better conferrer as a result. Remember, most drownings occur alone, and many people drown without any hint or sign of danger previously observed. Conferring often eliminates the danger of letting readers drown.

What Was the Question?

I can't ask so many stinking questions. I have to make conferring a time to discover answers to the important questions, the questions I am truly interested in knowing the answer to and those that will help the reader. If I bombard a child, he won't know what to say; this takes practice. I nudge him to consider his own questions.

I Did What?

Name it for the learner. If I see a student using a specific skill or strategy, I name it! If we are studying inferring and he uses a sensory image, I name it for him. It is important to plant the seeds of comprehension, to grow strategy language in the moment, to help readers understand the "so what?" behind their use of strategies.

ha.
When Mr.Allen confers with me I think it helps me understand more. Like he describes more of what something means or is. It also helps me understand the rest of my text.

Student Keystone Point

I Haven't Talked to You in Two Weeks

Relax; you're talking to them now. I do as many conferences as I can each day. And, although I don't have a side-by-side conference with each child daily, my students know that I will check in with them as readers *every* day sometime during crafting, composing, or reflecting.

Don't Waste My Time

I try to make sure other students are working on authentic experiences as I confer; I don't waste their time with stupid stuff (*stupid* is another cringer). If I thought that I had to "give them something to do" so I could confer, I would stop conferring. That's why strong instructional ashlars need to be in place.

You Need a Mint

What can I say? Coffee breath—it happens! Need I say more? Keep a mint handy.

So what is a premise? If we are talking about logic, a premise can be a proposition, a suggestion, or an invitation. The goal of a premise is to debate or support a conclusion or an assumption based on ideas or principles. And although the contentions on my *Conferring Ain't Easy* list are a bit tongue-in-cheek, each holds a place of great import in my coming to know conferring as an instructional keystone. It is my hope that you will identify with a premise; maybe even add one or two of your own to the list. This idea of conferring, or any other aspect of reader's workshop, is not about magic. Fred Rogers said:

> I like to swim, but there are some days I just don't feel much like doing it—but *I do it anyway*! I know it's good for me and I promised myself I'd do it every day, and I like to keep my promises. That's one of my disciplines. And it's a good feeling after you've tried and done something well. Inside you think, "I've kept at this and I've really learned it—not by magic, but my own work." (2003, 105)

PONDERING: What is a premise you would add to this list? What are you still wondering? What are you thinking about now that you weren't thinking about before?

So, it is through hard work and practice that we get better at conferring—managing our time, gathering information about readers, knowing which path a conference will take—and doing it well. There is no feeling like having a conference go well. I contend that any reading conference, no matter the course it takes, should have a positive impact on a reader.

Chryse Hutchins (coauthor of *7 Keys to Comprehension*) recently e-mailed me and said:

> What you develop with your class is a true interweave of learning. . . . We feel that place of security and fervor when we enter your classroom. . . . I always think of that visiting teacher from California who said after day one

> of observation [two-day observation] in your classroom, "All those kids did is read, write, think, and talk." She HEARD her own words, shook her head with laughter, and added, "Well, tomorrow I want to see how he DID that!"
>
> As I travel the country, we are moving farther and farther from your type of classroom. It's all about downloading and assessing. I'm very sad about where we are at this point . . .

We need to slow down and get back to the business of knowing children, of knowing readers. If we want children to remember, understand, extend meaning, and make their reading experiences memorable, they have to be in a classroom where there's time for that to happen. They need time to develop as readers with us sitting alongside them, nudging them over the hurdles and celebrating their successes. We have to do just the opposite of what Chryse sees happening: we have to move farther and farther away from the rhetoric and get back to teaching. It is our profession. Don Graves says, "You will observe that the volume of rhetoric by the experts is directly related to the distance the speaker is from the classroom" (Graves 2001, 2). And, conferring with readers holds all the other aspects of our reader's workshop together.

Once a group of national visitors were in town for one of the Denver-based PEBC's Thinking Strategy Institutes (one of many groups spending time observing in several classrooms throughout the Denver metro area), spending two mornings in my classroom. During the debriefing, one of the visitors said, "What Patrick does is like magic . . ." But my lab facilitator explained that it is really much more than magic! It is about knowing and codeveloping all the pieces of reader's workshop.

As they created a list of "What does Patrick believe?" from smack dab in the middle of the chart out popped the word *conferring.* Conferring. Conferring is one of the things that people frequently ask me about when they visit my classroom. That is why I chose to write about conferring, and that is why I have asked you to ponder and revise your own conferring practices. That is why I continue to re-vision mine.

Because, like Hush in *Possum Magic*, children really *do* mind. Our students (like Hannah, Mikayla, Sam, Jacob, Jaryd, Haley, Cole) want us to find the magic that will make their thinking visible. For my students and me, conferring is one way to make that happen. And, yes, all my children do is read, write, think, and talk (during reader's and writer's workshop, that is)! And I listen. To make thinking visible, "schools should ensure that thoughtful learning is pervasive, not sporadic" (Ritchhart and Perkins 2008, 58).

And it's hard work. It is taking something as intangible as "What are you thinking?" or "Tell me how your reading is going" or "Last time we talked you said you were going to _____; how is that going now?" and making it tangible. It is like a pirate's search for gold (remember Sara's words?). And discovering gold is hard work.

Reading should be left somewhat organic. When I confer, I am having the opportunity to talk one-on-one with the reader. About what he is thinking, in the moment. I am able to respond. I am able to listen, to question, to ponder . . . and he is able to beguile me with his thoughts as a reader—holding my attention, interest, and devotion to his *coming to know*. Conferring with a reader is the best time of reader's workshop.

Lingering Questions and Answers About Conferring with Readers

I conclude this chapter with a question and answer section. Perhaps a few specific questions may still be floating around in your head. Some questions might deal with the counterfeit beliefs Lori Conrad and I brainstormed. Some might linger from your own classroom experiences. Some might deal with the specifics of conferring. Some I have pondered as I've honed my conferring skills and strategies. Some are the questions that I have been asked about conferring.

I realize, of course, that you will have already answered them for yourself . . . It is my hope that as you read *Conferring: The Keystone of Reader's Workshop*, the ponderings you have dialogued about or written about have answered many of your questions. You've thought about how to bring conferring to the forefront of your daily work with readers. It is my hope that you are well on your way to exploring conferring as a *keystone* in your own reader's workshop, starting your own inquiry process.

How often do I confer with each reader?

As often as possible. Remember, there are two kinds of conferences, the actual sit-down, side-by-side conference and the touchstone, check-in, conference. I check in with every reader in the classroom every day.

During crafting, as we move through the gradual release of responsibility model, I am listening to children's voices, recording their comments about reading on anchor charts, in my conferring notebook, on sticky notes (crafting is the perfect time to listen in on children's thinking—often I'll have a brief one-on-one conversation with a child as part of crafting while the rest of the group observes and listens). The dialogue during crafting helps support and nurture the dialogue that may happen during an individual conference.

During composing, I try to confer with a minimum of five or six students each day. The number varies, workshop to workshop, but that is an average. I have to remember that there are other opportunities for readers to confer during composing time. Readers confer with each other (they know the RIP Model and often follow it as they are engaged in conversations with fellow readers or turn to a neighbor to talk about their reading). Readers, sitting in proximity, also listen in as I confer with a reader (remember, that's why I don't use a table anymore); it gives others an opportunity to eavesdrop (they often say things like, "When you were conferring with Cole, I was thinking ____").

During reflecting, I listen to children reflect on their reading experiences. Often students will volunteer to share: "Today while I was conferring with Mr. Allen, I noticed that ______." It is important to note that during the reflecting portion of the workshop, we talk in pairs, small groups, or as a whole group. Often a student's comments during reflecting will lead to an impromptu public conference. This gives other readers the opportunity to hear the language of conferring and provides another opportunity to get to know individual readers personally. We focus on that one-on-one conference knowing that, of course, there will be additional opportunities for other readers to reflect as well—in pairs, in small groups, as a whole group.

I often set a goal, "Today, I plan to confer with six children," and then see if I can meet that goal during the composing portion of the workshop. At the beginning of the year, my conferences tend to be shorter so I can build that faculty with more students (as we develop the five ashlars), and when our workshop is running smoothly and students are developing more independence (composing for approximately forty-five minutes), I try to confer with at least five or six readers in one-on-one conferences, leaving plenty of time to check in with others.

How long do conferences last?

It varies. Again, I set a goal. When I first started conferring I literally tried an egg timer sitting on the desk; it worked, but then I moved away from timing myself. I want conferences to be kept manageable, between three minutes and five minutes. There is no magic number. Recording my conferences and listening carefully to them gives me a chance to reflect on length. The length isn't as important as the content and the outcome, but trying to keep conferences running smoothly and following a specific structure has helped me be more efficient and effective. Sometimes if the **R** part of a conference takes some time (let's say I do a brief running record or think-aloud), I try to keep the rest of the conference to an appropriate length. I want students to return to their reading, so they have time to work on their plan or to apply what we have talked about in crafting. Having a focus keeps conferences more manageable. Ellin Keene recommends we vary the pace and purpose of conferences as our readers grow toward independence.

How do I confer with difficult students?

This is an intriguing question. First of all, I think we have to define *difficult*. Perhaps a reader is grappling with book choice and needs support. That's difficult. Perhaps a reader has been labeled a *struggling reader* and her level of trust is lacking—I think of Sahara, in *Sahara Special*, sitting in the hallway feeling like a "street person of the school" (Codell 2003, 5). That's difficult. Perhaps a reader needs support on a surface structure system and I need to

M.L.
When someone talks to me about my reading it helps me understand the book because when someone confers with me they explore what strategy I am using and tell me what else I could do.

Student Keystone Point

adapt our conference to support her acquisition of those needs. That's difficult. Perhaps a reader is mucking about with a new thinking strategy and needs some additional support in figuring out how it might be playing out for her in the text she's reading. That's difficult. Perhaps I need to say, "You know what, let's confer tomorrow; I can tell you just need some time to read." That's difficult. Perhaps there is *stuff* going on that I might not know about (a friend moved away, trouble at home, etc.) that's interfering with a reader. That's difficult. Perhaps the child is still learning to decode in a meaningful context. That's difficult. Perhaps a child is blessed to speak two languages (in those cases, this conversation is so important; they are hearing the language of reading). That's difficult. Perhaps a child has not developed a positive stance toward reading. That's difficult.

I need to define what *difficult* means for that reader. I have to be flexible, recognizing purpose as the catalyst. I may have to adjust my pace or my purpose. The student may need to step up to the plate and raise the level of expectations she has for herself as a reader. I think about the five ashlars; perhaps one of them needs to be revisited or re-visioned. I confer with a "difficult" student the same way I do with any other student; perhaps a bit more patiently, but with hope nonetheless.

How do I utilize parents and other staff members?

Parents and instructional support staff are trained to confer with readers. I teach them the RIP Model (I have a special conferring notebook for parents), and we talk about the purpose of conferring and meeting with readers. When parents confer with readers, I often have them focus conferences on fluency. Parents spend time listening to students read out loud. They record miscues and whether or not students made an effort to correct them. I encourage parents to ask general questions that help readers understand that they, too, are sincerely curious about the student as a reader. I ask parents to take notes and record any insights they might glean about the child's ability to comprehend, decode, make wise book choices, and so on. Parents enjoy spending time with readers, and having a conferring notebook ready gives parents something real and authentic to do with readers when they volunteer during reader's workshop. It is important that we teach parent volunteers and support staff how to confer with readers. Knowing how to confer makes their work with students more purposeful and meaningful.

What do I do with my notes?

The notes I take during a conference support me with documentation of student growth, providing me with meaningful data (the *D* word) for assessment and evaluation. My conferring notes are open while I complete progress reports or when I need to document reading growth or monitor progress. My conferring notes can be used as documentation to see how a reader is responding to an intervention or other instructional support she might be receiving. According to Richard Allington, "Reading is like virtually every human proficiency in that practice matters. Practice alone is not sufficient to develop proficiency; however, instruction is also required. But practice—reading volume—is an important factor in the design of reading interventions" (Cummins 2006, 130). I think conferring notes become evidence of instruction and interventions, especially when using the RIP structure.

In the same chapter, Allington (discussing interventions with struggling readers) states, "Enhancing classroom reading lessons first and then focusing on providing more intensive, more personalized, and more expert reading instruction to students who still struggle is the only solution" (Cummins 2006, 136). My conferring notes provide a record of the support I provide individual readers, struggling or otherwise.

Three simple things my notes do for me as a teacher: (1) They provide me with documentation of what readers are thinking during the reading process, (2) They document the one-on-one instruction that I provide to students, and (3) They provide data around the types of instruction I may need to consider for the whole class. My conferring notes give me a place to start next time I confer or as I plan a thinking-strategy study. My conferring notes give me something to compare to more formalized measures such as the DRA2 or a formal fluency measure.

During a conference, my students realize that the notes I take (1) show that what they say is important and deserves to be written down, (2) may serve as a talking point in the future, and (3) can be used in their own responses to reading in their reader's or writer's notebooks. I look for emerging patterns in my notes that I can bring to the whole group during crafting as well.

How do I balance focusing on rich conversation and a relaxed, peer-to-peer interaction while still pointing out the myriad of things that a reader needs?

I think about cueing systems, thinking strategies, curriculum, standards, and so on. I know that throughout our day, students will receive instruction in different instructional configurations and in different content areas. My crafting lessons may focus on a specific need that emerged. The same visitor who asked me this question said, "I believe in the power of conferring because I've repeatedly seen it work, and the philosophy of conferring you are espousing seems ideal." I believe it is. But, it is also tempered with the other instructional practices occurring in a classroom—think-alouds, repeated reads, fluency work, opportunities to reflect, demonstration of specific skills, and so on.

I believe that there is no better place to work on a graphophonics issue than while sitting with the reader who is dealing with it. When I ask, "How is your reading going?" even my less experienced readers feel comfortable enough to say, "Well, when I read _____, I was really confused." I can't think of a better place to work through that confusion than in a conference. It is important to know the essential learnings required for your grade level; conferences are a perfect place to see them materialize and prosper.

What do I do about small groups?

In reader's workshop, I spend most of my composing time conferring with individuals. If time is spent working with a small invitational group, it is with a very specific purpose in mind. As we gather for a crafting lesson, I may ask that students work together on a particular skill or strategy in a piece of short text; while they are working, I move in to support them as needed (I count this as small-group work).

During composing, I may pull together a small, needs- or interest-based group, to support readers with a specific reading skill or strategy. I might use my notes to say to myself, "These four kids are struggling with book choice, or My conferring is showing me that this group of readers needs support with this text structure" (semantics system) and then I pull them together to support their decision making. But only briefly and with a specific skill or strategy in mind.

The majority of my time is spent working with individual readers (remember, there are ears listening in as I work one-on-one with every reader). Lori delineates between *Capital G* Guided Reading and *small g* guided reading. *Capital G* being those small groups based on reading level, three or four groups a day, rotating through centers, teacher-controlled conversation, not much flexibility, and so on. *Small g* being groups that are flexible, needs- or interest-based, pulled together for short periods of time to work together through a particular skill or strategy. If I do a small group, it is of the *small g* variety. Data from conferring is used to form the group.

If a small group is working together, the main focus should be on the pragmatic system, the social construction of meaning. As a reader, I learn best in a group where together we construct knowledge, talking through our work. There are plenty of opportunities to build in group work that is meaningful. My readers meet in strategy-based book clubs, they meet with fellow writers, they work together as mathematicians, they make decisions as scientists, and so on. Students build the capacity for language development, vocabulary, fluency, awareness of how language works, and other necessary reading skills not just during reader's workshop, but also in other content areas and throughout the instructional day.

Now, if I were in a situation where small groups were mandated, I would be sure to keep them flexible and purpose driven. It all goes back to purpose. My colleague Janice Gibson (the first-grade teacher who sends her kids on to Troy Rushmore) says, "You know, I am reconsidering my work with small groups. When I am conferring, I learn so much more about what my students are actually doing as readers." Flexibility and purpose are key factors in providing small-group support. Debbie Miller always reminds us to "know the theory behind our work, when our practices match what we believe, and when we clearly articulate what we do and why we do it, people listen" (2002, 6).

I don't believe in grouping readers by level; just because the whole group is reading a level 38 doesn't mean they have the same instructional needs. I can better support them in one-on-one conferring.

I have a group of friends (we call ourselves the Friday Freaks because we meet on the first Friday of each month in someone's home—for conversation, for sharing, for fellowship, for food and drink) that gathers to discuss our teaching and learning. We don't gather because we're all at the same reading level, read the same books, write the same stories, and teach at the same school. We meet because we have important things to reflect upon, and we find that we are better teachers and staff developers if we have the opportunity to meet. Our group is flexible, and each month our purpose changes. If we were grouped by reading level, I would be placed in a different ward. But, we are grouped by interest and need. Sometimes we move about the room talking to different people, sometimes we sit as a whole group and learn together, sometimes we work alone; that flexibility is what has kept the group together.

What is the rest of the class doing while I confer?

I could answer this question with a one-word answer: reading. Here is a more detailed list that Cheryl Zimmerman and I created of what readers are doing while I am conferring:

- Developing stamina and endurance
- Putting strategy work into practice
- Conferring with peers or other adults as needed
- Responding to reading experiences in a reader's/writer's notebook
- Developing metacognitive skills
- Building fluency
- Improving vocabulary
- Solving problems that arise
- Evaluating book choice
- Demonstrating wise reading behaviors
- Maintaining long-term thinking and depth

When I am conferring with readers, the rest of the class is actively involved in the work that real readers and writers do; remember, the *lens of authenticity* is the lens through which we should plan. Readers may be talking to a peer about a common text they are reading. Readers may be responding to text in their reader's/writer's notebook. Readers may be trying to apply a new strategy or skill we explored during crafting to their independent reading. They are composing.

That is why the ashlars I mentioned in Chapter 3 are so critical. If I want time to confer, students have to work in a focused, learner-centered environment that supports and recognizes the importance of trust, respect, and tone during composing time. If I want time to confer, students have to develop a sense of endurance and stamina. If I want time to confer, students have to understand the purpose of composing time, the purpose of conferring, the purpose of response, and so on. If I want time to confer, students have to know where they are on the gradual release of responsibility and develop flexibility so that they are always doing the *work* of readers. If I want time to confer, students have to understand the ins and outs of reader's workshop, knowing that there will always be a time for support, questions, and developing understanding.

We have to make sure that students who are not meeting with us are actively involved in reading when we are meeting with another child or group of children. I don't do "activities" or fill-in-the-blanks. I don't do novel packets or study guides. During composing, students may be working on something from our crafting session that I've asked them to work on as readers (they might be coding a piece of poetry with sensory images or finding the big idea in a short narrative). The expectation is that they will move into their own reading after they finish. We must be mindful of what students do during composing, especially if we want them to have something mindful to share during a conference or when we come to reflect at the end of reader's workshop. Each day before students begin composing, we'll brainstorm and record a list of Reader's Responsibilities (an idea that Cheryl gave me). These responsibilities become a simple visual list that students can refer to when they are stuck during composing time. Right after crafting, I jot down their responsibilities so that they know how to spend their time most productively.

So, what are the other students doing? All the things on Cheryl's and my list. Of course, they are mostly reading and maybe recording their thinking in their reader's/writer's notebooks. I love the quiet hum of readers at work that occurs when I am moving around the room conferring with individuals.

What do I do about students with special learning needs?

I think that we have to hold all children accountable and have high expectations. I have to help them make wise book choices and teach them how to make those choices for themselves. I have to teach readers that repeated readings help strengthen fluency and stretch thinking (this can only come from modeling and demonstrating). I have to think aloud often, so that all students come to understand the notion of metacognition. I have to provide opportunities throughout the day for students to hear and discuss text other than the books they are reading during composing time (it is important that children listen to text read aloud often). I have to let all children know that what they have to say is important and provide multiple opportunities for their thinking to blossom.

Why teach a strategy if you're not going to give students time to practice, learn, and apply it in their own reading?
Patrick Allen

Teacher Keystone Point

It is always my goal to have students with special needs in the classroom for crafting. If support teachers must pull students,

I request they do so during composing time if possible and that students come back into the fold prepared to work on specific reading work. I teach children to read the room so that when they come back in after stepping out for a few minutes, either with a volunteer or a specialist, they come into the room and slip into the workshop with minimal distraction—and if need be, I have them check in quietly with me as they return.

How do you explain your belief in conferring to others?

Well, first you write a book about conferring. No, wait, that's too complicated.

When visitors come to our classroom, I provide a detailed letter that explains and describes what they should expect. Here is an excerpt from the letter I hand them:

> I have been using the thinking strategies as an instructional underpinning for approximately 20 years. Each year I try to refine and redefine each strategy. I look for the wisest ways to guide students to use them independently [and please hear this—it looks different *every* year]—sometimes with more success than others. I don't look at the strategies as a "philosophy, a lesson a minute, a program, the 'Denver model,' or 'doing' *Mosaic*." My goal is to be authentic, not cute. Deep, not surface [I mean depth in study—not surface versus deep structures]. Explicit, not implicit. Flexible, not controlling. Mindful, not mindless. And I've come to realize that teaching my students how learners *think not just* ***do*** has had an amazing effect on our learning lives.
>
> It is through our exploration of the strategies that we, as readers and writers and thinkers, develop a deeper understanding of our process as learners—that's it. Sounds like a simple idea—eh? Our explorations enhance our own comprehension of text as we consume and compose text. These strategies are taught explicitly over a long period of time—our goal is to go "a mile deep and an inch wide." I learn more about myself by applying the strategies to my own learning process and, in turn, demonstrate that learning for the students in my room. And moving the *language of strategy instruction* into other curricular areas has helped develop a constant that meanders throughout our learning.
>
> Of course, we're bombarded with "outside sources" telling us how to do our jobs. As professionals, we need to make the decisions about how our children should spend their time. We need to ask [as Don Graves so wisely asks us to do], "What's that for?" If you can't find the answer—you probably shouldn't be doing it. And, we are asked to do a lot of silly

"stuff," aren't we! Regie Routman says we need to view teaching with a wide lens—as expert and learner—and teach with common sense . . . she says, "If something doesn't make sense, I don't do it!" For me, the work of *thinking* makes the most sense. We need to move children back to the forefront of our profession, and as Shelley Harwayne says, "We need to relish the 'genius of youth' and bring our scholarship into our classrooms." Ellin Keene talks about "intellectual engagement," and I wonder how much of the stuff we are asked to do leads us down a path to "intellectual disengagement"?

It's a long haul, this work with thinking—a complex release of responsibility—that benefits students, makes my teaching more enjoyable [but not always easier], and keeps our learning fresh and thoughtful! And so far, we're just beginning the journey . . .

Please feel free to shadow me and "listen in" on my conversations with kids. I will spend some time conferring with individuals. The conversations are still developing at this point. However, I believe that conferring is absolutely necessary at EVERY grade level. It's my best time of the day! I gather my most important assessment data from conferring. I think it's the crux, the keystone, of successful reading/writing classrooms. It's a slow go, as they learn to make more appropriate book choices, learn to talk about their thinking, and so on. I will gain the most valuable assessment data possible—through conferring.

Conferring ain't easy. Learning to confer takes time. "Few children learn to read books by themselves. Someone has to lure them into the wonderful world of the written word. Someone has to show them the way" (Bradfield 2002, 47). Perhaps we need to dedicate more time in our reader's workshop to conferring. Perhaps it ain't that hard either.

From that time onward Hush was visible . . .
Hush stayed visible forever.

—Mem Fox, 1983

Conclusion:

Adieu

Tonight my daughter Lauryn was walking out the door to soccer practice and shouted up the stairs to me, "Dad, make an epilogue for your book . . . Goodbye, I love you!" Something in her voice told me it was time to wrap this project up, time to bid you adieu. Like the end of a conference, it's time to move my chair away from my desk, from my notes, and leave you with a plan.

I began with the words, "Conferring has always been at the heart of my reader's workshop, much like the keystone has been important to stonemasons and bricklayers throughout history."

And, so, conferring becomes the foundation of what we all do with the readers in our care. I hope that conferring becomes part of the conversations you have with your students:

- Purposeful conversations that provide meaningful instruction
- Purposeful conversations that stretch your thinking and monitor your understanding
- Purposeful conversations that make you want to learn more, to do more
- Purposeful conversations with a specific goal in mind

I hope that when you walk into your reader's workshop tomorrow morning, you will pull up a chair next to a child, open up your conferring notebook, and ask, "What do you think?" And then you will lean in, look into his eyes, and listen to what he says.

Maybe someday, for one of your students you will be his Mrs. Franklin, Mrs. Miller, Mrs. Johnson, or Mr. Ericson, and he will look back and say fondly, "Every time my teacher sat down next to me, he took the time to listen to my thinking. It mattered."

Let me close with a synthesis of what one of my former students, Mackenzie, said it meant to be a metacognitive reader:

> To be a metacognitive reader, I need to remember . . .
>
> To not just read the words out, but to also read my thoughts! I won't be a proficient reader if I don't do this! I need to think about what I'm reading and how my thoughts apply to the situation I'm in.

I need to get pictures in my head. If the author gives a blurry description, I can get a picture and understand what she or he is trying to tell me!

I need to question text because if I'm not questioning the text or getting confused then the text is way too easy and I shouldn't be reading that book! It's okay to read books that are easy, but it's almost like a requirement to ask questions in a book. It's like an elevator; you have to push a button if you want to go anywhere! You have to ask questions, infer, get sensory images, and monitor your comprehension or your thinking won't go anywhere!

I need to monitor my comprehension as a reader to understand text. M.C. [monitoring comprehension] is important because it involves a lot of the other strategies. To understand text is to monitor comprehension. Monitoring comprehension is like if I ask a question and I don't notice it, then I am not monitoring comprehension, but if I do notice it then I am monitoring my comprehension.

I need to infer! Inferring is essential. It is essential to infer because an author often leaves essential details out of the book. Inferring is like a guessing game. You have to gather clues from where you might think one of the little cards are to make a match! If your matches are right, it's like you fill in a piece of the puzzle!

I need to D.W.I. [determine what's important]! I need to determine what's important. I need to only remember the critical elements. I need to figure out what words or sentences are very important! Words and sentences are hard to choose because I want to remember every single detail!

I need to use my B.K. [background knowledge] and B.E. [background experience]. I need to use these because if I don't have enough B.K. in a certain situation then I'm going to be asking too many questions and I might not be able to find the answers!

I need to synthesize when I'm reading! I think synthesis is like cooking. You throw all the ingredients together, mix them together, and the end result is FOOD. In reading, you have all these thoughts and you combine them all together and you get one big new overall learning or thought.

Fixing Up is critical if I'm going to be a reader! I have to fix up meaning or a word. Rereading is a part of fixing up! To fix up you have to reread, rethink. You need to think about what you previously read.

Mackenzie knew herself as a learner—look at what she walked away with as a reader. Our conversations throughout the year, our conferences, centered on remembering, understanding, extending meaning, and making reading experiences memorable. I so clearly remember when Mackenzie was reading *Margaret's Moves* by Berniece Rabe and during one conference, she looked at me and said, "Today I learned that the longer you try, the more you get!" Such wise words from a wise reader. Marilyn Ferguson says, "It's not so much that we're afraid of change or so in love with the old ways, but it's that place in between that we fear . . . It's like being between trapezes. It's Linus when his blanket is in the dryer. There's nothing to hold on to" (Cionca 2007, 141). The longer you try, the more you will get; the more you confer, the more you'll learn!

I cannot imagine what would have happened if Dad had not invited me to sit with him at our kitchen table and asked, "What do you think?" It's a pretty darned good question. It led me to an important conclusion all these years later: Conferring is the keystone!

And, I leave you with a quote that reminds me of that initial conference with Dad. Think of it as an invitation to explore conferring as the keystone of *your* reader's workshop: "But for many, many men their souls still hang in the balance because no one, *no one* has ever invited them to be dangerous, to know their own strength, to discover they have what it takes" (Eldredge 2001, 79).

Appendix

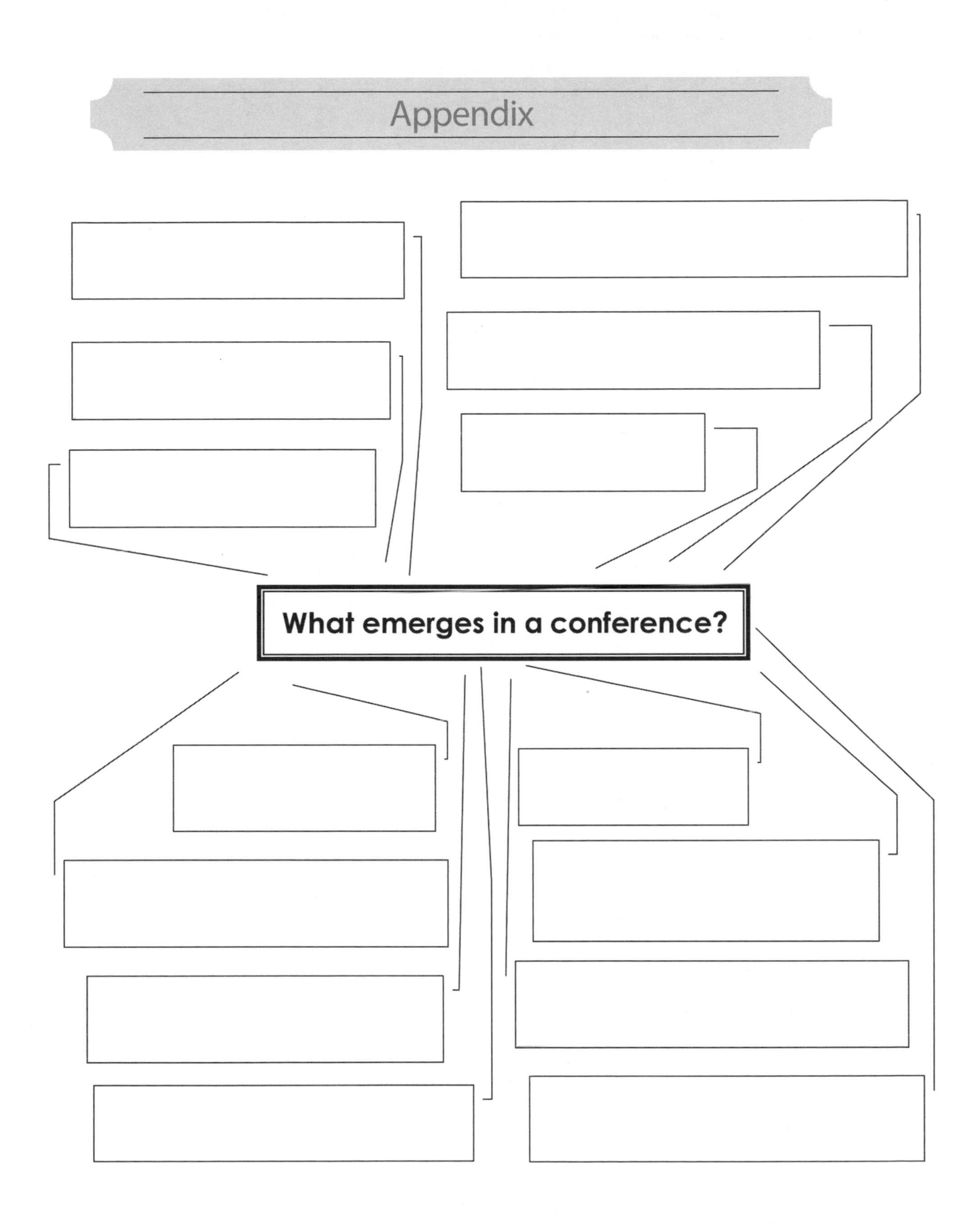

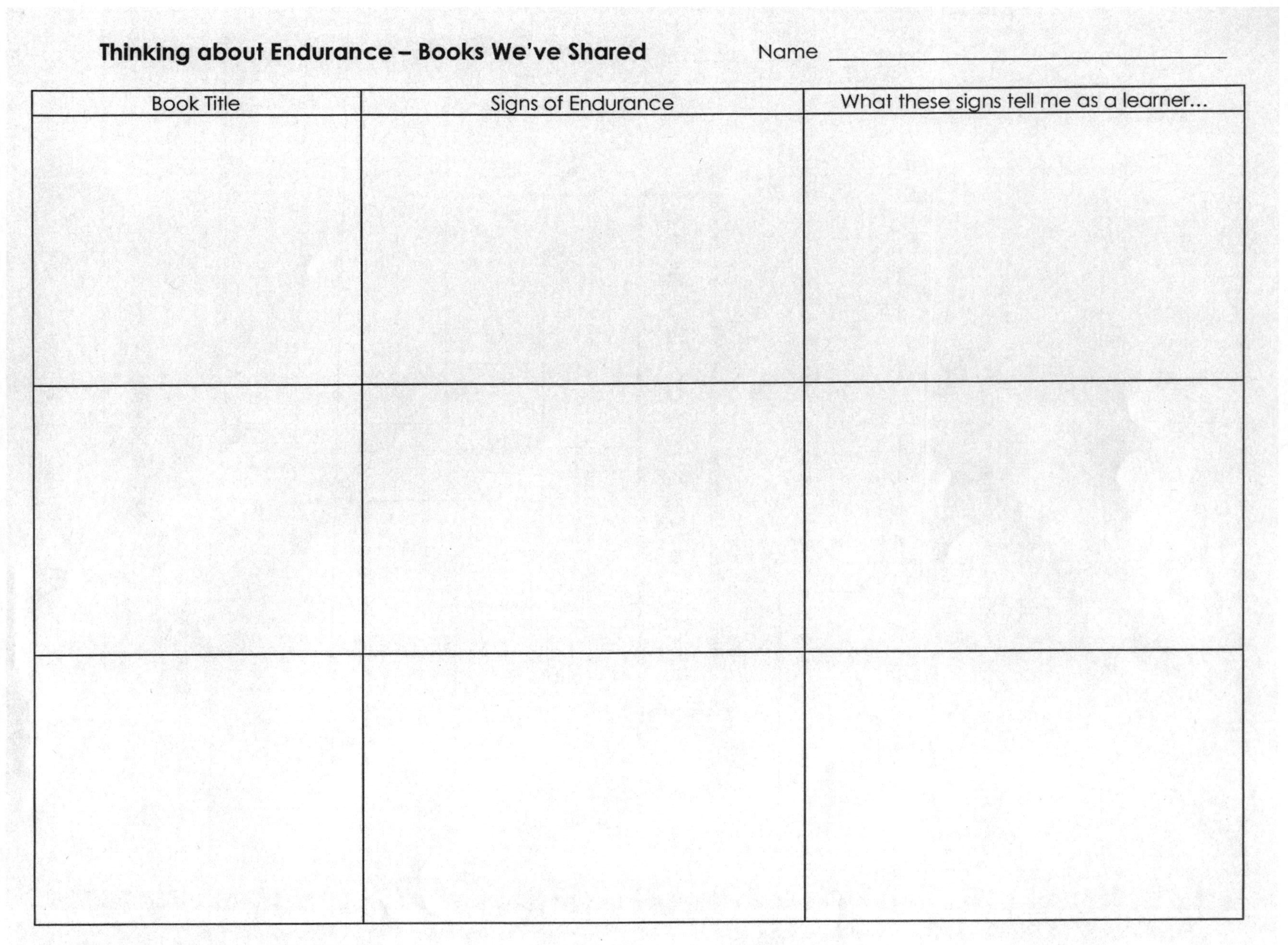

Thinking about Endurance – Books We've Shared

Name ________________

Book Title	Signs of Endurance	What these signs tell me as a learner...

Planning a Strategy Study – Reading or Writing

[based on the Gradual Release of Responsibility, Pearson and Gallagher 1983]

Planning for ______________________________
(Thinking Strategy or Unit of Study)

Assessment
(Specific evidence gathered to indicate understanding)

- ⇨
- ⇨
- ⇨
- ⇨
- ⇨

Thinking and Planning
(How will it be taught?
How is it used?)

Preliminary instructional considerations...

-
-
-
-
-

Think Aloud
(Modeling, demonstrating, sharing personal use of strategy)

Texts and Instructional Strategies

-
-
-
-
-

Shared Experience
(Inviting participation via whole-group experiences)

Texts and Instructional Strategies

-
-
-
-
-

Guided Experience
(Active participation in clusters or individually with support)

Texts and Instructional Strategies

-
-
-
-
-

Cooperative Experience
(Participation with peers, supporting growth and gathering evidence of understanding)

Texts and Instructional Strategies

-
-
-
-
-

Independence
(What learners know and do as a result of study—independently)

Texts and Instructional Strategies

-
-
-
-
-

Considerations
Links to Content or Standards

-
-
-
-
-
-

Personal Definition of Strategy or Study

Questions, Wonderings, Investigations

Defining Teacher and Student Roles - Gradual Release of Responsibility Model

1) THINKING AND PLANNING...

The teacher might be...
identifying the strategy to be taught
exploring his/her own use of the strategy
preparing the classroom and materials
collecting a variety of text
perusing resources for support
conferring with colleagues
preparing parent information

The students might be...
providing assessment data on "next steps"
continuing to practice and apply previous strategies

2) THINK ALOUD...

The teacher might be...
sharing models
demonstrating behaviors
orally revealing his/her thinking
thinking out loud about his/her process
being that "expert" for his/her students
choosing text to reveal thinking
using a variety of text to unpack his/her thinking

The students might be...
observing
noticing
listening
developing curiosity

3) SHARED EXPERIENCE...

The teacher might be...
providing models
demonstrating behaviors
visually revealing his/her thinking
thinking out loud about his/her process
inviting students to participate in thinking
asking questions to elicit thinking
nudging students to use strategy language
choosing text to elicit thinking

The students might be...
noting thinking behaviors
sharing noticings and wonderings
turning to talk or sharing with whole group
beginning to participate
"futzing" with strategy with support
asking questions

4) GUIDED EXPERIENCE...

The teacher might be...
visually revealing his/her thinking
shortening crafting lessons
recording student thinking
releasing more responsibility
meeting with needs-based clusters
choosing text for craft lessons

The students might be...
accepting more responsibility
providing evidence of their own thinking
actively participating during crafting
working in conversational clusters
applying thinking to carefully chosen text during crafting
attempting strategy in self-selected text during composing
providing assessment data

5) COOPERATIVE EXPERIENCE...

The teacher might be...
providing short, explicit instruction
recording student thinking
checking in with progress

The students might be...
moving toward independence
working in self-selected text
showing evidence of their own thinking
seeking support when needed
asking questions
working in small conversational clusters
utilizing strategies in reading responses

6) INDEPENDENT EXPERIENCE...

The teacher might be...
building student confidence
documenting individual growth
working with small needs-based clusters
beginning to think and plan for the next strategy
monitoring text choice

The students might be...
reading self-selected text
articulating understandings
working independently
demonstrating their thinking
creating models and records of their understanding
sharing their own think-alouds
responding to reading experiences

Reading Conferences for ________________________________

Date ______________ Title ________________________________ Page[s] __________

REVIEW/READ ALOUD/RECORD	INSTRUCTION/INSIGHTS/INTRIGUE	PLAN/PROGRESS/PURPOSE

Additional Comment(s):

Date ______________ Title ________________________________ Page[s] __________

REVIEW/READ ALOUD/RECORD	INSTRUCTION/INSIGHTS/INTRIGUE	PLAN/PROGRESS/PURPOSE

Additional Comment(s):

Date ______________ Title ________________________________ Page[s] __________

REVIEW/READ ALOUD/RECORD	INSTRUCTION/INSIGHTS/INTRIGUE	PLAN/PROGRESS/PURPOSE

Additional Comment(s):

Current Reads, Current Titles

Name	Date	Date

Reading Conference — Check Off Form

Name	Date								

Bibliography

Allen, T. 1991. *Walking to the Creek*. New York: Random House.

Armstrong, J. 2002. *Spirit of Endurance: The True Story of the Shackleton Expedition to the Antarctic*. New York: Crown Books.

Benson, L., ed. 2000. *Colorado Reads! Implementing the Colorado Basic Literacy Act: Thoughtful and Practical Responses*. Denver: Colorado Department of Education.

———. 2001. *Brain Waves: Cultivating the Disposition to Understand & Be Understood*. Self-published by author, Littleton, CO.

Bradfield, B. 2002. *Books and Reading: A Book of Quotations*. Mineola, NY: Dover.

Britton, J. 1970. *Language and Learning*. Coral Gables, FL: University of Miami Press.

Calkins, L., and L. Bellino. 1997. *Raising Lifelong Learners: A Parent's Guide*. Reading, MA: Addison-Wesley.

Caney S. 2006. *Steven Caney's Ultimate Building Book*. Philadelphia: Running Press.

Cionca, J. 2007. *Dear Pastor: Ministry Advice from Seasoned Pastors*. Loveland, CO: Group Publishing.

Codell, E. 2003. *Sahara Special*. New York: Hyperion Books for Children.

Conrad, B. (ed.), and M. Shultz. 2002. *Snoopy's Guide to the Writing Life*. Cincinnati, OH: Writer's Digest Books.

Conrad, L., M. Matthews, C. Zimmerman, and P. Allen. 2008. *Put Thinking to the Test*. Portland, ME: Stenhouse.

Costa, A. (ed.) 1991. *Developing Minds: A Resource Book for Teaching Thinking*. Alexandria, VA: Association for Supervision and Curriculum Development.

Cummins, C. 2006. *Understanding and Implementing Reading First Initiatives: The Changing Role of Administrators.* Newark, DE: International Reading Association.

Daniels, H., and M. Bizar. 2005. *Teaching the Best Practice Way.* Portland, ME: Stenhouse.

DiCamillo, K. 2000. *Because of Winn-Dixie.* New York: Scholastic.

Dictionary.com. 2009. http://www.dictionary.com.

Duke, N. K., and P. D. Pearson. 2002. "Effective Practices for Developing Reading Comprehension." In *What Research Has to Say About Reading Instruction,* ed. A. E. Farstrup and S. J. Samuels. Newark, DE: International Reading Association.

Eldredge, J. 2001. *Wild at Heart: Discovering the Secret of a Man's Soul.* Nashville, TN: Thomas Nelson.

Elkind, D. 1987. *Miseducation: Preschoolers at Risk.* New York: Random House.

Fox, J. 1997. *Poetic Medicine: The Healing Act of Poem Making.* New York: Penguin Putnam.

Fox, M. 1983. *Possum Magic.* Orlando, FL: Harcourt.

———. 1993. *Radical Reflections: Passionate Opinions on Teaching, Learning, and Living.* Orlando, FL: Harcourt.

Gadamer, H. G. 1989. *Truth and Method.* New York: Continuum.

Gallagher, M., and P. D. Pearson. 1983. "The Instruction of Reading Comprehension." *Contemporary Educational Psychology* 8 (3): 317–344.

Graves, D. 1994. *A Fresh Look at Writing.* Portsmouth, NH: Heinemann.

———. 1998. *How to Catch a Shark and Other Stories About Teaching and Learning.* Portsmouth, NH: Heinemann.

———. 2001. *The Energy to Teach.* Portsmouth, NH: Heinemann.

———. 2002. "The Energy to Teach." *Voices in the Middle* 10 (1): 8–10.

Guthrie, G. 2003. *1,600 Quotes and Pieces of Wisdom That Just Might Help You Out When You're Stuck in a Moment (and Can't Get Out of It!).* Bloomington, IN: iUniverse.

Hannigan, K. 2004. *Ida B . . . and Her Plans to Maximize Fun, Avoid Disaster, and (Possibly) Save the World.* New York: Greenwillow Books.

Harvard-Smithsonian Center for Astrophysics. 1987. *A Private Universe.* Videorecording. Washington, DC: Annenberg/CPB.

Harvey, S., and A. Goudvis. 2007. *Strategies That Work: Teaching Comprehension for Understanding and Engagement.* Portland, ME: Stenhouse.

Heuser, D. 2002. *Reworking the Workshop: Math and Science Reform in the Primary Grades.* Portsmouth, NH: Heinemann.

James, S. 2004. *Little One Step.* London: Walker Books.

Jensen, E. 1998. *Teaching with the Brain in Mind.* Alexandria, VA: Association for Supervision and Curriculum Development.

Jessup, H. 2001. *Grandma Summer.* London: Picture Puffins.

Johnston, P. 1997. *Knowing Literacy: Constructive Literacy Assessment.* Portland, ME: Stenhouse.

———. 2004. *Choice Words: How Our Language Affects Children's Learning.* Portland, ME: Stenhouse.

Keene, E. 2008. *To Understand: New Horizons in Reading Comprehension.* Portsmouth, NH: Heinemann.

Keene, E., and S. Zimmerman. 1997. *Mosaic of Thought: Teaching Comprehension in a Reader's Workshop.* Portsmouth, NH: Heinemann.

Keller, H. 2003. *The Story of My Life* (restored ed.), ed. James Berger. New York: Modern Library.

Kenison, K. 2000. *Mitten Strings for God.* New York: Warner Books.

Kujawa, S., and L. Huske. 1995. *The Strategic Teaching and Reading Project Guidebook* (rev. ed.). Oak Brook, IL: North Central Regional Educational Laboratory.

Lee, H. 1960. *To Kill a Mockingbird.* New York: Warner Books.

McKenzie, J. 2004. *From Now On: The Educational Technology Journal* 13(6): 1. http://www.fno.org.

Meier, D. 1995. *The Power of Their Ideas.* Boston: Beacon.

Meigs, C. 1995. *Invincible Louisa: The Story of the Author of Little Women.* New York: Little Brown Young Readers.

Miller, Debbie. 2002. *Reading with Meaning: Teaching Comprehension in the Primary Grades.* Portland, ME: Stenhouse.

———. 2005. *The Joy of Conferring: One-on-One with Young Readers.* Video series. Portland, ME: Stenhouse.

———. 2008. *Teaching with Intention*. Portland, ME: Stenhouse.

Miller, Donalyn. 2009. *The Book Whisperer*. San Francisco: Jossey-Bass.

Mooney, W., B. Mooney, and D. Holt. 1996. *The Storytellers Guide: Storytellers Share Advice for the Classroom*. Atlanta: August House.

Moss, J. 2003. "On the Other Side of the Door." In *Teaching with Fire: Poetry That Sustains the Courage to Teach*, ed. S. M. Intrator and M. Scribner. San Francisco: Jossey-Bass.

Murphy, P. K., and L. Mason. 2006. "Changing Knowledge and Beliefs." In *Handbook of Educational Psychology* (2nd ed.), ed. P. A. Alexander and P. H. Winne. Florence, KY: Routledge.

Murray, D. 1989. *Expecting the Unexpected: Teaching Myself—and Others—To Read and Write.* Portsmouth, NH: Boynton/Cook.

National Reading Panel. 2000. "Teaching Children to Read: An Evidence-Based Assessment of the Scientific Research Literature on Reading and Its Implications for Reading Instruction." National Institute of Child Health and Human Development. http://www.nichd.nih.gov/publications/nrp/report.cfm.

Parent, M. 2002. *Believing It All: Lessons I Learned from My Children*. New York: Back Bay Books.

Pennac, D. 1999. *Better than Life*. Markham, ON, Canada: Pembroke.

Perkins, D. N. 1991. "What Creative Thinking Is." In *Developing Minds: A Resource for Teaching Thinking,* ed. Arthur Costa. Alexandria, VA: Association for Supervision and Curriculum Development.

Ray, K. W. 1999. *Wondrous Words: Writers and Writing in the Elementary Classroom.* Urbana, IL: National Council of Teachers of English.

———. 2006a. "Exploring Inquiry as a Teaching Stance in the Writing Workshop." *Language Arts* 83(2): 246.

———. 2006b. *Study Driven: A Framework for Planning Units of Study in the Writing Workshop.* Portsmouth, NH: Heinemann.

Rief, L. 1992. *Seeking Diversity: Language Arts with Adolescents.* Portsmouth, NH: Heinemann.

———. 2003. *100 Quickwrites.* New York: Scholastic.

Ritchhart, R. 2002. *Intellectual Character: What It Is, Why It Matters, and How to Get It.* San Francisco: Jossey-Bass.

Ritchhart, R., and D. Perkins. 2008. "Making Thinking Visible." *Educational Leadership* (February 2008): 57–61.

Rogers, F. 2003. *The World According to Mister Rogers: Important Things to Remember.* New York: Hyperion Books.

Smith, F. 1987. *Joining the Literacy Club: Further Essays Into Education.* Portsmouth, NH: Heinemann.

Stafford, W. 2003. "You Reading This, Be Ready." In *Teaching with Fire: Poetry That Sustains the Courage to Teach,* ed. S. M. Intrator and M. Scribner. San Francisco: Jossey-Bass.

Sweeney, D. 2003. *Learning Along the Way.* Portland, ME: Stenhouse.

Szymusiak, K., F. Sibberson, and L. Koch. 2008. *Beyond Leveled Books,* 2nd ed. Portland, ME: Stenhouse.

Thoreau, H. D. 2005. *Walden.* Stilwell, KS: Digireads.

Tomlinson, S. R. 2008. *Suck Your Stomach In and Put Some Color On! What Southern Mamas Tell Their Daughters That the Rest of Y'all Should Know Too.* New York: Berkley Books.

Tovani, C. 2004. *Do I Really Have to Teach Reading?* Portland, ME: Stenhouse.

Vygotsky, L. S. 1962. *Thought and Language.* Cambridge, MA: MIT Press.

Wells, G. 1985. *The Meaning Makers: Children Learning Language and Using Language to Learn*. Portsmouth, NH: Heinemann.

Wilhelm, J. 2007. *Engaging Readers and Writers with Inquiry.* New York: Scholastic.

Zull, J. 2002. *The Art of Changing the Brain: Enriching the Practice of Teaching by Exploring the Biology of Learning*. Sterling, VA: Stylus.

Index

A

accountability, "Purpose Triangle" and, 62–67, 64*f*, 66*f*
agency, sense of, 27–28
Alcott, Bronson, 141
Alcott, Louisa May, 141
Alice Ramsey's Grand Adventure (Brown), 60
Allen, Patrick, 40, 62, 188
Allington, Richard, 185
Allison, Randi, 21–24, 29
Amber on the Mountain (Johnston), 61, 77
analytical context of conferring, 130–141, 131*f*, 134*f*
Armstrong, Jennifer, 55, 56
ashlars. *See* five ashlars
assessments
  encouraging inquiry and, 138–141
  walk-aways and, 158*f*
A Story for Bear (Haseley), 77
audience
  Discussing Purpose and Audience ashlar, 62–75, 64*f*, 66*f*, 67*f*, 71*f*, 72*f*, 74*f*
  "Purpose Triangle" and, 72–75, 72*f*, 74*f*
authenticity
  classroom environment and, 49
  classroom management during conferences and, 187–188
  creating a culture of thinking and, 40
  gradual release of responsibility and, 75–76
  purpose and audience and, 67
awe, classroom environment and, 49–50

B

beauty in the classroom, creating a culture of thinking and, 38–39
Becker, Jim, 51
Becker, S., 61
belief, Defining Trust, Respect, and Tone ashlar and, 50
beliefs about conferring, 8–11
Believing It All: Lessons I Learned from My Children (Parent), 80
Bellino, L., 137
Benson, Laura, 77, 149–150
Berg, Dana, 38, 39, 41, 92, 103
Better than Life (Pennac), 134–135
Beyond Leveled Books (Szymusiak, Sibberson, and Koch), 84
Bizar, M., 82, 152, 171
blank forms, 195–201
Bogart, J., 77
book choice
  classroom management during conferences and, 187–188
  ownership and, 150–152
  walk-aways and, 160*f*
Books and Reading: A Book of Quotations (Bradfield), 85, 190
Bos, Bev, 139–140
Bradfield, B., 85, 190
Britton, J, 41
Brown, D., 60, 61
Bryan, J., 61
Buddy, Colleen, 176
Bunting, E., 61, 77

C

Calkins, L., 137
Caney, Steven, 156
Carpenter, Mary Chapin, 177
challenges in conferring
  outcomes of conferring and, 18
  overview of, 175–182
  questions regarding conferring, 182–190
"Changing Knowledge and Beliefs," (Murphy and Mason), 9–10
chaos in the classroom, 48
Choice Words (Johnston), 129
Christopher, Matt, 142
Cionca, J., 193
City Foxes (Tweit), 77
classroom environment
  classroom management during conferences and, 187–188
  creating a culture of thinking, 38–40
  Defining Trust, Respect, and Tone ashlar and, 47–50
  overview of, 27–28
  where to sit during conferences, 152–153
classroom management during conferences, 48, 187–188
Codell, E., 183
colleagues
  importance of, 26–27
  learning from, 39–40
comfort during conferences, 178
community building, importance of, 26–27
composing
  frequency of conferences and, 182–183
  reader's workshop and, 83, 88, 89*f*, 90*f*–91*f*
  students with special needs and, 188–189
comprehension, walk-aways and, 161*f*

conceptual change, 9–10
condescending attitudes, 178
conferrer learning, 18–19
conferring notebook. *See also* note-taking systems; record keeping
  blank form for, 205
  conferring versus collecting, 107–116, 109*f*, 111*f*, 113*f*
  examples of, 166*f*, 171*f*
  inquiry and, 134*f*
  intimacy and, 146*f*
  overview of, 110
  rigor and, 122*f*
  RIP Model and, 104–107
conferring walk-aways. *See* walk-aways
Conrad, Lori, 8–11, 16, 24, 40, 42, 62, 117–118, 182, 186
continuity in education, 26–29
conversations
  balance and, 185
  developing intimacy and, 148–150
  encouraging inquiry and, 137–138
cooperative learning experience
  chart describing, 198
  gradual release of responsibility and, 79*f*
Costa, Arthur, 151
counterfeit beliefs about conferring, 8–11
crafting lessons
  encouraging inquiry and, 136–138
  frequency of conferences and, 182–183
  reader's workshop and, 83–86, 89*f*, 90*f*–91*f*
  students with special needs and, 188–189
  walk-aways and, 161*f*
culture of thinking, 38–40
Cummins, C., 185
Cummins, J., 61
Current Reads, Current Titles form
  blank form for, 200
  conferring notebook and, 110
  examples of, 111*f*

D

Daniels, H., 82, 152, 171
data collection, 138–141. *See also* conferring notebook
Dear Pastor: Ministry Advice from Seasoned Pastors (Cionca), 193
deep structure systems
  teaching during conferences and, 129
  walk-aways and, 161*f*
Defining Trust, Respect, and Tone ashlar, 42–50. *See also* five ashlars; respect; tone; trust
demonstration, 50
dePaola, T., 77
Developing Minds (Costa), 151
Developmental Reading Assessment (DRA2), 139
DiCamillo, Kate, xii
difficult students, 183–184
Discussing Purpose and Audience ashlar, 62–75, 64*f*, 66*f*, 67*f*, 71*f*, 72*f*, 74*f*. *See also* five ashlars
Do I Really Have to Teach Reading? (Tovani), 69
Drachman, E., 60
Duke, N. K., 76
duration of conferences, 183

E

"Effective Practices for Developing Reading Comprehension" (Duke and Pearson), 76
efficacy, inquiry and, 136
Eldredge, J., 193
elements of conferring, 117–118. *See also* inquiry; intimacy; rigor
Elkind, David, 172
endurance
  classroom management during conferences and, 187–188
  conferring notebook form regarding, 60*f*, 61*f*, 202
  overview of, 54–62, 56*f*, 60*f*, 61*f*
  Strengthening Endurance and Stamina ashlar, 51–62, 51*f*, 53*f*, 56*f*, 60*f*, 61*f*, 63*f*
environment, classroom
  classroom management during conferences and, 187–188
  creating a culture of thinking, 38–40
  Defining Trust, Respect, and Tone ashlar and, 47–50
  overview of, 27–28
  where to sit during conferences, 152–153
Ericson, Ross, xiii, 191
Ering, T. B., 61
examples of conferences
  complete, 163–171
  conferring notebook and, 166*f*, 171*f*
  discussion of, 171–174
expectations regarding conferring, 11–19, 12*f*, 14*f*
experiences
  chart describing, 198
  inquiry and, 135–136
  outcomes of conferring and, 16
explaining to others, 189–190
exploration, 50
Exploring the Gradual Release of Responsibility Model ashlar, 75–80, 79*f*. *See also* five ashlars

F

Farmer Boy (Wilder), 144–146, 151
fellowship, gradual release of responsibility and, 77

Ferguson, Marilyn, 193
Firefly Mountain (Tahomas), 60
fivc ashlars
  classroom management during conferences and, 187–188
  Defining Trust, Respect, and Tone ashlar, 42–50
  Discussing Purpose and Audience ashlar, 62–75, 64*f*, 66*f*, 67*f*, 71*f*, 72*f*, 74*f*
  elements of conferring and, 117–118
  Exploring the Gradual Release of Responsibility Model ashlar, 75–80, 79*f*
  Focusing on the Structure of Reader's Workshop ashlar, 80–92, 82*f*, 87*f*, 88*f*, 89*f*–91*f*
  list of, 41
  overview of, 41–42, 92
  Strengthening Endurance and Stamina ashlar, 51–62, 51*f*, 53*f*, 56*f*, 60*f*, 61*f*
fix-up strategies, walk-aways and, 158*f*
flexibility, 176
Focusing on the Structure of Reader's Workshop ashlar, 80–92, 82*f*, 87*f*, 88*f*, 89*f*–91*f*. *See also* five ashlars
forms, blank, 195–201
Fox, John, 153
Fox, Mem, 77, 84, 175, 181, 190
Franklin, Ben, 85
Franklin, Jo, xiv, 94–95, 191
Fraustiano, L., 60
frequency of conferences, 182–183
Fresh Look at Writing, A (Graves), 21
Frog Thing, A (Drachman), 60

G

Gadamer, Hans-Georg, 135
Gallagher, M., 75
Gibson, Janice, 151, 186
Gilkey, Judy, 127
Girl on the High-Diving Horse, The (High), 61, 77
Girl Wonder: A Baseball Story in Nine Innings (Hopkinson), 61
Gleam and Glow (Bunting), 61
goal setting
  outcomes of conferring and, 15
  walk-aways and, 159*f*, 160*f*
goals of conferring, 24–28, 26*f*
Golenbock, P., 60
Goudvis, Anne, 40, 68–69
gradual release of responsibility. *See also* responsibility
  Exploring the Gradual Release of Responsibility Model ashlar, 75–80, 79*f*
  frequency of conferences and, 182–183
  Strengthening Endurance and Stamina ashlar and, 55
gradual release of responsibility and, 198
Grandma Summer (Jessup), 166–171
Graves, Donald, 21, 29–30, 31, 42, 63, 77, 82, 84, 149, 181, 189
group work, 186–187
growth
  encouraging inquiry and, 136–138
  rigor and, 126
guided experience
  chart describing, 198
  gradual release of responsibility and, 79*f*
guiding principles, 23–24, 28–29, 34–35
Guthrie, G., 62

H

Hank Aaron: Brave in Every Way (Golenbock), 60
Hannigan, Katherine, 130–134, 136–137, 143, 150
Harvey, Stephanie, 40, 68–69
Harwayne, Shelley, 40, 42, 49, 190
Haseley, D., 77
Henry and Mudge (Rylant), 118–119
Hest, A., 60
Hickory Chair, The (Fraustiano), 60
High, L. O., 61, 77
history, outcomes of conferring and, 17
hope, creating a culture of thinking and, 39
Hopkinson, D., 61
How to Catch a Shark and Other Stories About Teaching and Learning (Graves), 77
humor in conferences, 178
Huske, L., 157
Hutchins, Chryse, 40, 47, 180–181

I

Ida B...and Her Plans to Maximize Fun, Avoid Disaster, and (Possibly) Save the World (Hannigan), 130–134, 136–137, 143, 150
independence
  gradual release of responsibility and, 77, 79*f*
  importance of, 14–15
  observation in conferences and, 156–157
  purpose and audience and, 72–75, 72*f*, 74*f*
independent experience, 198
information-transmission approach, 9–10
inquiry
  growth and need and, 136–138
  literacy craft and, 136–138
  mentors and, 141–143
  note-taking and, 138–141
  overview of, 130–141, 131*f*, 134*f*
insights
  blank form for, 199
  conferring notebook and, 109*f*, 113*f*, 122*f*

inquiry and, 134*f*
intimacy and, 146*f*
RIP Model and, 96, 100–101
instruction. *See also* five ashlars
blank form for, 199
conferring notebook and, 109*f*, 113*f*, 122*f*
inquiry and, 134*f*
instruction points, 16–17
intimacy and, 146*f*
RIP Model and, 96, 100
walk-aways and, 158*f*
instructional planning
assessments and, 139–140
conferring notes and, 107
gradual release of responsibility and, 79*f*
"Instruction of Reading Comprehension, The" (Gallagher and Pearson), 75
Intellectual Character: What It Is, Why It Matters, and How to Get It (Ritchhart), 28, 32
intimacy
listening and, 148–150
overview of, 143–153, 144*f*, 146*f*
ownership and, 150–152
sitting placements during conferences and, 152–153
walk-aways and, 162*f*
intrigue
blank form for, 199
conferring notebook and, 109*f*, 113*f*, 122*f*
inquiry and, 134*f*
intimacy and, 146*f*
RIP Model and, 96, 101
Invincible Louisa: The Story of the Author of Little Women (Meigs), 141
I Read It, but I Don't Get It (Tovani), 40

J

James, Simon, 76–77
Jensen, E., 96
Jeremiah Learns to Read (Bogart), 77
Jessup, Harley, 166–171
Johnson, A., 60
Johnson, Denise, xiii–xiv, 191
Johnston, Peter, 14, 27, 111–112, 125, 129, 143
Johnston, T., 61, 77
Just Like Josh Gibson (Johnson), 60

K

Keene, Ellin, 29–30, 40, 42, 75, 81, 83, 117–118, 128, 129, 148, 176, 190
Keep On! The Story of Matthew Henson (Hopkinson), 61
Keller, Helen, xv–xvi, 152
Kempton, Susan, 40
Kenison, K., 126–127
keystone metaphor
overview of, 1–4
reasons to confer and, 33–34
kindergarten, 123
Knowing Literacy: Constructive Literacy Assessment (Johnston), 27, 112, 125
knowledge, compared to wisdom, 25–26
Koch, L., 84
Kujawa, S., 157

L

LaMarch, J., 60
Laminack, L., 77
Language and Learning (Britton), 41
language of teachers, 39
Learning Along the Way (Sweeney), 176
learning needs of students, 188–189
learning of the conferrer, 18–19
learning to confer, 29–32, 31*f*
Lee, Harper, 6
L'Engle, Madeleine, 127
letter explaining conferring to others, 189–190
leveled groups, 186–187
Leyden, Leslie, 128
listening
challenges in conferring and, 177
developing intimacy and, 148–150
outcomes of conferring and, 17
reader's workshop and, 81
rigor and, 126–128
walk-aways and, 159*f*
literacy craft. *See* crafting lessons
Literate Kindergarten, The (Kempton), 40
Little One Step (James), 76–77
Lupica, Mike, 130

M

MacLachlan, Patricia, 48
"Making Thinking Visible" (Ritchhart and Perkins), 140, 181
management of classroom during conferences, 48, 187–188
Margaret's Moves (Rabe), 193
Mason, L., 9–10
Matthews, Missy, 40, 62, 78
Maxwell's Mountain (Becker), 61
McKenzie, James, 7
meaning making, 136–138
Meier, Deborah, 118, 123
Meigs, C., 141
mentor classrooms, 39–40. *See also* classroom environment
mentoring, gradual release of responsibility and, 77
mentors, matching students with, 141–143
metacognition
classroom management during conferences and, 187–188
elements of, 157
independence and, 156–157
intimacy and, 147

purpose and audience and, 72–75, 72*f*, 74*f*
reader's workshop and, 88
Miller, Debbie, 21, 38–39, 40, 41, 42, 76, 92, 96, 135, 156, 186, 191
Miller, Meredi, xiii
misconceptions about conferring, 8–11
Miseducation (Elkind), 172
Mitten Strings for God (Kenison), 126–127
modeling, gradual release of responsibility and, 77
Morgan, Joe, 52
Mosaic of Thought (Keene and Zimmerman), 40, 75, 128
Moss, Jeff, 140
Mr. George Baker (Hest), 60
Mr. Putter and Tabby (Rylant), 119
Murphy, P. K., 9–10
Murray, Donald, 42, 93
myths regarding conferring. *See* counterfeit beliefs about conferring

N

Necks Out for Adventure: The True Story of Edwin Wiggleskin (Ering), 61
need, inquiry and, 136–138
note-taking systems. *See also* conferring notebook
blank form for, 199
conferring versus collecting, 107–116, 109*f*, 111*f*, 113*f*
importance of, 179
inquiry and, 138–141
overview of, 105–107, 184–185
rigor and, 122*f*
Now One Foot, Now the Other (dePaola), 77

O

observation, role of in conferences, 156–157
Olsen, Lisa, 147–148
1,600 Quotes and Pieces of Wisdom That Just Might Help You Out When You're Stuck in a Moment (and Can't Get Out of It!) (Guthrie), 62
organization in the classroom
creating a culture of thinking and, 38–39
Defining Trust, Respect, and Tone ashlar and, 48–49
outcomes of conferring, 11–19, 12*f*, 14*f*
ownership
classroom environment and, 49–50
Defining Trust, Respect, and Tone ashlar and, 50
developing intimacy and, 150–152
"Purpose Triangle" and, 62–67, 64*f*, 66*f*

P

Pajeau, Charles, 156
Parent, Marc, 80
parent volunteers, 184
Park, Barbara, 142
patterns, outcomes of conferring and, 15–16
Pearson, P. D., 75, 76
peer-to-peer interactions, 185, 187–188
Pennac, Daniel, 130, 134–135
Perkins, D. N., 92, 140, 181
planning
blank form for, 199
chart describing, 198
conferring notebook and, 109*f*, 113*f*, 122*f*
gradual release of responsibility and, 79*f*
inquiry and, 134*f*
intimacy and, 146*f*
RIP Model and, 96, 102
Planning a Strategy Study–Reading or Writing form
blank form for, 197
gradual release of responsibility and, 79*f*
Plan/Progress/Purpose form, 108–110
Polacco, P., 77
Possum Magic (Fox), 77, 84, 181
Power of Their Ideas, The (Meier), 123
principles, guiding, 23–24, 28–29, 34–35
processes, outcomes of conferring and, 15
progress
conferring notebook and, 107, 109*f*, 113*f*, 122*f*
inquiry and, 134*f*
intimacy and, 146*f*
RIP Model and, 96, 102–103
proximity to students during conferences
comfort and, 178
frequency of conferences and, 182–183
overview of, 152–153
purpose
blank form for, 199
conferring notebook and, 109*f*, 112, 113*f*, 122*f*
Discussing Purpose and Audience ashlar, 62–75, 64*f*, 66*f*, 67*f*, 71*f*, 72*f*, 74*f*
examining, 11–19, 12*f*, 14*f*
inquiry and, 134*f*
intimacy and, 146*f*
overview of, 68–70
"Purpose Triangle" and, 62–67, 64*f*, 66*f*, 72–75, 72*f*, 74*f*
reader's workshop and, 89*f*
RIP Model and, 96, 103
"Purpose Triangle"
overview of, 62–67, 64*f*, 66*f*

purpose and audience and, 72–75, 72*f*, 74*f*
Put Thinking to the Test (Conrad, Matthews, Zimmerman, and Allen), 40, 62

Q

questions during conferring
challenges in conferring and, 179
Defining Trust, Respect, and Tone ashlar and, 45–46
developing intimacy and, 148–149
examples of, 30, 31*f*
overview of, 29–32, 31*f*
rigor and, 129
RIP Model and, 97–98
walk-aways and, 158*f*

R

Rabe, Berniece, 193
Raft, The (LaMarch), 60
Raising Lifelong Learners: A Parent's Guide (Calkins and Bellino), 137
rapport, 18
Ray, Katie Wood, 27–28, 42, 82, 85, 136, 176
read aloud
blank form for, 199
conferring notebook and, 109*f*, 113*f*, 122*f*
inquiry and, 134*f*
intimacy and, 146*f*
RIP Model and, 96, 97
Reader's Responsibilities chart
classroom management during conferences and, 188
Strengthening Endurance and Stamina ashlar and, 54
reader's workshop, 80–92, 82*f*, 87*f*, 88*f*, 89*f*–91*f*
Reading Conference-Check Off form
blank form for, 201
conferring notebook and, 110
examples of, 111*f*
Reading with Meaning (Miller), 38, 40, 76, 186
reasons to confer, 33–35
record
blank form for, 199
conferring notebook and, 109*f*, 113*f*, 122*f*
inquiry and, 134*f*
intimacy and, 146*f*
RIP Model and, 96, 97–99
record keeping. *See also* conferring notebook
outcomes of conferring and, 16
overview of, 184–185
RIP Model and, 101
red thread metaphor, 28–29
reflecting
reader's workshop and, 83, 88, 89*f*, 90*f*–91*f*
thinking and, 140–141
respect
Defining Trust, Respect, and Tone ashlar, 42–50
development of, 45–47
importance of, 44
response, 50
responsibility. *See also* gradual release of responsibility
classroom environment and, 49–50
classroom management during conferences and, 187–188
Exploring the Gradual Release of Responsibility Model ashlar, 75–80, 79*f*
review
blank form for, 199
conferring notebook and, 109*f*, 113*f*, 122*f*
inquiry and, 134*f*
intimacy and, 146*f*
RIP Model and, 96–97
Rief, Linda, 46, 124
rigor
listening and, 126–128
overview of, 118–130, 118*f*, 122*f*
teaching and, 128–130
uncovering students strengths, struggles, and genuine wonderings, 125–126
RIP Model
conferring notebook and, 104–107, 107–116, 109*f*, 111*f*, 113*f*
frequency of conferences and, 182–183
Instruction, Insights, Intrigue component of, 99–101
metacognition and, 157
overview of, 94–96, 140–141
Plan, Progress, Purpose component of, 102–104
Review, Read Aloud, Record component of, 96–97
Ritchhart, Ron, 28, 32, 140, 181
River of Words: The Story of William Carlos Williams, A (Bryan), 61
Rogers, Fred, 155, 180
roles of teachers and students
challenges in conferring and, 176
chart describing, 198
gradual release of responsibility and, 78
reader's workshop and, 88–89, 90*f*–91*f*
Rousseau, Jean-Jacques, 52
Routman, Regie, 190
Rushmore, Troy, 26–27, 38, 39, 41, 53, 78, 80, 89, 90, 92, 106, 107, 112–114, 139–140, 173, 186
Ruskin, John, 62
Rylant, Cynthia, 118–223, 125, 128, 142

S

Sahara Special (Codell), 183
samples of conferences
complete, 163–171
conferring notebook and, 166*f*, 171*f*
discussion of, 171–174
sarcasm in conferences, 178
Saturdays and Teacakes (Laminack), 77
scaffolding, gradual release of responsibility and, 75
Seeking Diversity: Language Arts with Adolescents (Rief), 46
self-assessment and self-evaluation, 162*f*
7 Keys to Comprehension (Zimmerman and Hutchins), 40, 180
shared experience
chart describing, 198
gradual release of responsibility and, 79*f*
Sibberson, Franki, 42, 84, 110
side-by-side conference, 125
silence. *See also* listening
challenges in conferring and, 177
walk-aways and, 159*f*
sincerity, creating a culture of thinking and, 39
sitting placements during conferences
comfort and, 178
frequency of conferences and, 182–183
overview of, 152–153
small groups, 186–187
social context of conferring, 143–153, 144*f*, 146*f*
Spirit of Endurance: The True Story of the Shackleton Expedition to the Antarctic (Armstrong), 55
spontaneity in conferences, 137–138
staff members, 184
Stafford, William, 115
stamina
classroom management during conferences and, 187–188
overview of, 51–54, 53*f*
Strengthening Endurance and Stamina ashlar, 51–62, 51*f*, 53*f*, 56*f*, 60*f*, 61*f*, 63*f*
Steven Caney's Ultimate Building Book (Caney), 156
Strategic Teaching and Reading Project Guidebook, The (Kujawa and Huske), 157
Strategies that Work (Harvey and Goudvis), 40, 68–69
strategy study
challenges in conferring and, 179
classroom management during conferences and, 187–188
gradual release of responsibility and, 75–80, 79*f*
mentors and, 142
overview of, 15
teaching during conferences and, 129
walk-aways and, 158*f*
Strengthening Endurance and Stamina ashlar, 51–62, 51*f*, 53*f*, 56*f*, 60*f*, 61*f*, 63*f*. *See also* five ashlars
strengths of students, 125–126
structure in conferring, 95, 140–141. *See also* RIP Model
structure systems
teaching during conferences and, 129
walk-aways and, 158*f*, 161*f*
struggles of students
challenges in conferring and, 183–184
students with special needs, 188–189
uncovering during conferences, 125–126
student roles
challenges in conferring and, 176
chart describing, 198
gradual release of responsibility and, 78
reader's workshop and, 88–89, 90*f*–91*f*
students, questions for, 29–32, 31*f*
students with special needs, 188–189
Study Driven: A Framework for Planning Units of Study in the Writing Workshop (Ray), 27–28
Sullivan, Anne, xv–xvi, 152
support staff, 184
surface structure systems
teaching during conferences and, 129
walk-aways and, 158*f*
Sweeney, D., 176
Szymusiak, Karen, 42, 84

T

Tahomas, P., 60
talk, outcomes of conferring and, 18
Teacher and Student Roles chart, 78
teacher roles
challenges in conferring and, 176
chart describing, 204
gradual release of responsibility and, 78
reader's workshop and, 88–89, 90*f*–91*f*
teaching
challenges in conferring and, 177
during conferences, 128–130
outcomes of conferring and, 17
Teaching the Best Practice Way (Daniels and Bizar), 82, 152, 171
Teaching with the Brain in Mind (Jensen), 96

Teedie: The Story of Young Teddy Roosevelt (Brown), 61
test tips, walk-aways and, 160*f*
text selection
  classroom management during conferences and, 187–188
  ownership and, 150–152
  walk-aways and, 160*f*
Thank You, Mr. Falker (Polacco), 77
The Story of My Life (Keller), 152
think alouds
  chart describing, 198
  gradual release of responsibility and, 79*f*
  rigor and, 126
thinking routines, 32–33
thinking strategies. *See also* five ashlars
  challenges in conferring and, 177–178
  chart describing, 198
  gradual release of responsibility and, 79*f*
  overview of, 40–42
  structure in conferring and, 140–141
  teaching during conferences and, 129
Thoreau, Henry David, 40, 104
Thoughts and Language (Vygotsky), 126
time, 50. *See also* duration of conferences; frequency of conferences
Tomlinson, Shellie Rushing, 117
tone
  Defining Trust, Respect, and Tone ashlar, 42–50
  development of, 45–47
  importance of, 44
touchstone conference, 125
To Understand: New Horizons in Reading Comprehension (Keene), 40, 81
Tovani, Chris, 40, 42, 69
transcripts of conferences
  complete, 163–171
  conferring notebook and, 166*f*, 171*f*
  discussion of, 171–174
trust
  creating a culture of thinking and, 39
  Defining Trust, Respect, and Tone ashlar, 42–50
  development of, 45–47
  importance of, 43–44
Tweit, S., 77

U

understanding, 173
Understanding and Implementing Reading First Initiative: The Changing Role of Administrators (Cummins), 185

V

vocabulary development
  classroom management during conferences and, 187–188
  walk-aways and, 161*f*
Vygotsky, Lev, 126

W

Wagler, Mark, 37
Walden (Thoreau), 40
walk-aways
  overview of, 156–163, 158*f*–162*f*, 171–174
  Plan, Progress, Purpose component of the RIP Model, 104
  transcripts of conferences illustrating, 163–174, 166*f*, 171*f*
Walking to the Creek (Williams), 163–166
Wednesday Surprise, The (Bunting), 77
Wells, Gordon, 137
Whale, The (Rylant), 118–223, 125
"What Creative Thinking Is" (Perkins), 92
What emerges in a conference? form
  blank form for, 195
  overview of, 11–19, 12*f*, 14*f*
"When Someone Deeply Listens to You" (Fox), 153
Wild at Heart: Discovering the Secret of a Man's Soul (Eldredge), 193
Wilder, Laura Ingalls, 144–146, 151
Wilhelm, Jeff, 9
Williams, David, 163–166
wisdom, compared to knowledge, 25–26
Women Daredevils: Thrills, Chills, and Frills (Cummins), 61
wonderings of students, uncovering during conferences, 125–126
World According to Mister Rogers: Important Things to Remember, The (Rogers), 180
writing and conferring
  guiding questions and, 46–47
  overview of, 8

Z

Zimmerman, Cheryl, 38, 39, 40, 41, 62, 64–67, 69, 92, 124, 127, 157–163, 187, 188
Zimmerman, Susan, 40, 75, 128
Zull, James, 24